John Emory Gray

**The family record and history of Rev. David and Naomi Gray**

John Emory Gray

**The family record and history of Rev. David and Naomi Gray**

ISBN/EAN: 9783337282912

Printed in Europe, USA, Canada, Australia, Japan

Cover: Foto ©Andreas Hilbeck / pixelio.de

More available books at **www.hansebooks.com**

JOHN EMORY GRAY.

# THE

## Family Record and History

OF

# Rev. David and Naomi Gray,

### Compiled and Written

FOR THE

### Benefit of Their Relatives and Descendants.

By *JOHN EMORY GRAY,*
Cambridge City, Ind.

INDIANAPOLIS:
WM. B. BURFORD, LITHOGRAPHER, PRINTER, AND BINDER.
1887.

# PREFACE.

While at Findlay, Ohio, to pass the Christmas of 1885, visiting father, sister Eleanor, and the family of Mr. Ruthrauff, the thought which has culminated in the production of a limited edition of our family chronology was first suggested to me. It impressed me as a matter of particular importance and interest to all connected with our ancestral line, that an account of our ascendants and relations should be put into some permanent form, for preservation, more comprehensive—especially as to our forefathers—than the isolated records of each family branch, and more reliable than the personal remembrances of what we have heard, relative thereto, at the fireside rehearsals of the home circle.

Also, it seemed to me to be of vital importance that whatever was to be done by way of accomplishing such a purpose, should be begun at once, while father was still with us, that we might have the benefit of his knowledge, and that the memoirs might be freed from errors, and duly authenticated by his word and approval. The fact that such a step has not been taken until after our mother's death, whereby we have already lost much that would now be valuable and interesting from her recollections, is very unfortunate. Father, now being eighty-six years old, suffering under the infirmities of age, his work done, and seemingly

"Waiting—only waiting, waiting for the end,"

prompted me to use all possible diligence in effecting an early completion of such a work.

But the time seemed opportune for another reason. By force of circumstances and the law of necessity, it is not within the scope of our design to attempt reaching further back, genealogically, than to our great grandparents, nor to include, except, probably by notation of births, marriages, and deaths, any below their great grandchildren. These—our own family—the children of David and Naomi Gray, are so far advanced in life that their immediate families are not subject to further growth: unless, indeed, like Sarah, the mother of Isaac, or Elizabeth, the mother of John the Baptist, some of them be blessed of the Lord and "bear a child" in their old age. Thus, while the work might not be full as to detail, it may be complete as to span, and a great benefit to our children and our children's children as a "family tree" from which to extend their branches.

The idea of making a transcript of our family chronology and of its importance, is not original with myself, except, perhaps, as to the form and extent in which it is now presented. Others of my brothers and sisters had the matter in view first, but contemplated, it is understood, only the preparation by each family of notes from which to prepare a manuscript account of our ascendants, and of what might be interesting of personal incident in their lives.

This seemed to incur so much difficulty in getting concert of action and uniformity in kind and amount of information, that the present plan was suggested and adopted.

To me, the chief incentive in suggesting and preparing a printed chronology, extending down to and including our own family, is the honor due our father for the noble example and work of his life, and to our mother for her fortitude and fidelity to him.

Their history we wish perpetuated among our children, their lives intelligently known, and their memories revered by them. Not being a professional biographer, not writing for the public, called, as it were, before an audience of my friends only, and acting as a brother employed in a labor of mutual concern, I do not anticipate severe criticism of my effort.

My being possessed of but few data in the form of episode or historical sketch with which to embellish the account of our forefathers, has rendered the part of the work pertaining to them almost devoid of interest, except as to names and dates. Much assistance, by letter and manuscript, has been rendered by different members of the family, and they likewise share in the affectionate regard which prompted it. I am, therefore, to be exclusively commended or entirely faulted with little else than the expression it bears, and in this I feel that the character and loving-kindness of my readers will make them charitable.

There is one circumstance, however, which has attended me all the way through, which invokes leniency, and which, I think, should be understood. The work was begun at a period too late to produce a record of many of father's personal experiences. In consequence of his extreme age, the names of many persons whom he met and with whom he became acquainted, as well as many interesting and important incidents of his life, can not now be recalled. Indeed, most of those reminiscences that will naturally be looked for and that would have been particularly valuable to me as data, in the work undertaken, have entirely faded from his mind. This explanation must be accepted as an excuse for one among other deficiencies that will probably be discovered, and, at the same time, as my apology for offering, instead, so much from my own store of remembrances.

I have thought proper to make special mention of sister Mary and family and brother David in separate chapters. No one of the family, I think, will question my action in this particular. However, let it not be regarded as detracting from the rest of my brothers and sisters, nor as in any way depreciating them.

My aim has been to make the book a reasonable attainment of the objects in view; to secure for it family approval; to make it a relief from embarrassment to our offspring, in preserving the genealogy of their ancestry; to inspire them with due respect and reverence for the same, and with resolution to honor them by their own conduct and success in solving the problems of life, remembering the responsibility implied in the answer of the Athenian general, Iphicrates, the son of a shoemaker, who, when reproached by Harmodius with his birth, said, "I would rather be the first than the last of my family."

Trusting that some proximity to this line of idea has been reached, that a family want has been supplied, and that the benefit to be derived therefrom will be commensurate with the labor performed in its writing and compilation, this book is now committed into the care and keeping of our relationship.

J. E. G.

CAMBRIDGE CITY, IND., 1887.

# INTRODUCTION.

A great regret we have had in entering upon this work—and which it is one of its main objects to avert hereafter in tracing the lineage of the family—is the entire absence of knowledge concerning the earlier people from whom we are descended. Beyond our great grandparents we have not even a record of names and dates pertaining to our ancestors. But we would not have this statement regarded as a censure upon our forefathers for not preserving some account of them, for it undoubtedly represents the condition of families everywhere, and arises, most excusably, from the fact that family biographies and historical manuscripts are not, and have not been, customary with people in ordinary life. Besides, they lived at a time when our country was comparatively new, when schools were limited in number, when wealth and its advantages were the inheritance of but few families, when the Revolution was in progress, when great hardships were to be endured, and when the question of how to get a living was a matter of such grave importance, that their attention must have been directed entirely away from a work of this kind. It would also seem inconsistent in us to be deeply pained at their neglect, when it is known that, with greater advantages and under much more favorable circumstances, we came very near repeating the error by omission of any detailed account of our own forefathers, having only recently caught the idea and been forcibly impressed with its importance. Nor has the statement been made to bring into prominence an inference the public might draw, that the names of our remote ancestors can not be written high upon the scroll of fame, else they would not now be resting in family oblivion; for, while such an inference would be based on the truth that only very great persons are given high public honor and distinction, and that histories of ordinary people are uncommon, it does not disprove that we have lost connection with our progenitive line, nor nullify the fact that there are many prominent and illustrious personages in history, bearing our ancestral names, to whom it is not impossible or improbable we are remotely connected.

We have made mention of the fact, however, because it is customary in works of this kind to go far back to remote ancestors, and in our not doing so there might seem, in the character and importance of our lineage, to be a strange defect which might provoke inquiry should it chance to meet the public eye, and must, therefore, be accounted for. In view of this fact, if no other, it was deemed best to be honest at the start and acknowledge that we don't know anything about them.

But all this is no argument against a family biography and autobiography. There are reasons, positive and negative, which show them to be suitable to kindred of every circumstance and condition in life—to the farmer and mechanic as well as to the warrior and statesman. Honor and credit to families are reflected from two directions—from ancestors down and from progeny up—and from neglect of family records and manuscripts, there has been as much difficulty in finding the obscure and unknown progenitor of some poor boy who has risen from poverty to honor and distinction as there has been to find an illustrious ancestry for offspring that have no other merit.

Many persons in their family pride, and consciousness of defect, forget and violate the scriptural injunction which says, "Think not to say within yourselves we have Abraham to our father," and are very anxious to prove their descent from heroes and great men. But in the world, and especially in the republic in which we live, it can not be told from what condition in life a great man will spring. He is as liable to be the child of the poor and unknown as of the rich and the distinguished; why not act, then, in view of what may come, as well as in consideration of what has gone before?

Moreover, it is not improper that we should have a family biography, just because we do not know anything of our people beyond our great grandparents, for in the absence of anything to the contrary, we have the loyal right to presume that our remote ancestors were quite respectable people, the privilege to demonstrate that our forefathers more recently figured in events of historical note, to preserve our family history from heart motives and reasons which do not concern the public mind; and if these be not sufficient, to hope that in the coming years some scion of our stock may rise to prominence and shed a lustre o'er our heads that will silence cavil and clear away all anxiety, if any exists, in our minds, by reason of an insinuated mediocrity.

The utility and importance, then, of every family having a written or printed chronology, may be deemed unquestionable, even though custom, so far, has not sanctioned it, and public opinion has not yet declared in its favor.

However, referring again to the matter of regret, that we know absolutely nothing pertaining to our early ancestors, there also exists a meagerness of information respecting many of our more direct lineal ascendants who come within the scope of our work. Their names are about all the account we can give of them. For a simple chronology this limited knowledge, perhaps, would be sufficient, and is really of much importance and interest, when compared with no information at all, and will serve as a starting point for something more in detail hereafter; yet to give such finish and interest to our undertaking as must naturally be desired, and which, under the circumstances, it is within our ambition to produce, something more would be required. But as stated, this embarrassment did not come upon us suddenly and unexpectedly in the course of compilation. It was previously recognized and considered, and the conclusion formed that a beginning must be made and that only additional obscurity would be the result of further delay. The intention was thus formed to do the best we could with what data we had, and hand it down to our posterity for preservation as the basis for a more extended family record in coming years, when those who are now fathers and grandfathers shall have passed away.

As "distance lends enchantment to the view," so age adds value and importance to a knowledge of persons and events. What, in the present, of our family life is an incident of the merest note, becomes to our posterity a theme of absorbing interest. So, too, what now seems to us so meager, from our nearer view, may, perhaps, seem to them of fuller mold, and satisfy expectation. We have, nevertheless, had some desire to discover a rational and exonerating cause for there being such a barrenness of incident or history in connection with the lives of our grandparents and great grandparents. It has seemed that we naturally ought to know more about them and be able to narrate more respecting them; but we are not, and by a contemplation of the matter we have become impressed, convinced, that it is almost entirely due to the fact of our father and mother migrating to Ohio at a comparatively early date, leaving all their relations in the then far east, and where they all, except our father's immediate family, ever remained. It was a wide separation, not only for the reason that it was five hundred miles of distance, and took weeks of slow travel to overcome it, but still wider for the reason that it precluded all idea of frequent visits to their native home, the time and expense involved being insuperable obstacles to a family of limited means. After leaving Delaware, in 1829, our mother never made but one visit to her old home, and that was in 1856, nearly thirty years from the time of her migration, and this when railroad communication had been established, and she had a son in the railroad service who accompanied her and bore the expense. None of her people ever visited Ohio except her sister Sophia, at a still later date, and only for a short time. Thus, family knowledge died out and family records were lost sight of. This theory is corroborated by the fact that we have some clear and interesting account of our grandfather Frazer Gray and his family, all of whom emigrated to Ohio, while, as to those ascendants of our family, on both sides, that remained in Delaware, we know but little besides their names. It may be asked, in this connection, why we know so little of our great grandparents, William and Elizabeth Gray, as their son—our grandfather—Frazer Gray, came to Ohio. This is answered by the supposition that they died when he was quite young, as our own father has no remembrance of ever hearing him refer to them.

From what has been said respecting the limited knowledge we have of many of our progenitors, it may be supposed that in taking up our own family history, where this want of information did not continue, that the limit of all our embarrassments had been reached; yet, this would show forgetfulness of the truth that every position we assume in life has its obstacles, and every office or vocation its inherent troop of difficulties. Human beings are so constituted that they often think that what they have not is all that they need, and not until they get the desired object do they realize that they need something else a great deal worse. Much so has it been with us in this work. When we had few data we were not mindful that we needed anything else, but on arriving at the point where information was plentiful, we found that the ability to put facts together and give them the character and dignity of history was a matter of quite as much desire and importance to us as a knowledge of the events we wished to narrate. Our mind has been beset with conflicting notions as to the propriety of relating this, and the impropriety of mentioning that, as to what we ought to say in order to be just, and as to what should not be said for fear of being considered egotistical or over important in our family estimate. Also, whether a record should be made presenting the family in Sunday garb and in import alone of our father's high calling as a preacher of the Gospel, or allow it to appear, naturally, that we belonged to the common brotherhood of man, with dispositions, passions, tempers, hopes, and desires, as other people, is a matter that came up for consideration. The latter question was suggested, no doubt, from the impress of an idea the public seem to entertain, that many things may be overlooked and condoned in the offspring of a layman, or person outside of the church, that would be highly censurable in the child of a Christian minister, and in consequence of the belief, on our part, that the idea is unorthodox, uncharitable, and untruthful.

In this connection we are reminded of the old saying that, "preacher's children are the worst children in the world." It scarcely merits attention for certainly no intelligent person has ever expressed it as a literal truth, and it may be regarded as simply on a par with the old saws that, "the tailor always wears a ragged coat" and that "the shoemaker's wife always goes barefoot." They all spring too, to some extent, from the same idea. The tailor being a maker and often a vender of clothes, the public have a notion that they cost him but little and that he ought to advertise his business by wearing the best goods and appearing ever dressed in the latest fashion. The shoemaker being a maker of shoes the same notion prevails as to him, and his wife, at least, is expected to have the neatest dressed foot in the community. Any variation from these anticipations attracts more than ordinary attention and excites remark and gossip. So with the Christian minister, the people infer that his family should be a daily exemplification of his profession and a living model and promulgation of his good work. No allowance is made for his children's having the natural impulses and propensities of human kind, and consequently any little misbehavior or childish difficulty they get into, otherwise unnoticable, is given great notoriety and grossly exaggerated.

These views undoubtedly account for the origin of this saying. But since this primary start, it has gained a wider significance and has more recently been used to give expression to prejudiced feelings of any and every kind not only against the minister and his family but also against the church and its cause. Human nature has a weakness which often tempts people, when they can not conceal their own faults, to try to lessen, obscure, or seek immunity from them by casting an imputation on somebody else and by claiming that they are no worse than certain other persons. In making these comparisons for their own benefit they never select individuals of low repute, but always compare with, or refer to, the most respectable people. It is this trait in human character of trying to show that somebody else bearing a good name is worse than we are, that has had much to do in widening the signification of this reflection and slander on ministers of the church and their offspring. The father of the boy who may have received a black eye or bloody nose from the minister's son for taunting him by saying "your father is poor and my father has to help support you," and the mother, whose jealousy may have been awakened by the minister's daughter outstripping her own at school, or for some other reason, will both respond aye to the declaration that "preacher's children are the worst children in the world." The bully and the brawler who may have heard that the preacher's boy had a quarrel with another boy on the street, and the scoffer, the person of atheistical views and tendencies—because he sees its force, if true, would be to show that religious training and education is useless, christianity a farce, and the Bible a lie—now never allow the opportunity to pass for endorsing the statement that, "preacher's children are the worst children in the world."

It is an assertion that no one has ever made any serious attempt to prove. History refutes it; the records of our jails and penitentiaries, our alms-houses and dens of infamy, pronounce it false; the seats of learning and the numerous positions of honor, trust, and usefulness occupied by the sons of clergymen give it a most emphatic denial, and it is known to all intelligent and fair-minded people to be as openly false as it has been extensively circulated.

But as to our own family history. We had some landmarks of thought and purpose which aided us in a solution of the doubts that crossed our mind and assisted us in deciding our course. We were reminded by these that the object in view was family interest and benefit, and not public instruction; that we were writing more for our posterity than for ourselves; that but a few short years at most could elapse ere it would cease to be of any value to the direct members of our father's household, and that we should be governed by considerations of future appreciation. The extreme lack of such information as would depict to us, in a measure, the daily life, the ingoings and outgoings of our forefathers, of something that would be a reflex of their circumstances and habits, and the pleasure and interest we feel such knowledge would now give, emphasized the desire to supply this want, as respects ourselves, to our children. The family narrative will, therefore, be found to contain something besides a record of father's church work. If an outsider chance to see it, it will not appear that any of our people were ever hung. Had such been the case, we believe the public scrutinizing enough to have found it out before this without our telling it.

It is natural to all to feel and speak the highest sentiment of love and regard for their parents, and what we express for our own is no limit of this privilege to others. We know, also, that however worthy the lives of our father and mother, it would be vanity to suppose that persons outside of the family will manifest as much interest in them as we do, or be induced by our estimate to give them more than a passing notice, even did we seek to direct their attention to them. But we know them "for ourselves, and not for another," and it is our delight, our glory, and our consolation, to pay them, as far as we can, the honor they merit. In this, the indifference of the world may not circumscribe or deter us. To Rev. David and Naomi Gray, the leading personages in this history, we, therefore, point with no limited degree of pride, no bonndary lines of respect, no feeble and shortened expressions of love and admiration. Although the names of our father and mother do not appear in the world's constellation of great men and women, and are unknown to fame, their virtues are highly worthy of commemoration, and to day are a richer legacy to us than wealth, and a sweeter solace than public praise.

As a Christian minister, our father, by the power of the Gospel, was the means of bringing hundreds "from darkness to light, and from the power of Satan unto God." In this work our mother was a constant support. Contemplating these truths, may we not felicitously inquire, what will be their distinction in the other world, as compared with many of the illustrious names in history, remembering that Christ has said, " Whosoever shall do and teach these, my commandments, shall be called great in the Kingdom of Heaven."

# DAVID GRAY'S GRANDPARENTS.

### William Gray—Elizabeth Gray.

William and Elizabeth Gray, father's grandparents, had four children, Joseph, Elizabeth, Polly, and Frazer. Their early life was spent in New Jersey, in which State all these children were born. Subsequently the family moved to Sussex County, Delaware. Joseph and Polly never married. Elizabeth married William Robbins. They raised a family of eight children —David, William, John, Joseph, Celia, Nancy, Elizabeth, and George. Seven of these raised families. George, the youngest, died in early manhood. David married a Quakeress, whose maiden name can not be recalled. Her Christian name was Nancy, and she was a very pious and exemplary woman. William's wife's name has also been forgotten. John married a woman whose Christian name was Lydia, maiden name unknown; Joseph married Mary Reynolds, a lady of excellent family; Celia married Abram Lynch; Nancy married William Tatman first, and John Sharpe second. Elizabeth was married three times—first to a Mr. Robbins, second to Ishmael Steel, and third to a Mr. Holland. Frazer Gray, the fourth child of William and Elizabeth Gray, became father's father by marriage to his second wife, Elizabeth Lockwood.

William and Elizabeth Gray were of English origin. We have no details respecting their history, and it is supposed that they died while Frazer Gray was quite young.

### Samuel Lockwood—Zipporah Lockwood.

Samuel and Zipporah Lockwood, father's grandfather and grandmother, were natives of Delaware. They had eight children, three sons and five daughters—Benjamin, William, Samuel, Zippa, Elizabeth, Rachel, Nancy, and Leah, all of whom married into first-class families. Benjamin married Louie Long, daughter of Colonel Long; William married Phœbe Dingle, daughter of Dr. Dingle, and Samuel married Patty Holland, daughter of a wealthy farmer; Zippa never married; Elizabeth married Frazer Gray; Rachel married Joshua Robinson; Nancy married William Schofield, and Leah married James Tingle. The Tingles were a noble family; most of them were Episcopalians and Methodists, and all very well off, financially, except James, who was rather poor. Elizabeth became father's mother by marriage to Frazer Gray.

Samuel Lockwood was a very respectable and prominent citizen of Dagsborough Hundred, Sussex County, Delaware. He was a member of the Protestant Episcopal Church, and, although a slave-holder, his record is highly honorable and creditable to his posterity. He was married twice. Elizabeth, father's mother, was by Samuel's first wife.

## NAOMI GRAY'S GRANDPARENTS.

### Lyttleton Lofland—Grace Lofland.

Lyttleton and Grace Lofland, mother's grandparents, were also natives and residents of Sussex County, Delaware, and of English descent. They had eight children, six sons and two daughters. Their names, in order of birth, were Luke, Elias, James, Hevelow, William, Jonathan, Grace, and Hannah.

Luke married Elizabeth Morris. James's wife's maiden name is not remembered; her Christian name was Polly. Elias married a daughter of Bivans Morris, a brother of William Morris, mother's grandfather. Hevelow, William, and Jonathan were all married, but the names of their wives can not now be ascertained. Grace married Boze Warren, and Hannah married Samuel Hurst. Luke became mother's father by marriage to Elizabeth Morris. Mother's grandfather, Lyttleton Lofland, was a slave owner, and a man of naturally high spirit. Of his family we know that he had at least two brothers, Isaac and Purnal. Isaac, by his third wife, Cynthia Virdin, was the father of Dr. John Lofland, the "Milford Bard," and Purnal, by his wife, Mary Robinson, was the father of Dr. James Lofland. Both Dr. John and James Lofland were born in Milford, Delaware. From what we have heard mother say, we infer that the Loflands were a warm and generous-hearted people, but proud spirited, and somewhat given to intemperance; and that their dispositions, when under the influence of liquor, would lead them to do things that they would be very sorry for afterward. They were undoubtedly of naturally strong intellects and noble impulses. This is affirmed, we think, by the history of the "Milford Bard," whose mental capacity was probably better developed by education than that of any other member of the family, and the only one of them of whom we have any complete historic account. Although, in consequence of the vice of intemperance, of which he vainly sought to rid himself, and from which he almost constantly suffered remorse, his history shows that he was a man of much brilliancy of intellect and of most generous spirit. In writing to a friend, with whom he had previously had some difficulty, he says, " To fall out with a friend is equal to a spell of sickness to me of a week's duration." This is a Lofland trait, more or less common to every one of our family, and is received from mother, whose disposition was much the same. Dr. John Lofland had a sister, the wife of Rev. Corry Chambers, of Wilmington, Delaware: she was a lady of energy and talent. A book, entitled " The Poetical and Prose Writings of the Milford Bard," was published in Baltimore in 1853. The author died January 22, 1849. We have a copy of this work in our hands. It contains a picture of the author, which resembles our sister Elizabeth very much. He was born on the 9th day of March, in the year 1798. We copy from the book two pieces, one of poetry and one of prose, to give an idea of his genius and the bent of his mind:

### THE CATHEDRAL BELL, BALTIMORE.

How sweetly sounds that evening bell; how soothing is its toll;
It comes like mellow music on the meditating soul.
It speaks as with a tongue from heaven, to every heart of care,
And, like an angel whispering, it calls the soul to prayer.

It speaks of Him who loved the world, of Him who deigned to give
His blessed Son to die, that man—ungrateful man—might live.
That glorious Son, who to mankind his gospel page unfurled,
And hung redemption's rainbow round a dark and dying world.

O, thou most holy, heavenly Church, at whose all-sacred shrine
The God of Heaven, in truth, pronounced devoted and divine,
What millions in all ages since have at thy altar knelt,
And all the luxuries of faith, of hope and love have felt.

The infidel in vain may strike; in vain the fool may mock;
In vain all opposition, too—'tis built upon a rock;
"The gates of hell shall not prevail" against its holy name;
When ages, yet unknown, have passed, the Church will stand the same.

From age to age, alas! the Church has been severely used,
By persecution butchered, and by bigotry abused;
But still she sends out from the ark of peace the gentle dove,
And holds out to the world around the olive leaf of love.

Ah! would that all mankind were thus inclined to live in peace;
The heart would be a heaven on earth, the storms of strife would cease;
The dagger would no longer drink the guiltless victim's gore,
And every man would go in peace, ay, go and sin no more.

O, happy day! it were indeed; the angels high in heaven
Would tune their harps of gold, and sing the truce of mercy given;
But man, because he will not join the holy church of God,
Gives vent to vengeance, and uplifts fell persecution's rod.

Her doors are open unto all: the tree of life is there,
And every one may of the fruit in rich abundance share;
Come, one and all, a mother she will ever truly prove,
Her ways are ways of pleasantness, her paths are peace and love.

Sweet bell, thy tongue in mournful tones speaks to my silent heart,
And bids me to prepare, for soon I must from earth depart,
And lie down in the grave alone like him who slumbers here,
And who, like me, could once in life thy mellow music hear.

I love to muse at evening hour, when thou art sounding far,
And, while I listen, gaze upon yon bright and blessed star;
And think of all the happy host that dwell, ye dead, with you,
Beyond the starry skies above—sweet evening bell, adieu.

## THE MARCH OF MIND.

Wrapped in the mantle of imagination the traveler stands, in gloomy meditation, amid the ruins of ancient Greece. He looks down the tempestuous tide of time and views the wrecks of ages and of empires. He stands with indescribable emotions upon the crumbling fragments of grandeur where the hall of wisdom once stood, and the thunders of eloquence were heard. There arose the sun on Athens' lofty towers, and there the sidereal orbs of learning illuminated the world. It was in Greece that the human mind emerged from the night of mental darkness and severed the galling chain of tyrannical ignorance. She flourished, and mankind stood astonished at the sublimity of her career. But where, now, is the glory of Greece? Where, now, is the land of science and song? Where, now, are her brave warriors; her illustrious statesmen; her immortal poets? They have gone down the rapid tide of time, and have ceased to exist but on the scroll of fame. The lamp of learning has been extinguished, and mental darkness rests upon the bosom of her land. Gothic ignorance now dwells upon the ruins of Oriental greatness.

In the march of mind, Rome arose on the ruins of Greece, to wave her sceptre over the subjugated world. There Virgil strung his lyre to sing Æneas' fame; and there Cicero shook the forum with thunders of his eloquence, and struck terror to the hearts of tyrants. Rome, then, was the mistress of the world, and on her walls waved the flags of all nations. The mighty Hannibal lifted his arm against her, but she crushed it; and Carthage, so long victorious, fell before her. Cæsar then lived; his path was conquest, and dreadful was the fate of that warrior that dared the vengeance of his arm. But where, now, is Cæsar? and where is Cicero? Alas, they have been murdered. And where, now, is mighty Rome? She has been thrown over the precipice of faction and lost in the whirlpool of anarchy. A barbarian torrent has overrun the blooming gardens of Italy; the Goth and the Vandal have prostrated her glory forever. The brilliant sun of science, that rose on the gardens of Greece, was destined to shine on the ruins of Rome, and then to go down in the night of time to arise in another hemisphere.

In the march of mind, France, plunging into the vortex of a bloody revolution, arrests the attention. Napoleon rose, like a giant from his slumber, and seated himself on the throne of the Bourbons. He pointed the thunder of his artillery at Italy, and she fell before him. He leveled his lightning at Spain, and she trembled. He sounded the knell of vengeance on the plains of Austerlitz, and all Europe was at his feet. He was greater than Cæsar; he was greater than Alexander. But where, now, is the French Emperor? Where, now, is Napoleon Bonaparte? He has fallen from the throne of the Czars, on which he seated himself in Moscow. The tremendous military drama has closed, and the great tragedian has left the stage forever. His race was short, but it was brilliant—like the bright meteor that flames along the horizon for a moment, then disappears. The Lion of England triumphed over the fallen Tiger of Corsica, but his fame is immortal.

The march of mind is now advancing on the shores of America. On the ruins of an Indian empire a great republic has arisen to illuminate the world. But where are the Aborigines of the western world? A pilgrim bark, deeply freighted from the east, came darkening on their shores. They yielded not their empire tamely, but they could not stand against the sons of light. With slow and solitary steps they took up their mournful march to the West, and yielded, with a broken heart, their native hills to another race. Before the victorious march of mind they have been driven from their native haunts to the margin of the great Pacific.

The great flood of time will roll on until the Aborigines are swept from the face of the earth forever. 'Ere long not one lone trace of them will remain, save the mausoleum of the warrior and the page on which his exploits are recorded. The last child of the forest will soon climb his native mountain to view the setting sun of Indian glory. And there shall he bow his knee, the last time, to the sun as he sinks behind his lonely cottage, and worship the Great Spirit of the waters and the genius of storm and darkness.

Where the council fires blazed, the tall temple, dedicated to God, now glitters in the setting sun; and the river, once unrippled but by the Indian canoe, is now white with the sails of commerce. The plowshare hath passed over the bones of the Red Man's ancestors, and the golden harvest waves over their tombs. The march of mind hath been to them the march to the grave. When ages shall have rolled away, and some youth shall ask his aged sire where the wigwam stood, he shall point to some flourishing city on the banks of the stream where once the Indian hunter bathed and viewed his manly limbs.

By wisdom, industry and valor, the Republic of the United States has arisen to stand against the world. The forest has fallen before her hardy sons, the yelling savage has been tamed, and the lion of England driven from her shores. Her government is superior to any in the world, and her country suffers not in comparison with any on the globe. The gardens of America are richly diversified with hills and dales, mountains and valleys, where Spring walks to strew the earth with flowers, romantic and beautifully sublime. Here are beautiful rivers, smoothly gliding through green meadows or pastoral elegance, where the shepherd hums to his fair one the song of liberty. Here, sparkling fountains roll down the flowery mountain side, and spread a thousand rainbows to the setting sun. Here, the roar of the headlong cataract is heard dashing its foaming billows down the rocks, like the crash of clouds, and stunning the ear with its clamors more tremendous than the roar of whirlwinds and storm.

It was in these scenes of poetry and romance that the Indian hunter once stood and gazed at his image. It was in these scenes that he heard the Great Spirit in the tempest and saw him in the clouds. It was on the banks of the lonely stream that he bowed down in adoration before the sinking sun. Alas! it was here that he read his doom in the evening skies, and dropped a tear upon his country's tomb. But the council fire has been extinguished, and the war-dance no longer echoes along the hills. In those beautiful scenes of poetry the Indian lover no longer bows down and wooes his dusky mate. They have retired before the march of mind, as the shades of night before the brilliant luminary of day.

Liberty has walked forth in her sky-blue cap to charm mankind, and the rays of science and philosophy are shed abroad in the land. The day is rapidly approaching when the glory and grandeur of Greece will be revived in the western world; when America, thrice happy America, shall be denominated the land of science and of song. The idea is irresistable that this land will yet be illuminated by a lamp of learning not inferior to those which shone on Greece and Rome. Another Homer may arise in the West, to sing the fame of his country and immortalize himself, and our history may, ere long, be as romantic as that of Greece and Rome.

There is a tide in human affairs, and there is a tide of empire. It flows in rivers of prosperity until it is full, but when it ebbs it ebbs forever. It would seem to the contemplative mind as if there is a certain hight to which republics shall aspire and then be hurled into midnight darkness. The march of mind seems to attain a certain extent, and then return again to barbarism. The sun of science sets on one shore to rise in a happier clime. But, my country, ere thou shalt lay prostrate beneath the foot of tyranny and ignorance, this hand shall have mouldered into dust, and these eyes, which have seen thy glory, shall have closed forever! The warlike sons of Indian glory sleep in their country's tomb, but that fate is not decreed to those who now tread where the wigwam stood and the council-fire blazed. American glory has but just dawned.

## WILLIAM MORRIS—SOPHIA LEMONDE MORRIS.

William and Sophia Morris, mother's grandparents, were residents of Broad-Kiln-Hundred, Sussex County, Delaware. They had four children,—William, Elizabeth, Polly, and Bivans.

William married Susan Hevelow; Elizabeth married Luke

Lofland and became mother's mother: Polly married Johnson Riley, and Bivans married the widow of Robert Collins. We have no further information respecting William than his marriage. Polly and her husband lived in Primehock-Neck.

Bivans, until he was fifty years of age, lived on the home farm, where mother's grandfather lived and died. He then sold it and bought a farm one mile from Smyrna, where, so we are informed, he died in poor circumstances, having met with financial misfortune by going security for his son-in-law. Mother frequently spoke of her uncle Bivans, who was, undoubtedly, a favorite of hers.

The Morris family were old-fashioned Methodists, and, financially, very well off. Mother's grandfather Morris was a man of sturdy character, and of much influence among his neighbors. His wife's surname, before marriage, was Lemonde. She was a sister to Samuel Lemonde, Esq.

# DAVID GRAY'S PARENTS.

FRAZER GRAY—ELIZABETH LOCKWOOD GRAY.

Frazer Gray, father's father, and youngest child of William and Elizabeth Gray, was born in the State of New Jersey, July 26, 1761, and subsequently, with the rest of the family, removed to Sussex County, Delaware. His boyhood days were passed on the farm. At the age of eighteen he joined the Revolutionary army for six months, as a substitute for his brother-in-law, William Robbins, in the then pending war for Independence.

At the expiration of this term he enlisted, for the war, in the Delaware Continentals, and served as one of the "Blue Hen's Chickens" until its close.

Although a private soldier, in his army life he was associated with one event of particular note in the history of that conflict, and one personal incident of more than ordinary interest. He was with his regiment on the Hudson at the time Major Andre was captured; was one of the soldiers that guarded him while in confinement, and stood near the gallows when the Major was hung. The following is his statement of the occurrence: "Andre was well and neatly dressed; was polite and courteous in his manners, never betraying the least emotion. When on the scaffold he made a beautiful speech, full of loyalty to his king, and denying any intention of enacting the role of a spy. He claimed that, under the circumstances, he ought not to be hung; but, if death was inevitable, a soldier's death by shooting should be ordered. As this his last appeal met with no response, he turned to the officer near him, and, with a smile on his face, signified his readiness to die in any way for his king and country."

Frazer Gray knew Washington, and had conversed with him. The following incident, in this connection, is related by him:

"A few of the 'Blue Hen's Chickens,' myself among the number, had leave to go out of the lines, chestnutting, on Sunday. While so engaged, Washington and his orderly rode near us, and the General called me to him. 'What are you doing here?' he said. 'Gathering some nuts, sir, by permission,' I replied. The General answered, 'It is right, then; but remember, green chestnuts are very unwholesome; be careful not to eat too many of them, for we can not spare any Delaware men,' and, with a regular military salute, he rode away."

At the termination of the war, he returned with his disbanded comrades to Delaware. On the 2d of March, 1785, he married his first wife, Mary Hevelow, of Broad-Kiln Hundred, Sussex County, Delaware. From this union there were five children—James, William, Nancy, John, and Elizabeth. All these lived to mature age and raised families, except James. William married Mary Tatman, Nancy married Philip Wingate, John married Mary Ponder, and Elizabeth married James Morris, first, and, after his death, John Long—all highly respectable connections. James never married, but his history deserves special mention. James was a young man of no ordinary promise. He went to sea when fourteen years old, learned to be an expert seaman, and at the age of twenty-one had gained the confidence of ship-owners to such an extent that he was given command of a vessel. He was very successful in accumulating money, and became the owner, or part owner, of two vessels—the schooner "William and Mary," and a sloop, the "Ann Maria." But before he reached the age of thirty-five years he became intemperate, sold his vessels, and migrated to Ohio, where he engaged in the fur trade, marketing his furs at New Orleans. While engaged in this traffic, about the year 1820, his family were attracted by a newspaper account of the murder of one James Gray, a passenger on a flat-bottomed boat, destined for New Orleans, owned by Edward and Howard Stone, and containing a cargo of slaves. The crew consisted of Edward and Howard Stone, and a white man named Cobb to assist in handling the boat, James Gray being a passenger. On a certain night, as the boat lay moored along the Kentucky shore, the slaves got loose and murdered the four white men. Nothing was ever heard of James afterward, and his identity as our uncle is not doubted.

In January, 1795, Mary Hevelow Gray, the mother of this family, died. December 19, 1796, Frazer Gray married his second wife, Elizabeth Lockwood, fourth child and second daughter of Samuel Lockwood, of Dagsborough Hundred, Sussex County, Delaware, born January 27, 1771. From this union there were also born five children—Rachel, David, Samuel, George, and Mary. Rachel died in childhood, December 11, 1806, aged nine years. David married Naomi Lofland, Samuel never married, George married Jane Barr, and Mary married John Postle.

In 1839, Frazer and Elizabeth Gray, their son Samuel, and John Postle and his family, all followed George and David to Ohio, and settled in Marion County.

Frazer Gray was a man of sound body and good morals, a patriot, and though from a slave State, and a democrat, he was opposed to slavery, and had frequently been heard to say that that part of the Declaration of Independence which says, "All men are created equal and have certain inalienable rights, among which are life, liberty, and the pursuit of happiness," is a lie as long as slavery exists in the United States. He died without pain or lingering sickness, October 11, 1849, aged 88 years, 2 months and 16 days.

His wife, Elizabeth Lockwood Gray, survived him nearly four years. She died June 23, 1853, aged 82 years, 5 months, and 4 days.

George Gray was born in Sussex County, Delaware, May 18, 1806. He worked on a farm with his father until he was seventeen years of age, at which period he left home to learn the carpenter and joiner trade. He worked three or more years at this trade. February 13, 1827, he was married to Mary Jane, daughter of William and Mary Barr. After his marriage he worked two years in a ship-yard near his home in Delaware. May 20, 1829, he emigrated to Ohio with his brother David, the latter stopping at Zanesville, and George coming on to Marion County. Here he worked a while at his trade, as carpenters were much needed at the time. In 1835 the Legislature elected him Associate Judge of Marion County, in which capacity he served seven years. He was next elected Justice of the Peace of Montgomery Township, and in 1858 was appointed postmaster at Cochranton postoffice. In 1860 he was elected Probate Judge of Marion County, and was re-elected to the same office in 1863. He was once chosen Mayor of the city of Marion, but resigned the office soon afterward. Of the many offices of honor and trust which he held, the last was Justice of the Peace of Grand Township, where he lived. He died in Scott-Town December 29, 1880, having been an active man all his life, and much loved and respected by all who knew him.

Aunt Mary Jane Barr Gray, his wife, was born in Sussex, County, Delaware, October 29, 1809, and died in Scott-Town, Marion County, Ohio, March 28, 1869. She was a Christian and a member of the Methodist Episcopal Church. They had seven children—William Henry, David, James, John, Sarah, Amos, and Mary.

William Henry was never married. He was born in Sussex County, Delaware, January 31, 1828, and died December 1, 1854, near Kosauqua, Van Buren County, Iowa, where he was also buried. He and our brother, David Simpson, were babes in their mothers' arms, respectively sixteen months and four months old, when our father and Uncle George, with their families, emigrated to Ohio. The rest of their children were born in Marion County, Ohio. James and Sarah never married; David married Lucinda M. Van Houton; John married Abinda Riley; Amos married Elizabeth Guthrie, and Mary married David Humphey. David died September 11, 1866, leaving a widow and two children.

Mary, fifth child of Frazer and Elizabeth Lockwood Gray, was born April 9, 1810, and married John Postle January 12, 1831. They had five children—Eliza Jane, George H., Hester Ann, Mary Elizabeth, and Rachel Ann.

Eliza Jane married Irvin Wheeler. She died April 9, 1867. She has two children living in Iowa, but we have not been able to get any further information respecting them. George H. married Ann Waples, and Hester Ann died in infancy. Mary Elizabeth was married twice—first to R. R. Cameron, and second to Henry Dulebohn. Rachel married J. A. Sappington.

Samuel Gray, son of Frazer and Elizabeth Lockwood Gray, was born in Sussex County, Delaware, August 1, 1803. He was a bachelor. He lived a very quiet and secluded life. His highest aim was to make money. He took good care, however, of his aged father and mother. They lived on his farm near Scott-Town until they died. He employed a girl—Mary Jones—to keep house for them; so they had no care whatever. After John Postle died he took care of his sister Mary also, and no husband could have been kinder to her or more thoughtful as to her wants than he. He was a good man. He died November 22, 1881, and was buried on Thanksgiving Day at Scott-Town. He had an exceedingly large funeral cortege. His estate was valued at $17,000, and, after paying all debts and providing tombstones for his father's, his mother's, and his own grave, his brother David, sister Mary and his brother George's heirs received three equal divisions of $5,200 each.

Frazer and Elizabeth Gray, John Postle, and Eliza Jane Postle Wheeler are buried in Union Cemetery, one and one-half miles east of Scott-Town, Marion County, Ohio; Uncle George, Aunt Jane, and Cousin David at Pleasant Hill Cemetery, three miles east, and Uncle Samuel at Scott-Town Cemetery, one mile south of Scott-Town.

Father and Aunt Mary Postle are the only children of Frazer and Elizabeth Lockwood Gray now living—May 1886.

# NAOMI GRAY'S PARENTS.

### Luke Lofland—Elizabeth Morris Lofland.

Luke Lofland, mother's father, was the eldest child of Lyttleton and Grace Lofland, and was born in Sussex County, Delaware, in 1770. He died in his native county, May 23, 1850. He was a farmer, and owned a family of slaves—Jesse and Lucy and their son David, who were manumitted in 1828. He was married twice. His first wife—mother's mother—was Elizabeth Morris. They had seven children—Morris, Naomi, Mary, Sophia, Luke, Elizabeth, and John. Morris married Jane Stokely, and died a few years afterward. They had one child, a daughter, named Elizabeth, who, after her father's death, removed with her mother to Chester, Pennsylvania, and there married. We have no further trace of her. Her mother is dead.

Naomi, our mother, married David Gray. They had eleven children—Mary, Elizabeth, William, David, Sarah, Samuel, John, Emily, Eleanor, Malinda, and Laura. Mary married Joseph Stubbs; Elizabeth married William Brewster first, and Dr. Gibson second; William perished by fire at Sandusky City, Ohio, February 26, 1851, at which time he was in his twenty-fifth year and unmarried; David married Louise Jackson first, and Eugenia Doolittle second; Sarah married Martin Luther Higgins; Samuel married Julia Druett; John married Jane Ramsey; Emily married John Ruthrauff; Malinda married C. C. Godman; Eleanor never married, and Laura died in infancy.

Mary, third child of Luke and Elizabeth Morris Lofland, married John Hevelow. They had eight children—Alfred, Jonathan, William, Sarah, James, Morris, Edward, and Anna. Of these, Sarah and Jane only are now living, and Sarah is the only one of the children that ever married. Her husband's name was Wallace Veazy. He has been dead nearly five years. Two of the children, William and Alfred, were cripples, the former from birth and the latter from about the time he was twenty years of age. Alfred's affliction was rheumatism. Previous to his becoming thus afflicted, he was a ship carpenter and sailor. He deserves special mention as a person of a very bright intellect, and as possessing happy conversational powers and much general information. He was a fine penman, and wrote most beautiful letters. He became deeply pious a number of years before his death, which occurred August 22, 1877. His physical condition has been thus described: He lost all use of his lower limbs from his hips down; he had no use of his arms nor of his hands excepting a use of his fingers sufficient to enable him to write; he could not feed himself; he had to be put to bed and taken up, dressed and set in his chair; in every way he was as helpless as an infant. His sister Sarah, now a widow, living in Ellendale, Sussex County, Delaware, was mainly his nurse. His mind, however, was sound and strong. His body seemed to be healthy, and he had a far more than ordinary ability for business. Physically helpless as he was, yet, with a hand to write, a mind to think, and a tongue with which to talk, he engaged with his sister and brother in the mercantile trade in Ellendale. He did the thinking, the planning, and the ordering of the goods, and the other members did the physical work. In this way they were enabled to lay by something for after life.

John Hevelow, the father of this family and son of Anthony and Rachel Hevelow, was born January 15, 1799, and died April 23, 1870. Aunt Mary Hevelow, the mother, was born April 15, 1803, and died November 1, 1870.

Sophia, fourth child of Luke and Elizabeth Morris Lofland, married John Rickards. They had two children, David and George. David lived to manhood and was married, but the name of his wife we are not able to give. He died when about twenty-five years of age. George died in youth. After the death of her husband Aunt Sophia made the house of our cousin, Alfred Hevelow, in Ellendale, her home. She died there July 4, 1883.

Elizabeth, sixth child of Luke and Elizabeth Morris Lofland, was married twice, first to Mr. Houghacre, and second to James Hevelow, having one child by her second husband.

Shortly after her second marriage the family moved to Cecil County, Maryland, where she and the child both died. We have no dates respecting the birth or death of our Aunt Elizabeth, but we know that she was about fifty years of age when she died.

Luke, second son and fifth child of Luke and Elizabeth Morris Lofland, died in early manhood, and his brother John, seventh child, died in youth.

Elizabeth Morris Lofland, mother's mother, died about 1815, at which time our mother was near sixteen years of age, and after which she went to live with her grandfather Morris.

Luke Lofland's second wife was Elizabeth Evans. They had one child, Lyttleton M., born in Sussex County, Delaware, September 5, 1820. He married Annie Truitt, August 9, 1842. They had six children—Elizabeth, Luke, Alfred, William, John, and David. Of these four are living—Luke, Alfred, John, and David. Elizabeth and William died when quite young. Luke Lofland's second wife lived only a few years after marriage, and when their son Lyttleton grew to manhood and was married his father made his home with him. In consequence of this when his father died, our uncle Lyttleton became heir to the small home farm in Cedar Creek Hundred, where he now lives and which has been in possession of the family for probably one hundred years or more.

1142964

REV. DAVID GRAY.

NAOMI GRAY.

# DAVID GRAY AND NAOMI GRAY.

David Gray, second child and eldest son of Frazer and Elizabeth Lockwood Gray, was born in Sussex County, Delaware, March 28, 1800. At the age of fourteen years he went to sea with his half-brother James, and continued the sailor's life for three years. When about seventeen years old he commenced the blacksmith trade with his half-brother John at Milton, Delaware. While here he was converted, and joined the Methodist Episcopal Church in February, 1819. After learning his trade he opened a shop at his father's home, about six miles from Milton, at a place called White's Cross-Roads. Here he met Naomi Lofland at the home of her grandfather, William Morris, in Broad-Kiln Hundred, and married her September 14, 1820.

Naomi Lofland, the second child and eldest daughter of Luke and Elizabeth Morris Lofland, was born in Sussex County, Delaware, September 9, 1799. She became a member of the church at the age of seventeen years. Our mother is reputed to have been very handsome at the time of her marriage, and the union a pure love affair. One thing is certain, for the life in which our father was destined to engage, for the care and economy it was necessary to have exercised over his household affairs, for all the privations and hardships that a Methodist minister's family must endure and provide against, and for fidelity to the church and to himself, it was a most fortunate and holy marriage.

They began housekeeping January 1, 1821, at White's Cross-Roads, where father carried on blacksmithing. Here Mary Jane, their first child, was born August 25, 1821.

In the following year they removed to a little farm belonging to mother's father, Luke Lofland, in Cedar Creek Hundred. At this place father farmed a little and smithed a little, and nothing of particular note is connected with their life here. The farm spoken of was retained by Luke Lofland until his death, and is now owned and occupied by his son, Lyttleton M. Lofland, mother's half-brother; and we learn from him that the cinders thrown out there from father's forge, sixty-four years ago, are still to be seen.

The father-in-law wishing to occupy the place, they next removed, January 21, 1824, to a farm at Slaughter-Neck,* on which there was a forge and a large patronage of blacksmith work. Here Elizabeth was born, April 26, 1824, and William Morris, July 27, 1826.

In the beginning of the year 1827 they moved to Broad-Kiln-Neck. While here, father was licensed to exhort, and

---

*The origin of this name is interesting. In the early history of Delaware there lived near Lewes, or Lewistown, then called Hoarkill, a party of emigrants, of whom one, Nicholas Brabant, was the leader. His wife had been educated in all the accomplishments, as well as the solid acquirements, of that age. They had one daughter, and in due time Mrs. Brabant commenced her education, and the Indians, excited by curiosity, came to see her teach her child. But they soon became afraid of her, and declared her to be a witch, she having amused them by reading and writing. She wrote upon a piece of paper what the Indians, through an interpreter, told her, and bade them take it to her husband, who was in the woods, and he would know what they said. Upon his taking the paper and reading aloud their thoughts, they fell down, yelled, and declared her to be a witch.

A young chief, Wawtawhrond, after witnessing the same, could not hide his emotions, and he and his followers fell down in adoration before Brabant and his wife. By such means these two acquired an ascendancy over the Indians, who, believing them to be inspired with the power of the Great Spirit, feared to offend them. They did not, however, feel thus toward the rest of the party, for it was not long before one was murdered, and a threat made to kill the whole number, save Brabant and his family. The Indians being numerous, this threat would have been carried into execution, but for an ingenious subterfuge. A vessel from Amsterdam had stranded on the shore of the Delaware Bay, on board of which was a cannon, an eighteen-pounder, with a vast quantity of powder and shot. A man by the name of Lander managed to get the gun on shore, and when a large number of the Indians had assembled around it, he told them it was the Great Spirit, and would speak whenever they did anything wrong. It was not long before another of the party was murdered, but it could not be discovered who did the deed. The cannon was loaded and fired, to prove that they had done wrong. At the thundering sound, they yelled and fell down before it, owning that it must be the Great Spirit, for nothing human could speak so loud. Lander then charged the cannon with shot, and bade the Indians take hold of a rope attached to and in front of the gun, and that it would punish the guilty. The fatal match was then applied, a tremendous roar rolled along the shore and reverberated through the forest, while numbers fell bleeding and writhing in death agonies. By this means many were slaughtered, and so great was their superstitious terror that they feared to disobey the order to take hold of the rope, being assured that the Great Spirit would punish none but the guilty. Those whom Lander and the colonists dreaded most were placed near the cannon, that they might certainly be blown to atoms. Those who were at the further end of the rope and were not killed were pronounced good Indians, whom the Great Spirit loved. That part of Sussex County where the poor Indians were thus slaughtered is now called Slaughter-Neck, in memory of the event. This story is not fabulous, but a part of the unwritten history of Delaware.

David Simpson was born February 8, 1829, and named in honor of David Simpson, the author of a small book entitled, "Simpson's Plea for the Christian Religion."

May 20, 1829, in company with George Gray and family, they bid good-bye to relatives, friends, and their native State, and moved to Ohio. Father and family stopped at Zanesville, and uncle George and family located further west, in Marion County. After remaining in Zanesville a short time they moved to Dresden, where they lived about a year, but finding much malaria there, they removed to West Carlisle, Coshocton County, where Sarah Catharine was born, June 24, 1831. While living in West Carlisle, David Gray was licensed as a local preacher. The license is dated April 16, 1831, and signed Leroy Swormstedt, P. E.

In the year 1832 he bought a small home in East Union, and removed thither, going into partnership with John Buxton, at blacksmithing. Here Samuel Frazer was born, December 16, 1833.

In the fall of 1835, while still living at East Union, father was recommended to the Ohio Conference, which convened at Springfield, Ohio, as a proper person to be taken into the traveling connection, and also to be given Deacon's Orders. By vote of the Conference he was received. He was then ordained by Bishop Andrew* and appointed to Danville circuit.

As father's recommendation and his application to Conference for admission were both induced by his friends, we will give his own statement of the facts connected therewith:

"Rev. William B. Christie,† I think, is the person who first

---

* Bishop James Osgood Andrew, who ordained him, was a very prominent personage, and has an important history in his connection with the Methodist Episcopal Church. From Simpson' Cyclopædia of Methodism we quote the following: "Shortly previous to the meeting of the General Conference, in 1844, he married a southern lady, who was the owner of slaves. This fact produced great excitement, inasmuch as no Bishop of the Methodist church had ever before owned slaves, or been connected with slavery. The Committee on Episcopacy waited upon the Bishop, who informed them that he had married a wife who inherited slaves from her former husband; that he had secured them to her by a deed of trust; and that she could not emancipate them if she desired to. The embarrassment of the case was deeply felt by all parties, but after a protracted discussion, the General Conference, by a vote of 110 to 68, adopted the following: *Resolved*, That it is the sense of this General Conference that he desist from the exercise of his office so long as this impediment remains." This is what led to the separation of the Methodist Episcopal Church into the two divisions— Church North and Church South.

† When Rev. William B. Christie left the district in which East Union was situated, he went in the direction of Cincinnati. Our subsequent knowledge of him is that he became the pastor of a congregation there, which, after his death, built a church and called it Christie

became interested in my behalf, and had more to do with the matter than any other man. I was a local preacher, living in East Union, when Christie came to that district. He was in the habit of stopping at our house and he manifested much friendship for me and the family. At quarterly meetings and at camp-meetings he would frequently invite me to preach or to take some part in the services. He was one of the most able and talented ministers of his day; yet he was so social, plain, and simple in his manners that it was less embarrassing to me to preach before him than it was when in the presence of others who were much his inferiors. He presided at the Quarterly Conference that gave me my recommendation, and took it with him to the Annual Conference, as I did not go. In consequence of the numerous applications which he found there on his arrival and because of my large family, he deemed it not advisable to present it. It was Christie's last year on the district, but Adam Poe, being his successor, he requested him to have it brought up the next year, which was done."

Following is a copy of father's certificate as Deacon:

---

Chapel. He was a Kentuckian by birth, but was a member of the Ohio Conference when father joined it. His personal appearance was fine, and his manners cultured. The people heard him preach with great interest and admiration. He died in Cincinnati, March 26, 1842, and was buried in the old burying-ground in the rear of the Chapel named for him. His remains were afterward removed to the Wesleyan Cemetery, near Cumminsville, Cincinnati.

KNOW ALL MEN BY THESE PRESENTS,

THAT I, *James Osgood Andrew,* one of the Bishops of the Methodist Episcopal Church, in the United States of America, under the protection of ALMIGHTY GOD, and with a single eye to his glory, by the imposition of my hands and prayer, have this day set apart *David Gray* for the office of a DEACON, in the said Methodist Episcopal Church; a man who, in the judgment of the *Ohio Annual* Conference, is well qualified for that work; and he is hereby recommended to all whom it may concern, as a proper person to administer the ordinance of Baptism, Marriage, and the Burial of the Dead, in the absence of an Elder, and to feed the flock of Christ, so long as his spirit and practice are such as become the Gospel of Christ, and he continueth to hold fast the form of sound words, according to the established doctrines of the Gospel.

IN TESTIMONY WHEREOF, I have hereunto set my hand and seal, this *twenty-third* day of *August,* in the year of our Lord, one thousand eight hundred and *thirty-five.*

*Done at Springfield, Ohio.*

SEAL.

*James O. Andrew*

---

The following family memoirs are from our sister, Mary Jane Stubbs. They cover the period from 1821 to 1840:

"My very first recollections are of my Grandfather Lofland being at our house and leaning back in his chair, and I climbing into his lap. He was asking me whose girl I was, and I suppose I said his, for I remember of father saying, 'No, you are my girl.' I think I was then about two years old, and the only child. (This must have been while the family were living on grandfather's farm at Cedar Creek Hundred.) I remember distinctly when Elizabeth was born. I was then two years and nine months old. The midwife's name (they had no doctors in those days on such occasions) was Coffin—'Granny Coffin,' she was called. I can see her yet, with memory's eye, as she uncovered and showed me Elizabeth's black head, and said she was my sister. She was born in Sussex county, and in what they called Slaughter-Neck. I think it was not far from the Delaware Bay. While Elizabeth was still a baby we moved from Slaughter-Neck, a few, maybe five, miles, into what was called Broad-Kiln-Neck. I do not know much about the geography of the State, but judge from the names of these places that they were narrow strips of land, lying between creeks or streams of water, either inlets or outlets to the bay. Another item in connection with Elizabeth's babyhood and life at Slaughter-Neck I forgot to mention in its proper place. Mother was out making some garden, in the early spring, and tied Elizabeth in a little chair and sat her near a very small fire in an open fire-place, and left her in the care of myself and Uncle Lyttleton, her half brother, then a little boy. Somehow, I don't remember how, the baby fell over into the fire and burned her head. Mother said I ran out and cried, 'My God, the child is in the fire!' While the burn was being dressed my grandfather Lofland looked at me and said reproachfully, 'Why did you let your little sister get burned?' I can yet remember how keenly I felt the blame, and the injustice, also, of the implication. I think, now, grandfather said it just to plague me, but I thought then it was all earnest."

Referring to this incident it is interesting to note that Lyttleton Lofland, mother's half brother, mentioned as having been left with sister Mary to watch the baby, was born in 1820, and was at that time near four years of age, and Mary, born in 1821, was about three. They have never seen each other since the family left Delaware, but in a letter from Lyttleton, who is still living, dated January 23, 1886, he says, " I remember your sister Mary; she was a pretty child—and Elizabeth and William. They visited father's house a few days before going west."

Our sister Mary continues: " We lived in Broad-Kiln-Neck until father and mother decided to move west. I was eight years old in August, after we arrived in Ohio in June. I can remember hearing father portraying to mother the advantages their children would have in this 'new country.' There would be no slavery influence there and their children would have a chance there to rise, etc. These were some of the arguments used to gain mother's consent to leave Delaware.

"Of course I was too young then to comprehend what this all meant; but O, how often I thought of it during the Rebellion, and thanked God that he put it into our father's mind to bring us away from under the influence of such an iniquitous institution!

"It was a great trial for mother to leave all her friends, relatives, and early associations, and bid farewell to them, never expecting to see them again in this world, and many of whom she never did see afterward, although she once revisited her native place. But, while this visit was a great satisfaction to her, it was one of those pleasures that is largely mingled with sadness. To revisit places familiar to her in her youthful days, and those of her early married life; the old home and most of those with whom she once took sweet counsel gone, and their places filled with strangers, could not help but recall sad memories. While contemplating these things, or events, we can realize that what was gain to us was not gotten without trial and sacrifice on the part of our father and mother.

"When I think of our traveling equipage, I wonder how we ever got through the journey. We had one wagon and two horses. There was Uncle George, Aunt Jane, and one child, Wm. Henry; father, mother, Aunt Sophia, and four children—ten of us in all. We brought nothing with us but our bedding and clothing. Walking was in order. The horses belonged to father and the wagon to Uncle George. Father walked by his horses, and Uncle George carried his gun on his shoulder. When we reached Zanesville we stopped, and Uncle George went on to Marion County.

"Father had one hundred dollars in money and his two horses when we got to Zanesville. We stayed there six weeks, and then moved to Dresden. There was a great deal of ague in and about Dresden, and we were all sick but mother. Father had an attack of bilious fever, and, getting homesick, resolved that as soon as he recovered and gained means enough he would go back to Delaware, but mother's pride came to our relief. She could not bear to return looking worse than when we left; and to be laughed at, too, as we would be, was more than she could endure; so she in turn persuaded father to remain in 'this new country,' at least until we could pick up and get into good shape and then go. By the time, however, we got to this point, father had become rid of his homesickness and did not wish to return. I forgot to say, in speaking of our journey from Delaware, that David Simpson was just four months old the day we crossed the Ohio River at Wheeling—the 8th day of June, 1829. Aunt Sophia became homesick and returned home in less than six weeks from the time we reached Zanesville. She went back by stage, lost her trunk with all her clothing, and never found it.

"I was twelve or thirteen years of age, can not remember which, when I joined the church, and fourteen the year father was admitted into the Conference and appointed to Danville Circuit. I was not a Conference claimant. The rule of the church then was that the minister should be allowed one hundred dollars for himself, one hundred dollars for his wife, and a certain amount for each child under fourteen years of age. I have always boasted that I never lived off the church."

As it will appear that father's salary as a preacher was sometimes less than this rule would make it, we will explain that the rule of the Conference referred to by our sister, was only disciplinary in character, and not binding on the churches, the minister being left to collect the amount it stipulated, if he could. We imagine it was only a hint of what was necessary for support—a kind of border line between privation and necessary comfort marked out by Conference. The rule was not closely followed by the churches.

"The first winter that father traveled Danville Circuit, we children, six of us, all had the measles. We had a time of it. The second year on this charge we moved into the country to Scank's Creek, one mile from Gambier, the seat of Kenyon College. That year I taught my first school. It was on the Mohican, four or five miles south of Danville, and was a very small school. I was paid twelve dollars and my board. I was then sixteen years of age. From Scank's Creek we moved to Dalton, Wayne County. The first winter we were in Dalton I taught a subscription school three months. The summer following I taught a district school in the country, a term of three months. In the fall of the same year, while father was at Conference, there came a pair of twin babies to our house, and then there was enough to do without teaching school.

"Father was reappointed to Dalton Circuit, and the following summer I taught another term of school in the same district in which I taught the summer before. In the fall of this year, 1839, we moved to Wooster. Here I taught a select school two terms of three months each. Sammy and John came to school to me, and were then spelling words of one syllable. I remember it was very difficult to get John to pronounce, and on one occasion, after several unsuccessful efforts, I said to him, 'Call it something, cow, pig; give it a name, anyhow.' So he commenced 'D-i-k-e' and called out 'Pide,' which was the name of our cow.

"I remember hearing father tell of the first time he attempted to talk from a text. He selected Hebrews, 4th chapter, 9th verse: 'There remaineth therefore a rest to the people of God.' This was in Delaware (in the old Smith's Chapel in Broad-Kiln-Neck), while he was yet an exhorter. Just as he had read the passage, a young lady came in and embarrassed him some, but he heard afterward that she said he had something else to do besides blacksmithing. Her name was Eliza Warren. She was the house-keeper for ex-Governor Painter, the man that father worked for. So strong was the confidence of the ex-Governor in our father, that he kept his shop in reserve for him for one year, having heard the report that he was coming back to Delaware. The last time father visited his mother she expressed a desire to hear him preach. She was then nearly blind. So an appointment was made, and he preached from the same text, at Aunt Mary's House in Marion County. It was the last time he saw his mother. In 1840 I was married. Since then many and varied have been the scenes through which I have passed. Cares, toils and anxieties, common to the human family, have been my portion. But I think I can plainly see the hand of the Lord in his dealings with me all along life's journey. Myself and Mr. Stubbs are now in the rank of elderly people. Sixty-six years have turned his hair and beard almost white, and sixty-four winters' frosts and storm have mixed and streaked my hair with grey. We are growing old. Our joint inheritance is ten children by birth and marriage, and sixteen grandchildren now living."

From 1827 to 1835, our father so naturally and so steadily gravitated toward the regular ministerial office that it seems, and it may be supposed, that his admission into the conference was the ultimate consummation of a purpose long contemplated by him, but such is not the fact.

It was to him something like Paul's definition of faith. As to his desire, it was "the substance of things hoped for," but as to his expectations, it was "the evidence of things not seen" much beforehand. He says "From the time I was converted, in 1819, I had a particular reverence and respect for the Christian ministry, and often felt that I would like to be a preacher of the Gospel, but had no anticipation of ever attaining to the position. I have always been a believer in the providences of God, and have endeavored to work along as the way seemed to open up. I never asked the church for an office, and when made a class-leader did not think of further advancement. And so it was from one step to another until I entered the ministry; then my prayer was for the Lord to direct me to that field of labor in which, in His hands, I could do the most good."

From the account of our father's early life and occupation as a smith, and because he did not personally solicit and seek his own promotion, it must not be inferred that he merely drifted, unfitted and unprepared, into this high and important office, and that his acceptance by the Conference was only a piece of good luck. On the contrary, while it was a result which he in no sense contrived, his fitness and qualifications were the arguments in his favor, and the natural circumstances which attracted the attention of members of the Conference and led to his recommendation for membership.

There are numerous facts and indications which go to show that, at the time he was taken into the traveling connection, he was fully up in line with the regular ministry of his day. He had begun in that way, which most certainly promises efficiency in any vocation in life, namely, at the foot round. Through a period of fifteen years he had been, successively, a class-leader, exhorter, and local preacher, all, in their nature, experimental and preparatory to the ministerial profession. It may also be observed that, while a local preacher, he was very frequently called to officiate in the pulpit and at funerals, the latter being, of all occasions, the most delicate and trying to the sermonizer, and the most difficult from which to escape criticism and dissatisfaction. Moreover, it was something especially creditable to our father to be received by the Conference, and to be given an appointment at that time and under the existing circumstances. Applications were numerous, and preachers with large families were not desired on account of the difficulty of securing them congregational support. So much was this recognized by the Conference that a rule of the same was then in force, pledging all unmarried preachers admitted, not to marry within four years from the time of their admission. Father's family then numbered eight members.

But that which tends to establish more definitely his fitness for the new position he assumed is the fact that after joining the Conference he was rapidly and successively appointed to the most important circuits, and within six years from his start was sent to the then principal charge in the Conference list. There is no single reason to be assigned for this marked advancement. He was not more learned or more eloquent than his compeers. It arose no doubt from a combination of qualities which he possessed, and which may be set down as requisite to pastoral success. Father was not merely a sermonizer. He was a careful, painstaking citizen, kind-hearted and obliging; also a good executive, methodical as well as pious, and had great ambition to succeed and to do good. If dissensions arose or existed among the membership he sought to heal them. If a brother went astray he expostulated with him kindly and plead with him to return. He was charitable and conservative, but not in the sense of yielding to wrong. Disciplinary measures were the last resort. He looked after the material as well as the spiritual welfare of the church, always encouraging a live faith and an open purse. When he entered the pulpit he preached the gospel of Christ, and not spiritually emaciated discourses on topics, only indirectly connected with the welfare of souls. The notion now extant that the preaching of years ago is not suited to our day, and that the present knowledge and enlightenment of the people make it necessary for spiritual food to be administered in a diluted form, quite different from the allopathic method of our fathers, we believe to be an erroneous one. It seems to support the idea that

4—History.

learning detracts from the truth of Christianity, and is faulty in its estimate of our educational superiority and appreciation, as compared with the people of forty or fifty years ago. It comes within our observation that, were the first proposition true, we are not yet far enough ahead of them to justify much change. However, while such notions are prevailing and the Church is making a great effort to furnish a highly educated ministry to conserve them, her spiritual strength appears to decline and congregational attendance to dwindle away. The situation is anomalous, but the fault seems to be in the direction of the Church. The success which the Rev. Sam Jones is achieving at this time evinces that the people are still susceptible to old time gospel preaching. Thousands are thronging to hear him and many more are being turned away; hundreds are being converted, and his sermons in the daily press are being read in almost every household in the land. On the other hand the Church, in her anxiety to keep up with what is termed the progress of the age, is sending forth scores of young preachers to occupy her pulpits who have never been soundly converted to Christianity, who have nothing but a theoretical belief in the divinity of the Savior, and no qualification for the sacred office they fill beyond their college acquirements. They preach topical sermons, give lectures to their congregations on literary subjects, and cater to the idea that the world needs something more intellectual than primitive religion and gospel sermons for spiritual food. Learning and eloquence are certainly strong elements of success in the pulpit, if wielded by a zealous Christian belief. Yet it does seem difficult, by the present hotbed method of turning out preachers from our theological schools, to find a combination of these qualifications. Since father was a boy nearly everything in a material sense has expanded. Our country has rapidly developed. Educational facilities have vastly improved. Science, manufactures, and art have made great progress, inventions have been numerous and wonderful, and the Church has extended her borders and built many beautiful edifices; but it cannot be truthfully claimed that there has been a commensurate moral and religious advancement. Sunday theatre, beer garden and show entertainments, base ball playing, and other bold and public desecrations of the Sabbath, the abandonment of many pious and wholesome restraints and requirements, imposed by the Christian fathers, and a general loosening of the reins in church government, with consequent results, conspicuously appear to dispute any notion of much religious progress. Whatever reasons may be given to clear the Church of responsibility for these evils, her facilities and organization are as able to check them now, if zealously used, as they were in an earlier day to grapple with the immoral tendencies then existing.

Father's boyhood education was limited, and was little calculated to fit him for the pulpit. However, it was such as the times, the neighborhood in which he lived, and the circumstances of the family afforded. His parents were poor. At that period the free common school system of our country was unknown. Then, to secure anything in the way of school training involved an expense that bore heavily upon all classes, but especially upon people in the ordinary walks of life. Indeed, at that time there were but few schools of any kind, and the best of them accessible only to the rich.

Contemplating the meager opportunities given the common people to obtain knowledge, when father was a youth, and comparing them with the school facilities of the present day, we may truly congratulate ourselves upon the great advantages we now possess. At the same time there exists a doubt as to our making an adequate use of them, and a certainty that we are not sufficiently grateful for them. It would now be interesting to know what the per cent. of illiteracy was in Delaware at that period, compared with the twelve per cent. record of Indiana * to-day.

Then, ignorance to a great extent was unavoidable, whereas now, not to be able to read and write ought to be regarded almost a crime, and, considering our opportunities, this large per cent. of ignorance in our State at this time should be much less.

The saying that "Necessity is the mother of invention" is only another way of declaring that without assistance we make

---

* It is commonly supposed that this large per cent. of illiteracy among us is on account of the foreign population in our State, but it is an error; for, deducting the foreign element, it increases to seventeen per cent., and when we consider that many are unwilling to admit their ignorance when the enumerations are taken, we may safely conclude that it is really greater.

great effort and become self-reliant. The question thus arises, is there not too much tendency to make matters go easy at the present day, to effect the highest mental and physical advancement? The labor-saving disposition of the age has not confined itself to the invention of machines to avoid manual toil, but has become desirous for the discovery and employment of methods for the easy acquirement of knowledge.

Will it eventually triumph and succeed in subverting nature's law, "There is no excellence without great labor?" We think not, for however physically helpful labor-saving inventions may be, they can not relieve the mind nor improve the human senses. These derive their greatest powers by self activity and can not otherwise be improved upon for the efficient accomplishment of their heaven designed purposes.

From father we have the following account of his early educational advantages:

"I was started to school when seven years of age, in Sussex county, Delaware. Among the teachers in the neighborhood where I lived, and to whom I went to school, I recollect Uncle William Robbins, who married my father's sister Elizabeth, and for whom my father went as a substitute to the war. He was one of my first instructors, and a member of the Episcopal Church. Another was Windsor Rollins, quite an old gentleman; and another was Samuel Hurt, an uncle to my wife. He married her father's sister, Hannah Lofland. We had no female teachers in those days, and the men who taught were generally well advanced in years.

"I remember we carried our dinners to school in little baskets, and at noontime were required to place them on our desks and all stand up while the school-master asked a blessing. For reading books we used the Old and the New Testament. There were two classes. The first, or higher class, read from the Bible, and the second, or lower class, read from the New Testament. We stood up before the teacher and read a verse turn about. We had an arithmetic, but I do not recollect the name of the author. Next we had Dilworth's Spelling-Book, in which there were about six pages of grammar. The book for beginners was a primer with the alphabet in large letters on the first page, and in small letters on the second. After the alphabet there followed words of two letters, then three, then four and words of one syllable, next words of two syllables, and so on. There were no free schools then. Those we had were all formed and maintained by subscription, a stipulated price being charged for each pupil. We never had more than three months of school in one year. Sometimes the term began in December, and at other times not until January. These were all the school advantages I had before I went to sea at the age of fourteen. After my sea-faring life I commenced blacksmithing in the fall of 1817, and found an opportunity to attend a high school at Milton for a short time."

The "high school" referred to by father was not what we term a high school at the present day, but was, probably, a select school, in which the higher branches were taught by a person of greater knowledge and acquirements than the ordinary school teachers of that time. Father further says:

"While these were all the opportunities I had of going to school, I did not fail to study various books, especially after I was converted. I gave much attention to religious history. At the time I became a convert to Christianity I do not think there existed a theological school in America under the patronage of the Methodist Episcopal Church.

"The Methodist preachers then received their books of study from England. Among those deemed essential were Clark's Commentary upon the Bible, complete, Benson's Commentary, Watson's Biblical Dictionary, in which the persons and places mentioned in the Scriptures were each historically sketched, Watson's Theological Institutes, and above all, King James' translation of the good old Bible. Dr. Adam Clark, the author of the Commentary, was one of the most, if not the most, popular of the Bible scholars of his day. He was the reputed master of thirty-two languages. Dr. Benson was also a very popular English author, and Richard Watson, the most orthodox theologian then known. From these I derived my literary education for the pulpit, but my spiritual qualification, which I deem most essential of all, I received from the Holy Spirit. After the time at which I entered the ministry I of course had access to later and more numerous authors." An important part of father's preparation for the ministry has not been sufficiently dwelt upon in the preceding statements. It began immediately after his conversion, and was before he had any thought of becoming a preacher of the Gospel. Father esteemed Christianity a great blessing, and, consistently with what we have often heard related as the experience of persons truly converted, was anxious that others should be made to know and enjoy the comfort and peace which it gave him. This natural desire of the new convert is expressed in the lines of the old hymn that used to be sung at Methodist revivals:

> "Then will I tell to sinners 'round,
> What a dear Savior I have found."

From the moment of his conversion he had a desire to do something in the work of the church. He was unwilling to be an idler in the vineyard of the Lord. This spirit and zeal soon caused him to be made a class-leader, then an exhorter, and then a local preacher. These were all promotions in recognition of the study and effort he made to be useful, and to fill these positions acceptably. His language in this connection is: " I was diligent in my studies, and in reading all the good books which were accessible to me, and which were calculated to qualify me for my work." Thus it was that his ultimate admission into the Conference was the consequent result, and not the motive of his early labors. Thus it was, too, that he was voluntarily recommended to the Conference, and at the time of his acceptance, fully prepared for the work given him to do.

We have called attention to father's meager boyhood opportunities, not only as a matter of family history, but also to show the amount of study which afterward must have been necessary to overcome his disadvantages, and to depict the force of character he must have possessed in achieving success.

Referring to the time he was a local preacher, and when, it is said, he had his appointments as regular as the stationed preachers, our sister Mary writes:

" When I look at the opportunities, advantages, and privileges of education that ministers have in this day, and compare them with father's, when he had no library besides his Bible, Wesley's sermons, and a few other books, no study but the woods and the blacksmith shop, I just think he is quite a wonderful man.

" Poor at the start, how he managed to raise his family, and raise them as well as he did, and to do as much good as he has, seems to me quite marvelous. Mother was an excellent economist, and one strong auxiliary that he had. Every now and then I meet somebody that claims father as the person instrumental in doing him great good.

"An old gentleman called to see me a few days ago. He formerly lived in Orange, when it was a part of Ashland Circuit, but now lives in Missouri, and has daughters in Ashland that he was visiting. He said father was the man that 'threw the net over him,' and he knew no one he would rather see than Brother Gray."

But it is not a mere inference in father's history that he had to study hard to acquire fitness for his ministerial office, and thus make up for his early educational deficiencies, nor is it only a supposition that he possessed a will and tenacity of purpose which tends to success. We may derive a strong idea of his studious diligence, method, and resolute disposition from the following fact related by himself: "I read the Bible as a Christian duty, but not systematically, from 1819 until I joined the Conference, which covers a period of sixteen years. When I entered the regular ministry, in 1835, I commenced reading it by course, making it a rule to read the Old Testament through once every year, and the New Testament through twice every year, besides my other readings. This I continued until 1882, when I left off reading the Old Testament. During the last three years I have read the New Testament through twenty one times. I have thus read the Old and the New Testament through, respectively, forty-seven and one hundred and fifteen times."

Our mother was a woman of fine mental and physical organization, with keen perception and an excellent sense of propriety. She was highly loyal to her husband and studious of everything that would tend to lighten his cares, lessen his family expenses, and soften his labors. Indeed, we only repeat family utterances and express family convictions in saying that her thrift and support made it possible for father to continue in the ministry and meet expenses with the salaries he received.

The story of mother's girlhood we cannot furnish, by reason of her death before this history was contemplated, but we are in possession of information which throws some light upon it. Her school education, like father's, was such as the State of

Delaware generally afforded at that time, and has been described in our notes of his early life and opportunities. They did not live then, however, at a period when literary acquirements counted for as much as they do to-day, and to offset her poor school advantages, she received that rich domestic training which afterward became so valuable to father in his close financial circumstances, and which contributed so much to his support, that it actually enabled him to carry out successfully the great purpose of his life. The account of mother's home education furnishes also a portrayal of the general sentiment of that day, with regard to the fitting of boys and girls for the responsibilities which devolve upon them in after years. Father says: "Then the young man or the young woman who was the best practical worker was considered the most desirable match. Every family had its own machinery for the manufacture of cloth or goods for wearing apparel. The little spinning wheel, the large spinning wheel, the winding blades, the reel, the hand carding machines, the warping bars, and the hand-looms. At that time there was not a yard of broadcloth or calico manufactured in America, and therefore it was necessary for wives, mothers and daughters to card, spin, and weave.

Then a calico dress was the first-class dress for good society, and a silk dress was almost as rare as a comet. Your mother was an excellent spinner and weaver. She could make dresses for herself and children, and shirts, pants, and every-day coats for her husband. She was a first class cook, and made a neat and valuable housekeeper for her grandfather Morris in his last days, who gave us this advice: 'Marry for love and work for money.'"

"In the twenty-first year of my age we were married, and commenced housekeeping with no capital besides our ability to labor. For several years I pounded on the anvil and she banged the loom until we earned money enough to pay our way to Ohio." Speaking of her personal attractions, father says: "Her cheeks were rosy, her eyes were very bright, and she was estimated the handsomest girl in the whole community, not only by myself, but by disinterested parties. She never curled her hair, but wore it perfectly smooth." From this account we may safely conclude that our mother was not only good looking, but also, that although she banged the loom, she never banged her hair. Her associations were mostly with Christian people, and she belonged to a Methodist family; her mother, grandfather and grandmother Morris, and many of her uncles and aunts being Methodists. Yet mother was not a loud professing Christian, and during her whole career as the wife of a Gospel minister, she never displayed an ambition to be president of any of the missionary aid societies, the ladies' sewing circles, nor of any of the various other minor organizations of the church membership, to which ministers' wives are always expected to belong, and in which they are so frequently invited and solicited to take a leading part.

Her family cares would not have permitted it, without neglect of them, even had she possessed the taste and disposition to lead in such enterprises, and to be thus prominent. But it was also something of a matter of judgment, we think, that she had no such desire. The prominence thus assumed would have caused little else than an increase of her responsibilities, while it might also have afforded additional opportunities for the charge of officiousness, and for adverse criticism by persons naturally envious, and sufficiently so disposed without aggravation. We believe it to have been her thought that the purposes of these organizations are better served under the leadership of the wives of laymen, for she was never willing to take more than an active, but modest and unpretentious part in them. But mother was none the less a moral as well as a physical support to father for the reason that she was not aggressive in church work. The minister and his family are always under strict public surveillance. Their conduct is rigidly scrutinized, their dress and expenditures presumptuously, and often dictatorially, commented upon, and their fallibilities magnified and frequently made out to be matters of grave importance to the temporal and the eternal welfare of humanity. There are at least two visible reasons for this attitude of the public, including the church membership, toward the clergy and their families. The first is that the minister, by virtue of his high profession, should be a person of unexceptionable character, and that the nature of his office properly subjects him to open criticism. The second is that in every particular he is responsible for his family, and as their support is deemed—most unjustly—a gratuity and a public expense, therefore, the people are resolved into a committee of the whole on the general supervision of his affairs, private as well as public. The former of these positions is unobjectionable and proper. The latter is a tyranny of human nature, a trammeling of private right, a support of the idea that his usefulness is not material, and that his labors are not an equivalent for his pay. For the same reasons, the public are particularly and inconsistently sensitive as to the style and appearance of the minister's family. If his wife be good looking, well and good. She is not permitted to improve herself much by art. An attempt to be dressy or fashionable would at once incite unfavorable remark, and cause the people to think that her husband was getting too much salary. On the other hand, the whole family must appear well, regardless of their means, else the management is poor, and they are pronounced shiftless and undeserving. Straight indeed is the way and narrow the path which they have to travel.

But it is not our purpose now to write a homily on the wrongs endured by ministers and their families. Neither would we mar the history of our father and mother by any complaint of bad treatment from communities or church congregations, during any of the entire period of father's ministry. Much less would we misrepresent them by conveying the idea that these peculiarities of public sentiment are the strongest impressions left upon them in their old age, and an offset to the many kindnesses received, warm friendships formed, and experiences enjoyed in their long public career and connection with the good people of the church. While we think the habit of the public of scanning the preacher's domestic affairs, scrutinizing the expenditure of the poor pittance he receives, and of making all his interests public property, entirely unwarranted; and, while we think his services should impose upon the members of the church a legal as well as a moral obligation to pay him his salary, we have mentioned these facts only to illustrate our mother's moral support to father in steering the family clear of public criticism, in shielding him from domestic embarrassments, and in strengthening him, in his church relations, before the world.

This moral support of our mother will appear naturally, but indirectly, as we proceed in noting some of the general features of ministerial life, and prominent facts connected with father's and mother's family history after he joined the Conference.

The first Sunday in a new place is always an event of importance and anxiety to the minister and his wife, and to his children,—if they are old enough to comprehend the situation,—and a matter of great curiosity with the congregational public. The former are strongly desirous of making a good impression upon the people, while the latter are on the *qui vive* to learn what kind of a preacher they have obtained, to note the appearance of his family, and to opinionate on the probability of their being pleased with them. In this ordeal the pulpit effort generally decides as to the preacher, and the manner, dress, and appearance of the wife and children determine as to the family; and both opinions must be favorable to induce a bright anticipation of a good and pleasant year's work. Father's sermons must be judged by the open history of his life. He was undoubtedly criticised, as the best of preachers are, but it is not known to us, nor to any of his children, that his piety or earnestness was ever distrusted. Mother always bore the test successfully. The most queasy and querulous looked in vain at her and the children for a sign of sloth or a notion of extravagance, and she had no mannerism to which they could take exception. At home the scene was not changed. Her house was a picture of cleanliness and thrift. Father and mother would not live beyond their means, and he never left a circuit or station owing any one, whether his salary was paid him or not, and sometimes it was not. Whatever stipend he received, by watchfulness, industry, and frugality it always served to support the family. It may be further remarked, in connection with these facts, that father never entered the pulpit shabbily dressed; that the family were always respectably clothed, and generally had enough to eat. Sometimes the supply was a little scant, on other than the regular fast days, but we usually had plenty, considering that there was no waste. We remember that we then had a table etiquette of our own, which was, never to take more upon our plates than we would eat, and this habit became so fixed that it prevails with us to this day, in spite of *a la mode*. On week-days, on the street, and in attending school, our clothing was often patched, but mother's needle never permitted us to go ragged, nor suffered us to carry a flag of truce. The first week, on a new charge, was occupied in putting down carpets, stretching the bed-cords, filling the bed-ticks with fresh straw, and in arranging the furniture. The second week the children were started to school. This event brought the family to the next danger-line,—to the point where any favorable impressions previously made at their Sunday *debut* might be destroyed by a collision between the preacher's children and boys of the town; for the sons of strangers, on their first arrival, are nearly always tested by a jeering, or by what may be termed a mild species of hazing, by the older resident youth of the ordinary country town or village. But we were well disciplined by our parents as to the importance of being circumspect in our conduct, and knew well the effect which any misdemeanor, on our part, bore toward father in his ministerial position. This knowledge, and the fear of being punished at home, in most cases would bring us safely past the danger, and save father from unnecessary embarrassment at the beginning of his new work. Occasionally, however, we had a fight, and probably, in consequence, incurred censure, and caused the family some chagrin and discomfort.

Father was a strict disciplinarian, and in his family rules and regulations he was unvarying. We believe he was practically more rigid with his children than he was naturally inclined to be, or would have been had he not joined the Conference, and realized so deeply the responsibility of his office, and the necessity of family circumspection. We believe this to be true, because he always prefaced his chastisements with the statement that it was no pleasure to him to punish us, but that he did so to make better children of us, and to make us remember our wrong-doing and not repeat it. He evidently believed with Paul: "Now, no chastening, for the present, seemeth to be joyous, but grievous; nevertheless, afterward it yieldeth the peaceable fruit of righteousness unto them which are exercised thereby." When the misconduct was bold and open he would tell us how chagrined he felt to have the public pointing at his children as a stumbling block to the Church and a detriment to his usefulness. Both mother and father were keenly sensitive to public or private criticism, and guarded their reputations with the utmost vigilance. So anxious was father to be just, and to show the people that he did not uphold his boys in anything wrong, that we think he sometimes leaned too far the other way, and did his own children injustice. His punishments, a good deal like his sermons, were always divided into three parts, namely: First, the exordium before whipping; second, the main subject—that is, the trouncing; and third, the peroration or winding up talk, in which we were advised, enjoined, and abjured to try to do better in the future. If the children were sick, father was very anxious and attentive; while they were in good health, he was indulgent to them in regard to their plays and innocent pleasures, provided these pastimes did not interfere with their daily chores or duties. These facts, with many others that might be mentioned, show that he was naturally kind-hearted, and at no time severe, except from a sense of duty, and then not to an extent beyond what he thought was necessary for the protection of his family and professional interests. We remember contemplating in those days that, should we live to get married and raise a family, we would make an improvement on our father's family discipline. That day has come, and what then seemed so far away is now a living present and an actual experience. With a maturer mind, and a better judgment, we would now hesitate to say that any of his children have equaled, much less improved upon, his methods. Naturally proud, sensitive, and combative, inclined to be persevering, and to do with all our might what we determine upon doing, it would be hard, indeed, to tell what the retrospect of our lives would show at this time, if we had had a more indulgent and less conscientious and discerning father. So far as is usually practicable with minor children, living in town and going to school, we were trained to habits of regularity, frugality, and physical industry. No outside help was ever employed, except, probably, in some instances, for washing and house-cleaning, when mother or our sisters were sick or overtasked. The family always rose early. The boys were called in the morning before 6 o'clock, and were required, first to build the fires, put on the tea-kettle and fill it with fresh water; second, to go to the stable and do all the chores connected with taking care of the horse and cow. In the meantime breakfast would be prepared.

From the breakfast table they were sent to the wood pile to cut and split enough wood to last during the day, and then, after the horse was watered, which was not done until he was through eating, they were ready for school. In the evening, similar duties were again performed, after which they could play or study until a reasonable bedtime. To aid in the support of the family, and to save the boys from too much idleness, father and mother always had a garden. In preparing the ground for the garden, we generally used the spade. It was the most laborious method, but it avoided an outside expense for ploughing, which was a material point, and afterward made it easier to lay off the walks and beds. The soil was enriched with manure from our own stable, saved for the purpose. As far as our skill could avail, we always had a tasteful and flourishing garden, because, under the watchful eyes of our parents, who were seemingly ever mindful of the parable, "A certain sower went forth to sow," no weeds were allowed to spring up and choke the good seed. But to us this agricultural employment was irksome and exceedingly repugnant. We do not remember that we were then disposed to be indolent, but think that our dislike for the garden work was because it was too hard for boys in school eight months out of the year and unhardened by regular toil. Our hands would be blistered by the shovel and the hoe, and the sun would almost make us faint. However, when the beans, and peas, and corn were ripe, our youthful appetite took revenge.

Father was a great lover of a fine and spirited horse—a trait more or less common to Methodist preachers—and the family all shared his pride and gratification in usually possessing the "beauty of the town." His particular interest in this direction manifests itself in the fact that, while he was urgent that his boys should perform all the other outdoor labor, he mostly took it upon himself to groom the horse. Some of the rougher of this work—as, for instance, when the horse would come home splashed with mud—he would assign to his boys, directing them to clean it off with a wisp of hay; but the customary daily currying he willingly took upon himself. We have reason to believe he did a good deal of this in an automatic way, his mind being actually engaged in the study of his sermons. This is confirmed by the fact that he would go to the stable at irregular hours, and brush and curry the horse when there was really no need of it. The idea, in such instances, we think, was to get entirely away from any disturbance, and to have an opportunity to be upon his feet, a condition specially conducive to thought. In traveling the circuits, father usually rode horseback, especially in the winter season and when the roads were bad. There were always certain preparations to be made before his departure for an appointment. The horse received an extra grooming, and, if not too soon after the regular time of feeding, or if the distance to go was quite long, he was given an additional feed of oats or corn. Next, father's boots were to be blacked and his leggins to be put in order. When he had shaved, and changed his clothes, and was about ready to start, he commonly gave us a little lecture as to our behavior while he was gone, and directions as to the care of matters in his absence. The horse was then brought round to the door and held until father was ready for departure. Mother usually accompanied him to the door to see him off, and, having an eye for the beautiful, was most always incited to some expression of admiration for the beautiful steed standing there with arched neck, distended nostrils, and spirited eye.

When at home father always had prayer twice a day—in the morning just before breakfast, and in the evening directly before going to bed. In conducting these services he usually read a chapter from the Bible or Testament, and after singing a verse or two of some appropriate hymn, in which the family would join, he would follow with prayer. Sometimes the exercises would be varied by the family reading from the Scriptures a verse about, and often the singing would be omitted. The reading was once in a great while dispensed with on account of some pressing necessity, but the prayers never. The following will be recognized as one of the familiar hymns of the morning family service:

> "Lord, in the morning thou shalt hear
> My voice ascending high;
> To thee will I direct my prayer,
> To thee lift up mine eye."

The evening services also consisted of reading, singing, and prayer, with some variation. But the most sacred things are ofttimes marred by the ludicrous, and there was an incident, we recollect, which ever and anon occurred at these devotions, that was calculated to disturb the solemnity of our thoughts, and always afforded amusement to the family. Father read very much by course and had certain hours for study, and while thus engaged allowed nothing to interfere with, or turn him from his purpose. The children were never permitted to go to bed until after prayer, and in waiting for father to get through his reading, they would often go to sleep in the chairs and on the floor. Mother would frequently say, "Father, do have prayers and let the children go to bed," but it did not avail until he finished, and then all the children had to be waked before the services were begun. When he prayed it was required that all should kneel. In some cases one or more of the children would go to sleep again during prayer, and when the family rose they would be seen remaining there on their knees. At this we always had to laugh, but none of the children had an advantage over the others, for in the course of time everyone of them was caught in the same predicament. At evening family prayers the following familiar hymn was frequently sung:

> "Thus far the Lord hath led me on,
> Thus far His power prolongs my days;
> And every evening shall make known
> Some fresh memorial of His grace.
>
> "Much of my time has run to waste,
> And I, perhaps, am near my home;
> But He forgives my follies past,
> And gives me strength for days to come.
>
> "I lay my body down to sleep,
> Peace is the pillow for my head;
> While well appointed angels keep
> Their watchful stations 'round my bed."

Father was ever strict and particular as to family observance of the Christian Sabbath. Saturday was always more or less occupied in getting ready for Sunday. We were not allowed to stroll the streets, roam the country or woods, indulge in any of the youthful week-day sports, nor to perform any unnecessary labor on the Lord's day. One requirement, illustrating the comprehensiveness of our parent's guidance and control in regard to family respect for the Sabbath, was that on every Saturday night all the boots and shoes worn by members of the family were collected together, by one of the boys, and cleaned and polished, ready for Sunday morning dress.

Our attendance at Sabbath-school, and at each of the other regular services of the church, was never excused except in case of sickness, or some other necessitous cause.

---

In father's day, when circuits were the rule and stations the exception, ministers' families commonly had more visitors, and were called upon to entertain more company than are those of the present time. This may not seem consistent with the smaller salaries paid the preacher then, but it is a natural sequence of circuit organization as contra to stations. A greater number of visitors is consequent to the greater number of congregations and to a comity which usually exists among the memberships of the different appointments of a charge. The quarterly and protracted meetings, being held in turn at the various places on the circuit, produce, at such time, an interchange of attendance and assistance among the members of the various localities. Thus, it used to be that when these meetings were held in the chief town of the circuit, where father lived, his house was more or less a center of visitation. The people from neighboring parts of the circuit attending the services would make it an additional point to call upon the family, even if they did not stay for repast. The Elder, too, and other ministers who were frequently present to assist in conducting these meetings, customarily made father's house their headquarters. It was not an unusual thing, under such circumstances, to have in our stable, at one time, three or four horses belonging to the preachers. The children, especially the boys of the family, enjoyed these "big meeting" occasions, because they distracted father's attention from themselves and gave them a better opportunity than common to have "a time." We would ride the horses out morning and evening for exercise, and sometimes try their speed; but we would never tell the preachers afterward which one had the best horse.

Another matter that made these occasions welcome to the children, both boys and girls, was the better table fare always provided when we had company, and as long as the meetings

5—HISTORY.

lasted. Mother never failed to have a supply of honey, jellies, preserves, and other delicacies in reserve for such times, and these, with the pies and cakes and extra cooking which accompanied them, were always joyously anticipated by the younger members of the family. We were, however, sometimes disappointed in our expectations of enjoying all these good things, for, after the guests had retired from the table, the delicacies would, not unfrequently, be removed. A strange *denouement*, this would seem, if to take place now at any of the family boards of those children, now men and women; and it may even be thought, by some of them, that it is a matter that should be forgotten. But we are willing to be true to history if at no greater risk than the discovery of those events that testify so truly to the virtues of our parents, who were prone to practice this necessary economy that they might properly honor and entertain their friends, and maintain a respectable standing in society. It may further be satisfactorily contemplated, and be reasonably supposed, that we are none the worse off at this time for not having then been the pampered youths of fortune, and indulged in all our childish notions and desires.

Quarterly meetings in those days always occupied both Saturday and Sunday, and were frequently continued longer in view of a revival and an increase of the church membership. The Presiding Elder appointed the time when, and the Quarterly Conference the place where, each quarterly meeting would be held. The services would begin Saturday forenoon at 11 o'clock, with preaching by the Elder, and the Quarterly Conference would take place in the afternoon at 2 o'clock.

As previously intimated, in alluding to the number of visitors the family received at such times, every society on the circuit would be well represented at the meeting. On Saturday evening a sermon, usually by the preacher in charge, followed with an exhortation by his colleague, or by one of the local preachers, would constitute the main part of the service. An effort at revival would then frequently be made and the meeting would hold until quite late, the congregation singing and praying in old-fashioned Methodist style. The first church service on Sunday morning was *love-feast. If it came in contact with

---

\* In the Methodist Churches in America, in early times, the love-feasts were strictly held. They were usually connected with Quarterly Meeting services, and conducted by the Prethe hour for Sunday-school, the latter was omitted. The next service was preaching again by the Elder, at 11 A. M., and following it, the communion. Class and prayer meetings were frequently improvised for afternoon exercises on Sunday, but the next regular service, after the forenoon exercises, was preaching at night, with exhortations and singing and prayer.

Father says: "In my time quarterly meetings were very important, both as revival efforts and for the temporal business of the church. There was always quite a little Conference attending them, made up of the Presiding Elder, the two circuit preachers, all the local preachers on the charge, together with visitors. Our great means and opportunities for revivals then were the quarterly meetings, and the camp-meetings held between June and September."

The old time love-feast is almost an institution of the past, and class-meetings, one of the most prominent, essential, and characteristic features of early Methodism, are now, in many places, obsolete, and in others only indifferently observed, although they are still embraced in the Methodist Church polity. We know of a number of Methodist congregations in which there is not a class leader appointed, and which have not had a class organization for years. In support of this state of affairs it is claimed that these social meetings were suited to an early day, when the church was weak, but that like the Red Men of the forest, they have given way before the advancing force of enlightenment and civilization. While this idea speaks either little for Wesleyan Methodism or much for enlightenment and civilization, it is generally regarded by the clergy and the eminently faithful as the subterfuge of a dead faith, and the certain evidence of a decline in the vigor and spirituality of the church in which it prevails.

Although the love-feast awakened much interest on account of its beautiful ceremony of fraternal love and devotion, as manifested in the passing of the bread and water, and, while it excited a natural curiosity in consequence of its closed doors,

---

siding Elder when present. The bread was divided into small squares, so it could be more conveniently passed around and received. When love-feasts were kept with closed doors, tickets were essential for admission; these varied from time to time. In their earliest form they had some picture or symbolical representation, but subsequently a single text of Scripture or verse of a hymn was plainly printed on them, and in all cases the names of the persons receiving were written upon them by the pastor. In recent years tickets are seldom used, and with the growth of the Church, love-feasts are no longer held as privately as formerly.—SIMPSON'S CYCLOPÆDIA OF METHODISM.

it can hardly be said that it was as demanding upon Christian fortitude as the open class-meeting. It appears to have been organized and maintained chiefly upon the opinion that its closed doors would encourage the timid ones to an acknowledgment of Christian belief, and strengthen them in their good resolutions. This notion never seemed to us to fully meet the Savior's requirement, " Whosoever, therefore, shall confess me before men him will I also confess before my Father which is in heaven." Neither does it seem to accord with what we have always been given to understand to be the feeling of the genuine convert, which is, that he is always happy, and constrained to tell of his newly-found peace and pardon. The class meeting and open congregational confessions do consist with this feeling, for " The Scripture sayeth, whosover believeth on Him shall not be ashamed."

At the present time there is no religious gathering which reminds us of the zeal, enthusiasm, and attendance of an old-fashioned Methodist quarterly meeting, unless it be the Yearly Meetings of the sect called Friends.

Our mother found special friends on every charge father served. She was plain and tidy, and had none of that pretentious air which intimates a superiority to others, an expectancy of deference from associates, and which society views with so much disfavor. She acquired close friendly relations with her neighbors and church members, generally, by virtue of her home manners and her strong common sense; while her domestic education, in many instances, was a recommendation to the friendship of good people, who thus recognized in her a kindred spirit.

Circuits were not only the rule in those days, but they were also larger in territory and more numerous in appointments than they are now. Outside of the chief town from which the circuit took its name, and where the preacher generally lived, the other appointments were usually in the country, or at very small villages with a country membership attached. Father always received pressing invitations to bring his wife with him to these outside appointments, and we believe he made it a point to do so to the extent of getting her acquainted with, or at least introduced to, all the members of his charge during his term of service. In turn the members were always invited to visit at the parsonage. In these visits mother and father frequently met people whose early history and experiences were consonant with their own, and in the presence of the spinning wheel and sometimes the loom, the old time scenes and recollections were rehearsed, and the foundation of a warm and lasting friendship formed. Women generally like to talk by themselves on commonplace subjects and about those affairs which are under their special management and control. In such interchanges of views and opinions, which often occurred during these visits, mother was always at home. She could talk intelligently and suggestively with the most skillful and economical of the housewives, and her intercourse with the country women on home subjects won their esteem and made her many friends among them. Moreover, her manner and conversation relieved their minds of any idea that she was haughty, vain, or conceited, a notion which country folk are so prone to have respecting town people, and which is an obstacle to cordial and friendly relations between them whenever it exists. The friendship of these people was evinced in a substantial way. Father and mother scarcely ever returned without bringing with them donations, more or less, of apples, potatoes, butter, molasses, pickles, dried fruit, honey, jellies, and so forth. Also, in repaying father's and mother's visits, these good country people hardly ever came empty handed, but generally brought with them more than they would naturally consume, indicating that they did not wish their friendly intercourse with the family to operate in a decrease of the preacher's larder. Furthermore, the family received many incidental visits from this class of parishioners. In coming to the principal town of the circuit to trade, they would frequently show their kindness by dropping in with a pair of chickens, a few dozen eggs, or other produce. It was these frequent and substantial additions to father's salary that always enabled the family to offer a generous repast to their many welcome visitors, and which should always be taken into consideration when estimating the compensation of ministers of his time.

During the whole period of father's connection with the Conference, his maximum salary was five hundred dollars in money, per year, and a parsonage to live in. His minimum salary was one hundred and ten dollars in money, per year, out of which he paid his house rent; and yet his travels embraced, with few exceptions, the best circuits. The highest fee he ever received for performing the marriage ceremony was one hundred dollars in money and a seventy-five dollar suit of clothes. The lowest was nothing, and the next to the lowest was that the contracting parties named their first child in honor of him.

We have often thought that in character and habits our parents were well adapted to their positions, and in mind and feeling especially suited to each other and to the nature of their life-struggles. They possessed several traits in common, with just enough difference between them to make their dispositions distinctive and to strengthen the combination. While father's judgment was good, mother's counsel was equally valuable. While he was slower in forming his conclusions, his second thought being frequently better than his first, she was quicker to perceive, and her primary opinions were generally corroborated by his more mature consideration. Neither was lacking in pride, but mother was the more spirited of the two.

While father was undemonstrative in his feelings, his emotional nature was strong and deep. Under trial, mother's feelings were tender and subdued. Both were economical and yet not stingy. The beggar was never turned wantonly from their door. Silver and gold they had none, but such as they had was given. Father was frugal from habit, and knew by necessity and experience the value of every penny. Mother had an aptitude for turning everything to the best and fullest account, and economy with her was an art. Father's temperament was even, his mind contemplative, and his reasoning logical. Mother was impulsive, her mind alert and her thoughts intuitive.

Many traits of their characters are distinctively impressed upon their children. As some of these traits were common to both, it is difficult to determine in which one of them they were most prominent. One peculiar and distinctive feature of mother's character was, that while little things annoyed and fretted her, in any and in all real trials she exhibited most wonderful fortitude. Although the breaking of a dish, a disarrangement of the furniture, or the tearing of a dress, owing to her love of order and her saving propensities, would be an aggravation to her, she was cool, patient, and heroic when it was necessary to be so. Father's most prominent and special characteristics were—a tenacity of purpose; an ambition to succeed; and, to do well whatever he attempted.

SARAH CATHARINE GRAY HIGGINS.

# THE FAMILY ITINERANCY.

## DANVILLE.

### Conference Year, 1836.

Danville circuit was what was called a three-weeks' circuit, requiring one preacher, without any assistant, to preach every day of the three weeks, except four, and twice on each Sabbath. The circuit embraced sixteen or eighteen appointments, all in the country except two, and it took the preacher three weeks to make the round of them. The preaching places were mostly country schoolhouses and private dwellings. There were no villages within the bounds of the circuit except Danville and Millwood. In the town of Danville, Knox County, the family lived in a house of only one room, which served as a study, parlor, sitting-room, bedroom, dining-room, and kitchen. Here John Emory was born on Sunday, May 15, 1836, just before the forenoon church service. He was named in honor of *John Emory, D. D. There seems to have been a grateful, if not a fitting remembrance of the honor which the Conference had bestowed upon our father in his naming this child, the first born after his regular engagement in the ministry, for one of the bishops of the church. On this circuit he received, the first year, a stated compensation of $110 in money, out of

---

\* John Emory was a very talented and highly educated bishop of the M. E. Church, elected to that office in 1832. He was killed by being thrown from his carriage, on Wednesday morning, December 16, 1835, near Baltimore, Md. His early death was a great loss to the church. Few ministers have equaled him in accuracy of scholarship, broad and comprehensive views, fertility of genius, and in administrative ability.—Simpson's Cyclopedia of Methodism.

which he paid $20 rent for the house, leaving $90 with which to clothe and feed the family. It is not to be supposed they could have lived, even scantily, on this meager salary; and yet we have heard people say, "Preachers preach for money!" But provisions were plentiful, the people were kind, and many donations of food were received. Also, our sister Mary taught school, and thus assisted in the family support. In those days another means resorted to by preachers to increase their yearly stipend was to buy a horse, thin in flesh but sound, and, after fattening him up with the parishioners' oats, to sell him at a profit. This may be regarded as the origin of the claim that Methodist preachers are great horse-jockeys. Although there was no junior, there were four local preachers on the circuit to assist father in his work. Their names were Absalom Waddle, Thomas Cursad, John Welker, and John Smith. Of the latter father says: "To show what Christianity can do for a man, I wish to speak of John Smith. He was an Englishman, and came, with a wife and several children, from Canada to Ohio. He was then a poor, dissipated shoemaker. At one time he lived in Wayne County, and had been known to come into Wooster on cold, frosty mornings, barefooted, and run foot races on the streets for liquor. I do not know where he was converted, but the change was powerful. Prior to his conversion he was very poor, and hardly earned bread enough for himself and family. Afterward all were well clothed and fed. He was a noisy, shouting man. The first time I met him was at a quarterly meeting at East Union, when I was only a local preacher. He came there to attend the meeting. He came forward to the altar to talk and pray with the penitents. He was a large, muscular man, and he got into a shout, and threw his arms around so wildly that we had to dodge our heads, like ducks in a hailstorm, to keep out of his way. I had seen and heard many shoutings, but that was the loudest and most powerful one I ever witnessed. I met him no more until I went to Danville Circuit. Here I found him living in a little home near the Scark's Creek meeting-house, working at his trade, and providing well for his family. On a calm night, on his way home from prayer meeting, he could be heard for miles singing and praising God. At a meeting, where they took up a collection for a poor widow, whose house and everything in it had been burned, he had no money to give, but, taking off a flannel 'wamus' which he had on, he folded it up, and, throwing it into the collector's hands, said, 'This will make one of the children a frock.' At another time, on a Saturday, he met a poor man who was barefooted, and he took off his own shoes and gave them to him. He had a neighbor, Philip Brown, and in the evening he went over to his house, and, after telling him what he had done, he asked Brown to lend him an old pair to wear until he could make himself new ones. Mr. Brown hunted up a very old pair and gave them to him. He put them on and went to church. During the evening he got up to tell his experience, and, turning to Philip Brown, he said: 'Brother Brown, I am very glad you lent me your shoes;' and every one looked down at his feet and saw the awfully old and ragged shoes that he had on. John Smith, after his conversion, was a man diligent in his business, fervent in spirit, serving the Lord. The last I heard of him he was doing well for the Church, providing well for his family, and was well-to-do for this world.

Father's first year on Danville Circuit witnessed a strong increase in the church membership. When he was first sent to Danville charge it was then in the Ohio Conference, which, as previously stated, met at Springfield, Ohio, in the fall of 1835. It was in September. In May, 1836, the General Conference of the M. E. Church convened at Cincinnati, Ohio, and organized a new Conference called the Michigan Annual Conference, which embraced the whole State of Michigan and several counties of Northwestern Ohio, including Knox. By reason of this change, Danville Circuit, and father, too, were transferred to the new Conference before his first year on the charge had expired, under the appointment made by the Ohio Conference at Springfield in September, 1835.

In September, 1836, the Michigan Annual Conference held its first session at Mansfield, Ohio, Bishop Soule presiding, and father was returned to Danville Circuit. During the second year here, in order to be better accommodated with house room, the family moved from Danville to Scank's Creek, to a larger house in the country. The church congregation at this place was stronger than at Danville, and the salary this year was somewhat higher than it was the year before, but just what it was, is not now remembered. Danville Circuit was in the Wooster District, and Adam Poe was the Presiding Elder. During this year, also, father's work was marked by a steady growth of church membership.

In the fall of 1837, at the close of father's second year on Danville charge, the second session of the Michigan Conference sat at Detroit, Bishop Roberts presiding. Here an incident transpired, pertaining to father and his admission to Conference, which possesses much interest for us at this time, and we scarcely know which we enjoy most, the story, or the modest and generous spirit in which father tells it. We give it in his words:

"Like all young preachers coming into the Conference on trial, I had a course of study appointed me for the first two years. I do not remember the different branches of that course, but mainly, it was a study of the doctrines of the Bible. The Conference previously held at Mansfield had appointed a committee of five to conduct our examination on this course at the end of the two years. At Detroit, the two years being up, I, with others, went before that committee, not in open Conference, nor in the presence of the Bishop, but privately, for examination on the course. I think it was in this meeting the question was asked me, 'To what kingdom does man belong?' I answered 'To the Animal Kingdom,' and one of the committee snickered and laughed as though I had made a big mistake. I do not think this man said anything, except what his laughing implied, but all understood that he did not agree with me in my answer. Now do not think that this preacher who laughed was an ignorant man, for he was considered one of the smartest men in the Conference, and was appointed to the most important places. I shall not give his name, but he still lives, and since that time has had D. D. added to his name. But at that time, Animal Kingdom, Mineral Kingdom, and Vegetable Kingdom were very seldom talked of by Methodist ministers. The kingdoms they mostly talked of and thought about were the Kingdom of Light, the Kingdom of Darkness, the Kingdom of God, and the Human Heart. The word animal then was mainly applied to the lower animals, such as horses, cattle, sheep, and hogs; and it is not marvelous that this good brother, looking at it from that standpoint, was at first a little startled at my comparing man to a brute. Adam Poe was chairman of that committee, and after a few moments' conversation he decided I was right in my answer. At this Conference, on the 10th day of September, and after the examination referred to, I was ordained an Elder, and appointed by the Bishop to Dalton Circuit."

### CERTIFICATE.

## Know all Men by these Presents,

THAT I, *Robert R. Roberts*, one of the Bishops of the Methodist Episcopal Church, in the United States of America, under the protection of ALMIGHTY GOD, and with a single eye to his glory, by the imposition of my hands and prayer (being assisted by the Elders present) have this day set apart *David Gray* for the office of an ELDER in the said Methodist Episcopal Church, a man who, in the judgment of the *Michigan Annual* Conference, is well qualified for that work; and he is hereby recommended, to all whom it may concern, as a proper person to administer the sacraments and ordinances, and to feed the flock of Christ, so long as his spirit and practice are such as become the Gospel of Christ, and he continueth to hold fast the form of sound words, according to the established doctrines of the Gospel.

IN TESTIMONY WHEREOF, I have hereunto set my hand and seal, this *tenth* day of *September,* in the year of our Lord, one thousand eight hundred and *thirty-seven.*

*Done at Detroit, Mich.*

| SEAL. |

# DALTON.

### Conference Year—1838.

It was in accordance with a rule of the Conference, at that time, which did not allow its members to stay more than two years consecutively on one charge, that, in September, 1837, father was appointed to Dalton Circuit, within the boundaries of Wayne and Stark Counties. There the family found a comfortable parsonage in the town of Dalton. This circuit embraced the villages of Dalton, Greenville, Brookfield, Doylestown, Canal Fulton, and Mount Eaton, besides a number of country appointments. It was one of the largest and wealthiest four weeks' circuits in the Michigan Conference. It lay on each side, east and west, of the line dividing Wayne and Stark Counties, and extended from Mount Eaton on the south to Doylestown on the north. Father's appointment to this charge necessitated the moving of his family, by wagon, a distance of more than fifty miles. His note of this says: "We had no family carriage and but few household goods, but a large family of children, who sometimes walked, and sometimes rode in the wagon, during the journey, which occupied two days. I received this appointment, I think, through the recommendation of Adam Poe, my former Presiding Elder, he being personally acquainted with this circuit, and it being the one on which his father and mother lived."

Dalton Circuit was also in Wooster District, but this year John H. Power was Presiding Elder, and Jesse Warner was father's colleague. Besides these regular Conference ministers, the circuit contained four local preachers, the same number as on Danville Circuit. Of these, Father Wolfe was the senior; the next was a middle-aged man named Albertson, and the other two were younger men, whose names are not remembered.

Father's work at Dalton the first year was moderately successful, but there were no extensive revivals. During the first year there, sister Mary, to help support the family, taught school in both the winter and the summer, and, to reduce family expenses, it was arranged for brother William to live, during the winter, with Judge Henry, at Brookfield, and to go to school and do chores for his board. This left Elizabeth and Sarah to help mother in attending to the housework and in caring for the children, and David for chore-boy and general help to mother in father's absence. In the summer William hired to work on the farm of John Bowman. We relate these facts, not as matters of special interest, even in a family history, but of value in showing the turns which had to be made to keep father from sinking under the weight of his family responsibilities and necessities, and from being forced to abandon his chosen labors.

In September, 1838, the Conference convened at Tiffin, Ohio. At this session Bishop Waugh presided, and father was returned to Dalton with Charles B. Brandebury and Dr. Deming* as juniors. To explain why father had two assistants this year instead of one, it is only necessary to state that the same Conference which made these appointments had changed Dalton from a four to a six weeks' circuit, with three regular preachers instead of two. However, Dr. Deming took sick immediately after Conference adjourned, and died before reaching his ap-

---

*Dr. William N. Deming lived at Orange, an appointment of Ashland Circuit, afterward so well known to our family. He was a brother of Charles Deming, a merchant of Ashland, whose family were neighbors to us there. Before Dr. Deming's conversion he was skeptical, but while perusing "Bishop McIlvaine's Evidences of Christianity," he was brought under conviction. One evening, shortly afterward, while reading in the Bible, he suddenly rose from his chair and began walking the floor, excitedly exclaiming "It is true, it is true!" His wife asked, "What is true?" He replied, "The Bible, the Bible is true!" He continued for some time walking and praising God. The passage of scripture he was reading at the time light thus broke in upon him was the seventeenth verse of the last chapter of Revelations—"The Spirit and the bride say come, and let him that heareth say come, and let him that is athirst come, and whosoever will, let him take the water of life freely." How long after Dr. Deming's conversion it was until he was licensed to preach we are not informed, but he was appointed with father to his first charge on Dalton Circuit. He had reached as far as Wooster on his way to Dalton when he was taken sick, returned home, and, after a brief illness, died. His death was a severe stroke, not only to his family, but to the church, for it is said he was a man of much promise.

pointment. To remedy the effect of this unforeseen circumstance, it was arranged by Rev. John H. Power, the Presiding Elder, so that a south portion of the work was laid off into a new two-weeks' circuit. This was named the Mount Eaton Circuit, and for this part of the work a new preacher was supplied. Father and Rev. Brandebury took the regular charge. We can not relate the following incident connected with father at the close of his first Conference year at Dalton, without having our sympathies awakened, and without almost realizing how he felt under the circumstances. Already pressed down with the weight of a large family, he started for Conference, leaving our mother in a delicate situation, but after making all due preparations for her care and comfort, and for special watchfulness over her in his absence, he left, entertaining a hope that the "coming event" would not transpire until he returned. The remainder we will give in his words: "I got through my Conference business, and understanding that I would be reappointed to Dalton Circuit, I left for home before Conference was over. But while on the way I met a friend from Dalton, who informed me that my wife had been sick and was delivered of twins, and was doing well. This information impressed me deeply, for as much as I loved the ministry and gloried in preaching Christ to sinners, I felt that my large and growing family would compel me to go back to the anvil again to support them. But when I reached home and saw the friendship and interest manifested by my friends and neighbors, I was greatly relieved. Among the many kind and special friends the family had in Dalton and at other points on the circuit, I recall the English, McCully, and Duck families, the Moffits and the Wolcots. The Franks, who lived at Doylestown; the Hattans, at Greenville; and Judge Henry's family, of Brookfield. The twins were named Emily McCully and Eleanor Wolcot. Emily McCully was the wife of a merchant in Dalton, and Eleanor Wolcot was the wife of a lawyer there, both not only kind friends of the family, but good sisters in the church."

Father's second year at Dalton was one of great success in the history of the charge, there being revivals in all the towns in the circuit. While on this circuit, at Adam Poe's father's house near Greenville, father preached the funeral of Adam Poe's father, son of the Poe that killed Big-foot Indian, and the gun with which Big-foot was shot stood near him in the corner of the room.*

The salary allowance on Dalton Circuit was four hundred dollars a year, which, however, was not quite all paid.

---

* Adam Poe, who was the Presiding Elder during the first year father was on the Dalton Circuit, was a near descendant of the Poe family who were such great Indian fighters, and who figured so prominently in the defense of the pioneer settlements of Western Pennsylvania and Eastern Ohio, from the attacks of the savages. As a preacher he was not so argumentative as his successor, John H. Power; nevertheless he was strong in the pulpit, and probably of equal influence in the Conference. He was more social in private conversation, and consequently of greater influence in social life. He served several terms, as Presiding Elder, in the Michigan and North Ohio Conferences, and did more than any other preacher of his time toward starting the Wesleyan University at Delaware. He served a term in the book-agency at Cincinnati, and during his ministerial life was a delegate several times to the General Conference. We remember visiting him, with father, at his home in Cincinnati, a year or so before his death. We were invited to dine with him. During the time we were there he related a controversy which he had witnessed between an old Jew and his wife on the street that day. It demonstrated very powerfully his ability to amuse and entertain, and we there had personal experience of his strong social qualities. He died in Cincinnati, June 26, 1868.

## WOOSTER.

### Conference Year, 1840.

Father's labors on Dalton Circuit closed in September, 1839. At that time the fourth session of the Michigan Conference met at Ann Arbor, Michigan, Bishop Soule presiding. From this Conference, father was sent to Wooster Circuit, Wayne County. Cyrus Sawyer, an eminently pious, gifted, and popular young preacher, was appointed his colleague. This charge, being in the same county in which Dalton is located, did not occasion the family much inconvenience in moving from one place to the other. And while it was favorable in this particular, it was also a promotion, and was what might be termed an agreeable surprise to father, notwithstanding it entailed grave responsibilities upon him.

The closing hours of a Conference session, when the appointments are to be read, are of unusual interest to the members. Within such a time there are moments which bring with them much anxiety to the many hearts waiting in anxious suspense for a verdict which is portentous to their families and to their future ministerial labors. Especially is this so with those who know that by the rules of the Conference and by the expiration of their limit of time upon a circuit or charge, that a change is inevitable. Still more may it be regarded as a time of mental disquietude and heart flutterings with those younger members of the Conference, who naturally anticipate from the announcements some indication of the favor or disfavor with which their primary efforts in the ministry have been received.

It was the case in those days, and it may be so with the Conference of the present day, for aught we know to the contrary, that, as a rule, and except for some important cause, it was next to impossible for a preacher to obtain any intimation of his future appointment in advance of the regular announcement. One good reason for this was, that, at almost the last moment and after a list of the appointments had been made up, a necessity for a change would sometimes occur. It was seen, therefore, that it would lead to confusion, and, not unfrequently, to displeasure and disappointment, to disclose them beforehand, even though it may be truly said that Methodist ministers generally accept their appointments without complaint. Of course this rule, or adopted custom, did not tend to weaken the anxiety of the preachers to learn where they were to go, when the time arrived for the appointments to be made known. Consequently, when the Bishop rose to read them, a perfect stillness reigned; every eye was fixed upon him and every head bent forward to hear him.*

The scenes and the hour have been thus described in verse:

### READING THE APPOINTMENTS.

I was sitting in a wing slip, close beside the altar rail,
When the Bishop came in softly, with a face serene, but pale,
And a silence indescribably pathetic in its power,
Such as might have reigned in Heaven through that "space of half an hour,"
Rested on the whole assembly, as the Bishop rose and said:
"All the business being finished, the appointments will be read."

Not as one who handles lightly merchandise of little worth,
But as dealing with the richest, most important, things of earth.
In the fellowship of Jesus, with the failings of a man,
The good Bishop asked forbearance, he had done his best to plan,
For the glory of his Master, trusting Him to guide his pen
Without prejudice or favor; and the preachers cried, "Amen!"

"Troubled Waters"—"Nathan Peaceful"—how that saintly face grew red,
How the tears streamed through his fingers as he held his swimming head;
But his wife stooped down and whispered—What sweet message did she bear?
For he turned with face transfigured as upon some mount of prayer.
Swift as thought in highest action, sorrow passed and gladness came
At some wondrous strain of music breaking forth from Jesus' name.

"Grand Endeavor—Jonas Laggard"—blessed be the Lord, thought I,
They have put that brother Laggard where he has to work or die,
For the Church at Grand Endeavor, with its energy and prayer,
Will transform him to a hero or just drive him to despair.
If his trumpet lacks the vigor of the Gospel's charming sound,
They will start a big revival and forget that he's around.

---

*It seems that right here is a point in the ministerial life where Conference ministers might, protectively, exercise the plan of carrying in their minds small anticipations. Indeed, it would not be unwise for persons generally to exercise this precaution, for then they would never be found in a condition of mind to be much disappointed, and would always be prepared to enjoy, if it should come, something better than was naturally expected.

"Consecration—Jacob Faithful"—hand in hand the two will go
Through the years before them, bringing heavenly life to earth below.

"Greenland Corners—Peter Wholesoul"—but he lost his self-control,
Buttoned up his coat as if he felt a cold wind strike his soul,
Saw the dreary path before him, drew a deep breath, knit his brows,
Then concluded to be faithful to his ordination vows.

In the front pews sat the fathers, hair as white as driven snow—
As the Bishop read appointments they had filled long years ago;
Tender memories rushed upon them, life revived in heart and brain,
Till it seemed that they could travel their old circuits o'er again.

Then a mist came o'er my vision as the Bishop still read on,
And the veil that hides the future, for a moment was withdrawn;
For I saw the world's redeemer far above the Bishop stand,
On his head a crown of glory, and a long roll in his hand;
Round his throne a countless number of the ransomed listening, pressed—
He was stationing his preachers in the City of the Blest.

Some whose names were most familiar, known and reverenced by all,
Went down to the smaller mansions back against the city wall.
One who took the poorest churches, miles away from crowds and cars,
Went up to a throne of Splendor with a crown ablaze with stars.

How the angels sang to greet him! How the Master cried "Well done!"
While the preacher blushed and wondered where he had such glory won.
Some whose speech on earth was simple, with no arguments but tears,
Nothing novel in their sermons for fastidious, itching ears;
Coldly welcomed by the churches, counted burdensome by all,
Went up to the royal mansions, and were neighbors to St. Paul.

Soon the Master called a woman, only known here in the strife
By her quiet, gentle nature, though a faithful preacher's wife;
Praised and blessed her for the harvests she had garnered in the sky.
But she meekly turned and answered, "'Twas my husband, Lord, not I."
"Yes," the Master said, "his talents were as stars that glow and shine,
But thy faith gave them their virtue, and the glory, child, is thine."

Then a lame girl—I had known her—heard her name called with surprise,
There was trembling in her bosom, there was wonder in her eyes.
"I was nothing but a cripple; gleaned in no wide fields, thy king;
Only sat, a silent sufferer, 'neath the shadow of thy wing!"
"Thou hast been a mighty preacher, and the hearts of many stirred
To devotion by thy patience without uttering a word,"
Said the Master, and the maiden to his side with wonder pressed—
Christ was stationing his preachers in the City of the Blest;
And the harp strings of the angels linked their names to sweetest praise
Whom the world had passed unnoticed in the blindness of its ways.

—[Rev. Alfred J. Hough.

It was at such a time, and under its attendant circumstances, that father, while listening to the reading of the appointments by the bishop, heard his name announced for Wooster Circuit. He was greatly astonished. But, inasmuch as it was a compliment to him, and a strong commendation of his previous four years' work on Danville and Dalton circuits, we must suppose that he was none the less gratified. Father was not expecting this compliment on his past work, and was much surprised that one so young as he should be appointed to a charge attended by so many difficulties and responsibilities. Father found no relief from his surprise by contemplating the appointment as unstudied or accidental, for his presiding elder, Rev. J. H. Power, was fully acquainted with the condition of the church at Wooster, and had, after due deliberation, recommended him for the place. Describing the appointment at that time, father says, "Wooster was one of the oldest and most important charges in the Conference. There was a good parsonage there, but the church, a little old brick building, was ready to fall, and its front gable end was propped up with maple trees. Moreover, the spiritual condition of the membership was in a low state, owing to fierce debates among them over the questions of abolition and colonization. Rev. Power was a strong colonizationist, and had had a two days' discussion with an abolitionist there the year before my appointment, which discussion caused great excitement."

"The congregation had long been talking about building a new church, but this was a very unfavorable time to do so on account of the bad state of the bank currency. One might get a bank bill passable to-day and to-morrow it would not be worth half its value. During the time I was at Wooster there was a presidential election. It was the campaign of 1840, when William Henry Harrison was elected. This campaign produced great excitement, which made the time unfavorable to church building, and which naturally operated against the spiritual growth of the church membership. I was mostly aware of this state of things at Wooster before my appointment, and, learning this fact, you will not wonder that I trembled when the Bishop announced me for that charge. I knew, however, that the Presiding Elder was a man of ability and great influence in Wooster, and I had heard that my colleague was a pious and talented young man. The appointments were read about the middle of the afternoon of the day Conference adjourned. There was no way for us to get from Ann-Arbor to Detroit, on our way home, but by stage, and that would not leave until the following morning. We were, therefore, compelled to stay the remainder of the afternoon and over night in Ann Arbor. Brother Sawyer and myself met soon after the adjournment of Conference, and we took a walk to a neighboring wood, near the city, to talk over our plans and purposes for the coming year's work. I informed him of the state of things upon the charge which we were just about to enter. I told him there were two prime objects which, God being our helper, I desired to see accomplished. The first was a revival, the second the erection of a new church at Wooster. These two things I desired we should keep in daily remembrance. He most heartily agreed to my proposition. We then knelt down and prayed together for the accomplishment of these two purposes, and that our general labors might be crowned with success. He was to use his best endeavors to be in Wooster on the following Sabbath, my family's being at Dalton making it more convenient for me to be at Edinburgh and Fredericksburg the same day, and thus we began our year's labor. The next week I moved my family to Wooster. Brother Sawyer and myself agreed that we would lay the two matters pertaining to a revival and to the building of a new church before the local preachers, exhorters, class leaders and members, as far as possible, and ask them to unite with us in our efforts to attain these objects. And I have no doubt many of them heartily did so, for never in all my life have I seen answer to prayer more plainly given than in the results obtained. The growth of spirituality commenced very early in the year. It became manifest during the first meeting at Millbrook. The second quarterly meeting was held in Wooster about the holidays, and was protracted for several weeks. The little old church was crowded to its utmost capacity every evening during the continuance of the meeting. I do not now remember the number of conversions and accessions, but it was large. Later during the winter, at other points on the circuit, we had meetings which were marked by like results. Early in the spring we got out subscription papers and appointed officers and building committees to secure the erection of a new church. The old church was torn down, and services were, for a time, held in the court house. Thus the work continued until the close of the Conference year."*

---

*Speaking of the quarterly meetings and revivals on Wooster circuit during that year, brings to our mind a recent newspaper article, written by one William Graham, under the subject head "The Old-Time Quarterly Meeting." It is so corroborative of our recollections of the past, so full of truth and interest to those who have not forgotten those old-time religious scenes and events, and withal so appropriate to the work we have in hand, that, notwithstanding its length, we feel justified in reproducing it here. The writer says: "We live in an era of changes. Methodism has shared in these changes, generally for the better, but sometimes for the worse. Old Methodists are prone to recall the past, and compare things as they were with what they now are. They thank God for many improvements in their cherished church, but sigh for some old land-marks now lost. They hesitate to utter their convictions, lest they should be pronounced old fogies by this fast age, which imagines all change is progress. They have always been loyal to the church, and in conflicts many have kept her rules and not sought to mend them; and they deprecate the idea of the least appearance of disaffection, preferring to endure their grief in silence. They are not opposed to necessary changes, and rejoice in legitimate progress; but they are pained to see the heritage of the church wasted by mere novelties. Legitimate causes for change in the polity and methods of the church will arise from time to time, to which no one can reasonably object. When the times and surroundings of the church become so different as to render the old methods no longer efficient and successful, then a change is necessitated by the times; and Methodism has been successful in the past because it has had the wisdom and grace to adapt its methods to its changed surroundings. Then, when some necessary changes have been made, others have to be made in order to harmonize the system and preserve its organic unity. One change may necessitate another. We rejoice that Methodism can be changed: that it is no procrustean bed, insisting on changeless forms and traditions. Doctrines and principles do not change, but forms and methods may be changed without departing from fundamentals, and Methodism has always been sufficiently pliable for any proper adaptations, without losing its identity and essential characteristics. The intention of this paper, however, is to refer to the old-time quarterly meeting. It was a noted feature in Methodism, and a great public affair where it was held; but, alas, it is for the most part among the things of the past! It extended over at least two days, including a Sabbath. There was much preaching, exhortation and song, a love-feast, quarterly conference, the Lord's supper, and usually baptism, all in consecutive order. These services were under the direct supervision of the presiding elder, who was the master spirit, and whose presence was deemed as essential to the meeting as that of a bishop to an annual conference. The meeting could be held without him, but in that case one important element of power was wanting. The districts were so arranged, as to the number of appointments, that the presiding elder could attend all the quarterly meetings of the year, and personally oversee all the temporal and spiritual affairs of the church in detail. The bishops appointed to the office the ablest men in the conference, representative men of Methodism, of commanding ability and influence—marked men above the average of those occupying circuits and stations—and required them to report quarterly the state of the work to the bishop having charge, and confer with him in reference to any changes in the appointments or other special matters. Nothing was done in haste, but with due deliberation. When the business of the annual conference had been concluded and the appointments were read, the presiding elders had all been advised of the places they were to fill, and had the appointments for the first round on their districts already made out. And, after the conference had adjourned, each one of these pastors called his men together, had a cordial greeting, gave them the time of their first quarterly meeting, and the time and place of the district stewards' meeting, so that all things might be in order when he should visit them and their charges. On the charges, the quarterly meeting was announced several weeks in advance, and the notice was repeated afterward, so that the whole community was apprised of the coming event, for which great preparation was made, and from which great results were expected. The presiding elder made it a point to be present at the first service on Saturday morning, and, if necessary, he started one or two days before. The leading citizens and best minds of the community, outside of the church,

In May, 1840, subsequent to the meeting of the Michigan Annual Conference at Ann Arbor, and previous to the close of father's first year at Wooster, the General Conference again convened. At this session the territorial boundary of the Michigan Conference was changed, and made to include only the State of Michigan, and the northern counties of Ohio previously connected with it were formed into a new Conference, called the North Ohio Conference. This made the second time, during the first four years of father's regular work in the ministry, that he had been changed from one Annual Conference to another, by action of the General Conference, and in each instance it was done before the year for which he was appointed had closed. The North Ohio Conference, of which he was now a member, held its first session at Norwalk, Ohio. Bishop Hedding presided. The membership at Wooster sent a petition to this Conference for father's return to them, which was granted. Rev. J. H. Power's time, as Presiding Elder of the Wooster District, having expired, he was succeeded by Elmore Yocum, and Charles B. Brandebury was appointed junior preacher in place of Cyrus Sawyer. In consequence of these changes, father began his labors, the second year at

---

made it a point to be at the meeting and hear a representative man of the church, and they were not disappointed, but were often won to the church. All flocked to the meetings, making large and imposing congregations, and the effect was a lasting benefit to the church. The elder, realizing the importance of his position, preached with power and unction, presented the doctrines and set forth the polity of the church, sometimes controversially, and the people were made to understand Methodism, and usually to approve and accept it. The officers of the church were instructed in their several duties, and parts of the Discipline were read to enforce the advice. The pastor was personally advised concerning his work, and plans were arranged for aggressive movements. Meantime, devotional meetings were held at every opportunity. The revival spirit was fanned into a flame, and usually souls were converted before the elder left. A new inspiration was given to every department of church work. The meeting was regarded as a Godsend, and the presiding elder left for his next appointment with the benedictions of a grateful and a happy people. These were precious seasons to all—the presiding elder, pastor, and people—and they went forward in their work with renewed inspiration, enthusiasm, and hopefulness. There is inspiration even in the memories of those times and occasions. Now, since the marked changes, which have been made in the old-time quarterly meeting, were not necessitated, we may be allowed to ask, Are the new methods better than the old? and, if not, ought not the old plans be restored? If mistakes have been made in the administration, ought they be persisted in? Ought they not be corrected? It there are more old ministers and lay members than younger ones who deprecate these departures from the old paths, it is because the older have seen both methods work, and the younger have not. Our quarterly meetings nowadays have not only ceased to be occasions of great interest and importance to the church, but they are minified and have fallen into contempt. The presiding elder is cramped for the want of time, and can not give a solid service to any one of his numerous appointments, so that his influence for good is not felt. In short, our districts are too large in the number of their appointments to allow a presiding elder to render a satisfactory service. Twelve charges are about as many as one man can do justice to, and meet all the requirements of the Discipline.

Wooster, under different but, apparently, under little less embarrassing circumstances than he did the first. Then, the church, distracted and divided, cold and indifferent to its weak physical state, and spiritually enervated, was altogether in a very cheerless and disheartening condition. But during the year its spirit had revived, and its energies had been aroused to such an extent that before Conference again met, everything in connection with the church looked bright and promising. Now, in consequence of the new appointments, the outlook had again suddenly become almost as discouraging as before. The members were dissatisfied because the Conference had deprived them of two ministers, who had witnessed with them a happy change, and whose aid and influence were deemed essential to the attainment of further good results, and to the completion of other necessary work already in progress. The murmurings were not as limited as those that frequently succeed a change of ministers by the Conference. Such complaints are natural, and more or less common, and are often unpleasant enough to form one of the objectionable features of the itinerant's life. In this case the complaints were loud and general, and caused much despondency among those who felt a strong interest in the welfare of the church. A brother, whose name was Church, a merchant in Wooster, said to father: "You may as well give up at first as at last in trying to build that Church. The Conference has taken away Brother Sawyer and Brother Power, and has sent us men that can't fill their places." Father replied: "Brother Church, we must trust in God and not in man," and the erection of the church went on. As previously noted, congregations not unfrequently criticise the new preacher and fret over the change of a talented or favorite minister for one whom they estimate as having less force and ability. With such congregations it matters little, that in the pulpit, as in all other vocations, the highest talent is represented by the few. It is human nature to want the best. It argues little, under such circumstances, that the bright lights of Conference are not sufficient in number to go around, and that therefore the method of changing preachers about is the most fair and beneficent toward all. Reasons are plentiful in every church society to show that with them the people are peculiar, and that a first-class preacher only can do them any good. If the congregation is small, the salary meager, and the church in a weak condition, these facts show all the more forcibly a need for the best talent. Many pious people there are who mix enough philosophy with their religion to make them content with whomever the Conference sends them, but many there are also who have not this philosophy, and who, like the children of Israel, seem to need a constant manifestation of the Divine Spirit, or of the Bishop's favor, to keep them from grumbling. As suggested by father's remark to Brother Church, too much faith in man and not enough in God is often the cause of congregations' being dissatisfied with their preacher. Elmore Yocum, who succeeded John H. Power as Presiding Elder of the Wooster District, at the beginning of father's second year on Wooster Circuit, was a very good man and an ardent worker for the salvation of souls, but not so popular a pulpit man as John H. Power.*

Cyrus Sawyer, during his year's labor, had won the hearts of all the people, and was exceedingly popular. We are

---

*Elder John H. Power was a man of good talent, of strong intellect, and of much force of character. His style was argumentative, and his manner sincere. He was a great debater. It was the custom among the various denominations in his day to have discussions on fundamental questions of religion on which they differed. Unitarianism, Calvinism, Universalism, and Baptism, or Immersion, were the common subjects for these controversies. Power had nine debates on Universalism with preachers of that denomination, the last and most prominent of which was the one with Rev. N. Doolittle, of Akron, Ohio. This debate took place at Laporte, Lorain County, Ohio, in 1845, and was published at Columbus, Ohio, in 1846. John H. Power sustained to the preachers of the North Ohio Conference much the same relation that Richard Watson did to the earlier preachers of Methodism. Watson was a great theologian and logician, and it has somewhere been remarked of him, in a comparative way, that, while he was best fitted to guard the outer fortifications and bulwarks of Christianity, it was reserved for Fletcher to conduct you into the interior of its temple and show you its beauties. Out of the pulpit and off the rostrum Power was not much inclined to talk, the most of his time being given to study. He was over six feet tall, was sparely built, and had a grave and thoughtful countenance. His influence in the Conference was leading. Although a presiding elder could not remain more than four years in charge of the same district, it being customary that he should then give way to some one else, usually to some new man, yet Power was in such favor as an elder, that he was continued in the office for three or four terms successively. As soon as his term on one district expired he was appointed to another, thus avoiding any technical infringement of the rule. In this particular his case bore some resemblance to that of Cromwell's. Cromwell was a member of Parliament, and at the same time an officer in the Parliamentary Army. While occupying these two positions Parliament passed what was called the "Self-Denying Ordinance." By this ordinance all members of Parliament were excluded from commands in the army. Yet afterward Cromwell was found to be so essential to the army that the ordinance was quietly ignored as to him. Elder Power was many times appointed a delegate to the General Conference, and spent a term of four years in the book-agency at Cincinnati. He afterward went west. His connection with the North Ohio Conference closed at Tiffin, Ohio, in the fall of 1854. It is supposed that it was by his advice, there given, that father was appointed elder of the Maumee district. He was a strong friend of father's, and manifested his regard for him in many ways during their life together in the ministry. His death occurred in Burlington, Iowa, January 26, 1873.

almost certain that he was once afterward returned by the Conference to Wooster. He was relieved, however, of his spiritual labors, by death, at an early date. Rev. Brandebury, his successor, not being in good health, and seeing how popular Sawyer was, became discouraged, and, at the first quarterly meeting, asked for leave of absence for three or four months, to visit his friends in Pennsylvania. To take his place, during his absence, a local preacher named John Kimber was secured. He lived on a farm near Wooster. Though not a great preacher, he was an excellent revivalist. But dark clouds sometimes intervene the brightest sunlight. The gloom which had suddenly spread over the bright outlook at the close of the previous year was only temporary. The barren results which, it was predicted, would follow the new Conference appointments, were not realized, and greater success was attained during the second year than the first. In two years the church gained over four hundred accessions. The new chapel was finished in time to hold Conference in it at the close of the year. Father was much gratified by these second-year accomplishments. They were a credit to all the preachers of both years, a praise to the people, and a testimony to the Lord. It would, indeed, have been a reflection on the efficiency of the ministerial efforts of the preceding year, and an indication that the revival during the first year was illusive, had the building of the new church been abandoned, and had the spiritual interest suddenly relapsed for a cause no more serious than a change of preachers. The finale showed that the laity were sincere, and that their hearts were truly swayed by religious influences, and the Lord was honored by evidence that it was His Spirit and not man's eloquence that wrought the change.

While the family was living at Wooster, our sister Mary Jane was married to Joseph D. Stubbs, by Elmore Yocum, Presiding Elder, November 5, 1840. Also, here, sister Malinda Ann was born January 9, 1841, and named for Malinda Ann Spear, an intimate and warm friend of our mother, and wife of William Spear, a merchant of Wooster, and a member of the M. E. Church.

We mention it here, because there is a little novelty in the fact, that the family at this place reached its maximum number, eleven, including parents and children, all living at home at one time. Here was the point, too, at which the family poised and did not increase, but from that time on diminished. From the time father joined the Conference, in 1835, until he arrived at Wooster, the children had increased in number from six to nine, and the family from eight to eleven. There had also been an increase of one at Wooster, namely, Malinda, but a decrease of one, by the marriage of our sister Mary, left the number the same as before, and as Mary was married before Malinda was born, our statement that eleven is the highest number of the family living at home at any one time, holds true. The family left many warm friends in Wooster, among whom may be mentioned the Thomson family, consisting of Dr. (afterward Bishop) Edward Thomson, his mother, and two sisters. His mother was a member of the Baptist Church, and his two sisters, Elizabeth and Matilda, were members of the Methodist Church. Dr. Thomson also had a younger brother living there, who was studying law. The family of Jesse Warner, who had been father's colleague during his first year on Dalton Circuit, and who was again his colleague during the second year father was on Ashland Circuit, also lived near Wooster, and were warm friends of ours. Unlike the majority of junior preachers, Warner was a married man of middle age. While connected with the Conference he never moved his family. They lived all the time in his own house, on the old homestead farm, about three miles west of Wooster. The old homestead house stood back from the road, and was occupied by his father and mother, and a bachelor brother, who took care of them.

# NORWALK.

### Conference Year, 1842.

By the Conference which sat at Wooster in the fall of 1841, and at which Bishop Roberts presided, father was sent to Norwalk Circuit, Huron county, Ohio. This appointment occasioned another fifty miles' removal of the family and their effects, which transfer was accomplished mostly by wagon—about the only available method for such purpose then in vogue. Father's circumstances, however, were somewhat better at that time than they had been when the family left Danville for Dalton, for, in the meantime he had bought a buggy, in which himself and mother and Linda, the baby, made the journey from Wooster. Our brother William, having secured a clerkship in a store at Wooster, did not accompany the family to Norwalk, but the rest of the children, seven in number, followed father and mother in the moving wagons with the goods. Imagine that you see at this period of time, one or two covered wagons, containing the preacher's household goods, arriving at one of the principal towns in the Conference, a large family of children peering out from under the wagon-covers at the strange objects around them, and you may realize the change which a period of forty-five to fifty years has made in our country and in the itinerancy. Now railroads traverse almost every county and extend to nearly every city, town, and village in the land. The inventions of the age have accomplished so much toward overcoming the obstacles of labor, time, and space, that fifty miles of passenger travel, instead of being a tiresome ride of more than a day, in a carriage or buggy, as it was then, is now only a pleasant trip of two hours in the railway coach, attended by nearly all the comforts and conveniences of the drawing-room or parlor. Also, the facilities for the transportation of goods are improved as much as are the means of travel, and the day of expensive railroad transportation has passed. Nowadays the preacher, though without much money, avails himself of the railway cars to remove his family and goods to a new location. He goes in a shorter time than by the old wagon method, without additional cost, and in as respectable a manner as is afforded the wealthiest citizens of the country. Every place at which the family lived while father was a member of Conference, excepting one, is now on a line of railroad. Then only three were thus located, and they were father's last three places—Republic, Findlay, and Maumee City. These the family did not reach until toward the close of father's active career, when, it may be said, affairs were rapidly changing from old methods to new, and the country had strongly begun its development of railroad, telegraph, and other new enterprises. In this connection curiosity has led us to make an estimate of the outlay necessary to move the family and household goods a distance of fifty miles by rail at this time, basing the same on the status of the family as it was at Wooster in 1841. We find that it would not exceed twenty dollars.

The large decrease in the number of circuits and the corresponding increase in the number of stations, is another change that distinguishes the past from the present, and one which has produced for the ministers of this day a condition materially different from that which existed forty years ago. Father's Conference appointments were all circuits but two, and with two exceptions—the first and second—embraced important towns, usually county seats, where the family lived, and by the names of which the circuits were designated. These towns, with possibly one or two exceptions, have now all become stations. Indeed, at present there are no Conference circuits which in magnitude and importance represent those of the past. The few charges, so-called, which do exist are small in territory and limited in the number of their appointments. There are many charges now, in character between a station and a circuit, comprised of two or three small towns where the congregations would not be able separately to support a preacher. These are generally accessible by the cars, and to reach them the preacher requires no other traveling conveniences than a clergyman's half-fare certificate from the railroad company. The expense to preachers of keeping a horse, and the investment of several hundred dollars for traveling conveyances and outfit, are now generally obviated by the changed condition of affairs in the country and in the Church. But this is not all. Every grand and valuable improvement made in one direction seems to have, more or less, a reformatory influence over matters in other directions, thereby harmonizing all. Therefore, to keep pace with its clergy, whose condition has been so changed, indirectly, by railroad enterprise, it is not surprising to observe that the Church has also simultaneously advanced. Religious sentiment has undergone a change. From the aristocratic influences of the age it has acquired a culture and a polish which, we can fancy, would now cause a Church community to be very much shocked at the spectacle of a preacher moving into their midst in the old-time style, as represented by the family entrance into Norwalk. Such scenes are now reproduced only by the fortune-telling gypsies, and occasionally by some poor family traveling to the far, far West. Father's appointment to Norwalk was, in a measure, another surprise to him, but the reasons which made it so were different from those that had caused his astonishment when sent by the bishop to Wooster. Norwalk was then a seat of learning. The Norwalk Seminary, a school conducted under the patronage and auspices of the Methodist Episcopal Church, was then in full operation there, and it, with other denominational influences, made Norwalk, at that time, the choice charge of the Conference. The seminary at Norwalk was to the Methodist Church then what the Ohio Wesleyan University, at Delaware, is to the same Church now. Its location there gave to the place a denominational interest and importance, drew to it a population socially attractive, and made it a centre of intelligence and culture. The town was then blessed with Methodist divines. A number of them, having retired from the pulpit, were making the place their home, on account of its society and educational advantages; and others of them who were not in the regular work were living there for the same reasons, and also because of their having church business relations with the school. Among the former were Samuel Allen and John Janes, two superannuated ministers. Among the latter was

Thomas Dunn, agent for the Norwalk Seminary. Rev. William Gurley, commonly called Father Gurley, an old Irish preacher of some note, who was licensed to preach by John Wesley, and who had been a witness and sufferer in the Irish rebellion and Roman Catholic persecutions in Ireland in 1798, was another ministerial resident of the neighborhood Leonard B. Gurley, son of Father Gurley, and presiding elder of the district, and William B. Disbro, father's colleague, a young unmarried man, also at that time made Norwalk their home. These preachers, with their families, the faculty of the seminary, Dr. Thomson, Professor Dwight and wife, and Professor Nelson and wife, with the students, many of whom were studying theology with a view of entering the ministry, added to the regular membership of the church, and made up a congregation of strong intellectual merit and intelligence. Norwalk, therefore, was at that time an inviting appointment, likely to be desired by the most learned and eloquent preachers, and one which would naturally draw from the Conference its best talent. There was a number of strong men in the Conference, who were older in years and in membership than father, and who, probably, would have felt no timidity in accepting the charge; but father, from a consciousness of not having had a collegiate education to start with, was naturally surprised at receiving the appointment. Father attributes his fortune in being sent to Norwalk to two causes. One was the sincere friendship of Dr. Thomson, president of the Norwalk Seminary, who, it is supposed, recommended him to the bishop, and the other was the effect of the good results attending his own labors at Wooster.

Dr. Thomson, whose parents, we have noted, lived at Wooster, knew of father's large family, also that he needed a strong circuit for their support, and that he then had five children that ought to be going to school. He was also familiar with the marked change which had been wrought in church matters at Wooster during father's stay there. It is not known positively that he advocated sending father to Norwalk, but there are strong reasons for the conjecture that he did.

There was no parsonage at Norwalk, notwithstanding the other favorable conditions of the appointment; and the church building, though not poor, was smaller than would be anticipated after what we have said of the place. The audience room, however, had a gallery extending round three sides of it—east, west, and south—which gave it a good seating capacity. On the top of the edifice was a little belfry containing a good-sized bell, the only one in the town, which fact, applied to that day, is entirely sufficient to sustain all claims of high character for the congregation. We have often heard mother speak of the peculiarly solemn and impressive tone of the Norwalk church bell. There being no parsonage at Norwalk, and no house having been engaged for the family previous to its arrival there, father found it necessary to rent two or three rooms from a man named Owens until he could find a more permanent home. The rooms were situated near the church. Rev. Thomas Dunn, who has been referred to as agent of the Seminary, and his family, were old friends of ours from East Union, where both families had lived in 1832. He and father were local preachers there at the same time, Dunn being a merchant and father a blacksmith. Dunn joined the Conference a year or two before father did, and had subsequently received the appointment he was then filling at Norwalk. Although in the interim he and father had probably met at Conference the families had not been together since they parted at East Union. This meeting with old friends, in the midst of strangers, was a pleasant feature of our family introduction to Norwalk, and was enjoyed as a relief from the lonesomeness that is usually felt by itinerants on their arrival at a new place. After occupying the rooms in Owens' house several weeks, a new home was secured, located west on Main street about a half mile from the church. We can see the old place now—an unpainted, one-and-a-half-story house with a grassy front and side yard, in which we used to hold the mare to let her eat grass. The back end of the lot, on which the stable was located, bordered on a high steep bluff, at the base of which ran a sand-and-rock-bottomed stream of water, a branch of Huron River, in which, and back of our stable, the boys sometimes went a swimming. The location of our house was peculiar to a number of others situated in line with it. Norwalk, at that time, was built mostly on one long street (Main), shaded on each side with maple trees, which gave the town quite a cultured, college-like appearance. The creek comes into the town from an easterly direction, flows westward south of and nearly parallel with Main street, veering a little north until reaching the west end of it, only the space of a lot there separates them.

The family being settled, father entered upon his work with vigor. At that period of time there was much prejudice existing in the Methodist Episcopal Church against choir singing and instrumental music as a part of the religious congregational services. The opposition to them was strong among the clergy, as well as among the laity, and comprised all classes of the church membership. Bishop Soule was very antagonistic to instrumental music in the church services. Dr. Adam Clark, the great commentator, wrote against choir singing, regarding it as a source of trouble to the church. It was a vexatious question, and created dissensions in many congregations. We remember some of the arguments used against choir singing and the church organ. It was held that singing praises to the Lord was as much a devotional exercise as was prayer, and that, in choir singing, only those members who could sing by rule and note would be able to participate, while those who could not would be thus debarred from a part of the services. It was further held, that in forming choirs it would be frequently necessary to go out of the church for some skilled person to lead, and for good voices and musical talent, and that it would be changing Divine worship into a mockery thus to have persons without Christian profession performing the religious exercises of the church, and scientifically rendering praises to the Lord which could come appropriately and devoutly only from the hearts and tongues of His professed followers. Attempts to change from congregational to choir singing, in many instances, caused bitter feeling among church members, and often threatened the disruption of congregations. The opponents of choir music regarded it almost a sacrilege, and in some cases their objections to it were increased and their opposition intensified by the notion that those who wished thus to monopolize the singing exercises were anxious to get the rest out of the way. Carleton's poem, "The New Church Organ," humorously represents, in regard to this matter, much that took place, and the feeling that existed, in many church congregations forty years ago:

"They've got a brand-new organ, Sue,
    For all their fuss and search;
They've done just as they said they'd do,
    And fetched it into church.

"They've got a chorister and choir,
    Agin my voice and vote;
For it was never my desire
    To praise the Lord by note.

"And now their bold, new-fangled ways
    Is comin' all about;
And I, right in my latter days,
    Am fairly crowded out."

The congregation at Norwalk was no exception to the rule, in showing a divided sentiment on the subject of choir singing, when the time came to test it, which occurred while father was pastor there. But the matter was handled with such due consideration for the feelings of every one, and in such a fair, dispassionate, and conservative manner, that, in the settlement of it, harmony was maintained, and great benefit accrued. The customary manner of conducting the singing in the public worship of the Methodist Episcopal Church at that time was for the preacher to first announce and read the hymn. He then lined it. Lining the hymn, was to begin with the first verse and read two lines; the congregation would then sing them, the preacher or some member of the church starting the tune; then the next two lines would be read, and the congregation would again sing, proceeding this way through the entire hymn, or the specified number of verses to be sung. We understand that the custom of lining a hymn in early times, was adopted on account of the scarcity of books. By this means all who felt disposed to sing could do so, whether they were familiar with the hymn or not. In his notes of Norwalk, referring to this subject, father says: "There were brethren there who felt it to be their privilege to start the hymns on all occasions of public service, and not being acquainted with the principles of music, they would often pitch the tune so high that the voices of the congregation could not follow them. Again, they would pitch it too low and have to make a new start. They would also frequently get out of time and meter, causing great confusion and destroying the solemnity and enjoyment of the exercises. John Janes,* who had been a prominent man in the church and in the Conference, felt it his duty to advise me in the matter, and said to me, 'Brother Gray, if I were you, I

---

*John Janes was an able preacher and was noted for his eccentricity. We have in mind two anecdotes respecting him which we have heard father relate. On one occasion, he had just reached the place he was first appointed to by Conference, and, being a stranger in the town, he stopped at the hotel. He had eaten his supper and was quietly sitting on the porch in front of the hotel, in the dusk of the evening, when he noticed that a building, not far off, which had the appearance of a church, was being lighted up. He asked of some one near him what that meant, and was informed that the Campbellites were going to have a meeting there. He concluded that he would go and hear what the preacher had to say. He waited until due time for the meeting to open, and, on entering the church, found it nearly full, which necessitated his taking a seat near the door. During his sermon, the preacher attacked the Methodists and other denominations severely, and, at the close, said that if there was any one in the audience who wished to reply to his remarks, let him come forward and he should have an opportunity to do so. It is not likely he was expecting any one to accept his invitation, at least, not a minister from another church. Janes rose up by the door, and, as soon as the preacher saw him, he beckoned him forward. Janes went as far as the altar, and, turning to the audience, stated that he was a young Methodist preacher who had just been appointed to that place by the Conference; that it was merely incidental that he happened to be present then, but, if they would give him their attention, he would endeavor to make reply to some things that had been said concerning his denomination. The preacher then invited him into the pulpit. Janes accepted the invitation, and, opening a hymn-book first, remarked, "We Methodists always sing and pray before we preach." He then announced the hymn commencing,

Jesus, great shepherd of the sheep,
To Thee, for help, we fly;
Thy little flock in safety keep,
For O! the wolf is nigh!

As he read the last line he turned and pointed his finger at the Campbellite preacher, and, throughout the hymn wherever it refers to the wolf, as it does in many places, he would turn and point at the preacher. The effect on those present may be imagined. Janes at once gained their favor, and it is said that he gave the other preacher such a scoring that he never after attempted to preach there. At another time, when on his way to an appointment, he noticed a number of horses and buggies around a little church, or school-house, in a grove by the roadside, and indications of a meeting either about to be held or then in progress. Having plenty of time to reach his destination, he made up his mind to see what was going on at the place in the grove. Hitching his horse to the fence, and taking his saddle-bags on his arm, he went in, securing a seat on the end of a bench near the aisle, about midway between the door and the pulpit. Just as he entered, the preacher in the pulpit rose to begin his sermon. After reading his text, his first remark was: "Brethren, I have a hard job on my hands to-day, I have four horses to curry—the Episcopalian horse, the Presbyterian horse, the Lutheran horse, and the Methodist horse." He then launched out in a merciless tirade against the denominations he had mentioned. He wound up by saying that he had felt it his duty to make some severe criticisms against certain other churches during his sermon, but if any one present felt aggrieved by what had been said, he would pause a few moments before closing the exercises to give any such one an opportunity to reply. As he said this, he cast his eye toward the man with the saddle-bags. Janes got up and said: "My friends, in the outset of his sermon, your minister told you that he had a hard job on his hands to-day; that he had four horses to curry—the Episcopalian horse, the Presbyterian horse, the Lutheran horse, and the Methodist horse. Now, I have a much harder job on my hands—I have this jackass to curry." This convulsed the audience with laughter, and the friends of the preacher, who were mostly members of his church, seeing that their minister had caught a tartar, rose up from all parts of the congregation and entered protests against such an unwarranted disturbance of a religious meeting. In the midst of the uproar, Janes took up his saddle-bags, and remarking, "Why, you don't call this a religious meeting, do you?", he left the house.

would appoint some one to lead the singing. You are preacher in charge, and it is your prerogative to do so.' I replied to him, 'Brother Janes, I do not feel like taking that responsibility entirely on myself, but if you will help me I will suggest what I think is a better plan to remedy the difficulty. I will allude to the subject from the pulpit, and make an appointment for the whole membership to meet and discuss it in a Christian spirit. This I advise to be done to preserve harmony and obviate dissatisfaction.' The announcement was made, with an earnest request for all to be present. When the appointed time arrived there was a full attendance. The meeting was opened with prayer. I then stated the object in view, and that all should have an opportunity of presenting their opinions on the question at issue, and, after a full discussion, the matter would be decided by vote. It was further stated that all political parties and organized societies settle their differences in that way—the minority yielding to the majority—and it was hoped that whatever the result, the minority would, in good spirit, abide by the decision. The meeting was lengthy, and the discussion was largely participated in by the church members. When all who so desired had expressed their views, the vote was taken, and there was a fair majority in favor of the appointment of some one to lead the singing, but not to take it away from the congregation. Professor Nelson and his wife, belonging to the faculty of the Seminary, were appointed leaders, and it was arranged that they, and all others who wished to sing with them, should take seats in the front gallery. To help still more in the matter, Professor Nelson and his wife organized a Church Singing Circle, which met once a week for practice. From that time on the singing improved and the attendance at church greatly increased. The choir sang tunes which were familiar to the members in general, thus leaving no room for complaint. The change referred to, occurred in the fall, soon after I went to Norwalk, and the second quarterly meeting, which took place in the early part of the winter following, found the people reconciled to the new order of things and in good spirit to enjoy the occasion." Continuing, father says: "The quarterly meeting was protracted for seven weeks, and awakened much interest among the people of all denominations. The Baptists and Presbyterians took part in the services, and there was a great revival. As a result of the meetings, there was an increase of one hundred and fifty members in the several churches. Of these, the Methodist Church gained over one hundred, the Baptist about thirty, and the Presbyterians a number less than twenty. There were also revivals and accessions at various other points on the circuit. The salary allowed me that year I do not recollect, but it was all paid. Besides, the people made us the largest family donation we ever received, and which amounted in value to one hundred dollars. To offset that, however, I had the misfortune to lose my riding animal—a gray mare—from an attack of fistula. My year at Norwalk was one of great prosperity to the church there, and one of the happiest of my ministerial life."

The question may be asked, Why was father not returned to Norwalk Circuit for a second year under circumstances which gave him a natural right to expect it, and which made his transfer at the end of the first year seem very unjust? The reason is not obvious, for his labors there had been successful, and he enjoyed the favor of his congregations. But jealousies are sometimes exhibited by ministers as well as by other people, and log-rolling for good places is often indulged in by some of them, much after the manner of politicians seeking for the fattest offices. We are confident, however, and happy in the belief that father never condescended to such a course, that he always, readily and willingly, accepted whatever charge Conference gave him, without murmur and without intrigue. Had he been less circumspect in this way, we do not believe it would have added any credit to his history, while it would have destroyed the consolation we now have from knowing of no word or act in his whole career that detracts from his Christian profession, or shows him to have been moved by unworthy motives.

The family remained at Norwalk but one year, for the following reason: James McMahan, an aged and able minister in the Conference, felt aggrieved that father, a young man, who had been a member of the Conference but six years, should have been promoted over him to the best appointment, and presented a complaint to the Bishop, at the same time asking for the Norwalk Circuit. This complaint and application were made privately and in person by McMahan, and the result was favorable to his wishes; father being sent to Ashland, and Mc-

Mahan from Ashland to Norwalk. The cause of the change, then unknown to father, he afterward learned from Adam Poe, one of the Bishop's Cabinet. While at Norwalk, our brother, David Simpson, was apprenticed to a tailor, named S. D. Carkuff, for six years, during one of which he was to be sent to school. But at the end of four years, Carkuff took the gold fever, sold out his shop, and left for California, giving David the balance of his time. William did not stay long in Wooster after the family moved to Norwalk, but returned home and attended school at the Seminary.

Among the many friends and acquaintances of the family in Norwalk, there was one whom we remember with special interest. Her name was Mary Henry. She was a poor girl, an orphan, we think, who supported herself by sewing. She at first became known to us as a member of father's church, but by visiting at our house, and by occasional employment to do sewing for the household, she was afterward drawn into close and warm friendly relations with the family. As she possessed an attractive disposition, with ways and manners pleasing toward every one, we all became much attached to her. While we lived at Norwalk she was married to a man named Jarvis, who was a painter, and who, at times, was intemperate. Her contemplated marriage was talked of, with many misgivings, by her friends, and when it was consummated we all felt as if one of our family had gone out from among us. Mother often allowed us to go to see Mary at her home after her marriage. We now have in our mind the picture of one of these visits, in which she is sitting in an upper room sewing, and a little boy at her feet is listening, with childish interest, to her talk. The misgivings with respect to her marriage were prophetic. It was an unhappy one. We have no subsequent trace of this Norwalk friend; but, in speaking of her, we are reminded of the fact that, in the list of acquaintances formed during our family travels, there were two Mary Henrys. The other one was the daughter of Judge Henry, who lived at Brookfield, near Massilon, on Dalton circuit. She is beyond our recollection, but we get the following account of her from sister Mary: "She was a dwarf, or, at least, quite diminutive in size. She had been afflicted in her childhood, had been raised very tenderly, and had a very affectionate and sweet disposition. She visited us frequently while we lived at Dalton, and was a great favorite with us all. In after years Judge Henry moved to Wooster, and Mary died there."

Norwalk is bound to us by one hallowed association, and contains one spot which will remain green in the memory of every member of the family while life with them lasts. It reverts their minds to one whose life was cut off in the bloom of manhood by a fate undeserved, remorseless, and cruel, and which was attended by circumstances so seemingly unrelenting and determined in forcing it on him, that we fear to dwell in thought upon them lest we be persuaded to distrust the wise providences of God. That spot covers the charred remains of a doted son and an affectionate brother, who possessed their hearts' fondest love, and for whom, until that time, life seemed budded with joy and promise. In the cemetery there, at Wood Lawn, is a grave, now distant from friends, and over it stands a white marble shaft, bearing this inscription:

WILLIAM M. GRAY,

Son of

REV. DAVID AND NAOMI GRAY,

Who perished by fire at Sandusky City, February 26, 1851, in the twenty-fifth year of his age.

Our loved one has gone.

"The ways of God are righteous, altogether."

The details pertaining to the sad event referred to above will be currently related in our review of Bucyrus Circuit.

# ASHLAND.

### Conference Year, 1843.

The family moved to Ashland in September, 1842. The Conference which sent father there convened at Delaware, Ohio, Bishop Morris presiding. Father's colleague was Philip Wircham, who had been at Ashland, with McMahon, the previous year. Wircham, however, left his charge a short time after his appointment and was succeeded by Myron T. Ward. Ashland belonged to Wooster District, and Elmore Yocum was the Presiding Elder. Ashland Circuit was a very large four weeks' circuit, having eighteen or more appointments. These embraced, besides the town of Ashland, the villages of Jeromeville, Haysville, Orange, Sullivan, Bryan (now called Polk), Mohicanville, Rowsburgh, and Perrysburgh; also, the country appointments of North Orange, Hill's Meeting House, Strickland's Meeting House, Sherradden, McGuire's, McKay's, Wylie's, and Tyler's Bridge. Ashland was then in Richland County. It was not a county seat, but it contained about sixteen hundred inhabitants, being fully as large as Norwalk, and surpassing it in business importance. It had some manufacturing interests, and being situated in one of the best agricultural districts of Ohio, it possessed one notable business feature—a large country trade, which it still retains. The school advantages of Ashland were also excellent. The Ashland Academy, a school organized in the year 1838, open to students from abroad, and unsectarian in character, was then in the zenith of its glory. There was a long, two story frame house, painted white, situated on Cottage street, near the Academy, intended to serve its interests, and in which were furnished board and lodging for the students from other places. It must have been fully occupied, for when the students were engaged in pitching quoits and in other college pastimes, in front of this building, they appeared very numerous. The community was wide awake in educational matters, and we remember that there was a strong ambition among the students to excel. We were not old enough nor far advanced enough, at that time, to attend school at the Academy, but this feeling was so glowing then that it attracted our notice and impressed even our youthful mind. In the weekly literary exercises at the Academy, which were given much attention, there was strong competition for superiority, and there many a brilliant intellect gave early promise of future honor and renown. Those times, under memory's enchanting vision, seem to us now almost like a miniature of the days of ancient Greece, when "Cecropias pillared state" trembled with the eloquence of Grecian oratory. Among the students attending school at the Academy, at that time, who were noted for their genius and oratorical powers, was a young man named John Jacobs, the son of a tailor who lived in Ashland. Young Jacobs gained distinction at the school on account of his fine compositions and oratory, and was regarded in the community as a person who would, in time, reach a high position in some profession, or in the halls of state. After leaving school he studied law, and bid fair to fulfill these predictions. But, "Go read the history of genius; it is a history of sorrow which no eye can trace without being moistened with tears." He became dissipated, and filled a drunkard's grave at the early age of thirty-seven. The first principal of this Academy was Rev. Robert Fulton, a Presbyterian clergyman, who died in 1841. He was succeeded by Samuel Johnson, who resigned in 1844. Johnson was succeeded by Lorin Andrews, one of the most noted educators that Ohio has ever had. It was while we were living in Ashland that Andrews became principal of the Academy, and it was during the time he was connected with it that the school reached its most flourishing condition. He retained the position until 1847, when he resigned to become principal of the Union Schools at Massillon. In 1859 he accepted the presidency of Kenyon College, and was the first lay member of the Episcopal Church who had ever been invited to fill that position. Of Andrews the "History of Ashland County" says, "In an unfortunate hour the citizens of Ashland permitted him to retire from the Academy, an institution which had been an ornament to the town and a source of profit to her people." After the resignation of Professor Andrews this institution rapidly passed away, and a Union School sprung up in its place, occupying the old Academy buildings and site.

At the time we lived in Ashland there was a peculiarity belonging to a number of the church edifices, public buildings, and business houses there, so marked that it formed a distinguishing feature of the place, but which the changes of time have entirely swept away. They were built of flat, undressed stone, taken from the bed and banks of a small stream called Fulkerson's Run, which then bordered Ashland on the south, but now divides it in about the center. The M. E. Church, the Presbyterian Church, the district school house, Resnor & Deming's store, and Graham's store, were among the buildings of this kind. Also, they were all centrally located, and closely situated to each other. The Methodist church was low and oblong, and stood where the court house now stands. It was without bell or belfry, or any architectural ornamentation whatever. The Presbyterian church, which was then nearly new, was rather a pretentious structure for that day. In the selection of the stone for its wall facings, it showed that more care had been taken for it than for the other mentioned buildings of the same material, and the masonry work had been well pointed up. It had a high steeple, a good bell, and its interior was quite polished.

The old district school house, in which we first attended public school, and for which, consequently, our memory has a naturally patriotic reverence, was located on the northwest corner of Hard Scrabble* and Church streets. It was a plain clon-

---

\* Hard Scrabble, we think, was a nickname for this street, although at that day we never heard it called anything else, and if it had another name we do not know what it was. Also, as we remember it, the appellation more strictly referred to a certain portion of the street, Second street, running east and west, comes up to and terminates at Church street, which runs north and south. What was then known as Hard Scrabble is a natural continuance of Second street. Beginning at Church stree', where Second street ends, it continues directly on west, as if all one street, for about one square further and then angles off towards the northwest. It is this angle ine of the street that was especially identified by the name Hard Scrabble, and so called because of the dilapidated buildings that fronted it on both sides. Cottage street, in a general course north and south, crosses what was Hard Scrabble, at the angle point mentioned, and terminates in an inter-ection with Main street, at the foot of a little hill. Old Hard Scrabble is now called Sandusky street, but is entirely changed in ap-

gated structure, one story high, and contained two rooms. There was, however, a sharp declension northward in the site on which it stood, and the walls, deepening as they extended in that direction, elevated the north room high above the street. A large air chamber, or cellar, was also thus formed under both rooms, which, from the nature of the ground surface, grew larger toward the north end. A hallway, which itself was partitioned across the middle, separated the two rooms. The entrance to the south room was on the west side of the house, first into the hall, the outside door being about two steps from the ground. The entrance to the north room was on the east side, first into the hall, up a flight of eight or ten steps from the street below.

The seat and desk arrangements were both comfortable and convenient, and embraced, even more strictly than at present, the plan of locating pupils singly. Each pupil had a separate seat, with front and side desk, to which there was no access except by the aisle or passage down and at the left of the row in which they were situated. All the side desks, in a line, were framed together by taking two long, wide boards, one for the top and the other for the bottom, and enclosing a space between them, on the right side and at the ends, in box fashion, with other boards about eight inches deep. The left side was open and was divided by cross pieces into as many distinct desk apartments as there were seats in the row. To this open side, and opposite these apartments, were joined the seats and front desk boards, the latter being grooved into the side desk board, the top of both side and front being on a level. The seats, which, like the desks, were made of plain poplar lumber, were square, upright, and chair shaped, with solid backs. We have seen modern school seats and desks of handsomer style and finish, but none which excelled those old time ones for convenience, and none which could be more inspiring to pupils by reason of individual care and unshared possession. The interior of each desk was large enough to contain not only the books and slate, but also the dinner basket, head covering, and all the

---

pearance, and, at this day, compares favorably with other parts of the town. On the northwest corner of Cottage and Sandusky streets is located the new M. E. church, the largest and most costly church edifice in Ashland. On the southeast corner of the same streets is the new Ashland county jail, a handsome and expensive structure.

out-door wraps of its occupant, together with as many apples and nuts as could reasonably be disposed of during the school intermissions. Webster's Elementary Spelling Book was then the text-book for beginners, and McGuffey's Readers, Olney's Geography, Ray's Arithmetic, and Kirkham's Grammar were used in the advanced classes. For literary exercises, Porter's Rhetorical Reader contained the most popular selections. Like Kirkham's Grammar, it was bound in sheep, and we think it was the text-book at the academy. Steel pens had not then been introduced, and it devolved upon the teacher to make writing pens for the pupils out of goose quills. It was an essential qualification then for the teacher to know how to make a pen.

But there were some edifices there that were not of stone, which, on account of old time associations, deserve a passing notice. The Academy was one. It was a high, two-story brick, painted red, with an open, two-story, wooden, portico front, painted white, which extended from the ground floor to the top-most ceiling under the projecting gable roof. Over the portico was an open, square-shaped belfry containing a bell. The location of the Academy was good, being on high ground near the west line of a grassy plot more than one-fourth of a town square in extent. The boarding-house for students was situated northwest, and the larger and business portion of the town, southeast of the academy. Chiefly owing to this fact there were two gates to the ground, similarly located. The soil about Ashland is very sticky in wet weather, and consequently board walks were made to extend from the two gates, one northwest reaching to the boarding-house and to the residences of a number of merchants and business men living in that part of town, and the other southeast, past the Presbyterian Church and the district school house, to the postoffice and business center of the place. The hypothenuse line thus formed through the Academy grounds was a great thoroughfare for pedestrians—both students and citizen—passing backward and forward between the several points named. The Hopewell Church was an old-time frame structure, with a little polygon-shaped, shutter-enclosed, round-topped dome. We believe it had no bell. It stood on Cottage street, north of the Academy boarding-house, and set a little back from the street, thus leaving a small bit of ground in front. It extended back into the village church-yard, which was lower than the street border, and which gradually sloped backward towards a ravine, called Gamble's Hollow. It had a high foundation at the rear to set it up on a level with its front. We remember this old church in connection with an incident in which, like poor Tray, we suffered for being found in bad company. Back of the pulpit was a window overlooking the church-yard. One day, after strolling about with a neighbor boy, Howard Deming, we had come up from Gamble's Hollow, and had stopped behind the church, under this window. We were about separating for our homes when suddenly our companion picked up a short, heavy stick, that happened to be lying there, and said, " Well, before we go, let us give the preachers a little fresh air," and, throwing it through the window, broke the sash and several panes of glass. Just at the moment, old Mother Robbins happened to be passing along the street. She was at such a distance from the church that she could see us in the rear of it. The noise attracted her attention, and recognizing both of us, she exclaimed, "Oh! you bad children." Without pretense of being a real good boy, we can say that that act of young Deming very much exceeded our own wantonness of disposition, and the thought of what would be said and of what would happen in consequence of it, frightened us greatly. We do not recollect that we were punished in this case, but think it likely that we were. One result, however, was that father paid half the damages. It appeared, under inquiry, that glass had been broken out of different windows of the same church at other times by some person or persons unknown. Therefore, nothing was more natural than that we two boys should be pronounced guilty of the whole, and our fathers settled with the church authorities on the basis of such an inference.

The Graham mansion, at that time the most aristocratic private residence in Ashland, stood near the Hopewell Church, a little north, and on the opposite side, of Cottage street. It was the last house, within the town limits, on that street. It was a common subject of awe and wonderment among the youths of the place, who invested it with fabulous proportions, One speculation among the boys concerning it was that it contained a hundred rooms. But this may be regarded only as an extreme illustration of the Munchausen tendency of young minds and of the magnifying powers natural to youthful vision.

The dwelling will be remembered as a wide, square, one-and-a-half-story brick, with a hip roof, balcony top-center, and piazza, extending round the front and sides. A fine lawn spread out before and to the right and left of it, reaching several hundred feet down to the street. In the summer season the air around it was wont to be filled with the music of birds and the perfume of flowers. It also had other extensive grounds, including an agricultural garden, an orchard, pasturage, and large barn accommodations. Its location and connections united many comforts of the farm with the advantages and social pleasures of the village to make it an attractive home. 'Squire Graham, its owner, was one of our neighbors, a prominent merchant of Ashland, a deacon in the Presbyterian Church, and an excellent man.

Father left the family at Norwalk, and went to Ashland the first Sunday after Conference adjourned. He there found a protracted meeting in progress in the M. E. Church, under the leadership of Rev. Solomon Ritz and Rev. Sloan, two new school Lutheran preachers. Father says, "They held their meetings very much after the manner of the Methodists. On Sunday they allowed me to preach the morning sermon, commencing the work on my new charge. In the afternoon I left for Orange, to fill an appointment there, and they continued their meeting. On Monday following I returned to Norwalk, and, during the same week, brought my family to Ashland. The old parsonage being in a rickety condition, we did not move directly into it, but occupied, for a few months, a brick house on Second street, a short distance east of the Methodist Church."

The house referred to by father had a two-story, or double porch, in front, much after the style of the portico of the Academy. It was almost adjacent to the old, weather-beaten frame house that Joseph and Mary Stubbs lived in when they first came to Ashland, and which stood on the northeast corner of Church and Second streets, directly opposite the district schoolhouse. Only a large shed separated the two residences. While living in Norwalk, Sister Elizabeth had been promised in marriage to William Brewster, and in the brick dwelling, temporarily occupied by the family as stated, they were married, in the fall of 1842, by Elmore Yocum, Presiding Elder. Brewster owned a farm just south of Norwalk, and on that farm he and Elizabeth went to housekeeping. At the time of their marriage Brewster was a widower, and had two little boys, named Willie and Platte, but they died in early boyhood. Their mother's name before marriage was Benedict.

In the family removal to Ashland, brother David had been left at Norwalk with Carkuff, under conditions previously mentioned. William, although older than David, had not yet been settled to any business, and therefore came with the family to Ashland. He there attended school at the academy during the first winter and spring following the family transfer from Norwalk, after which he was apprenticed, for three years, to Christian Rissor, a tailor of Ashland.

Father's note of Ashland further says, "The second Sabbath after conference found the Lutheran protracted meeting still in progress in the M. E. Church, and awakening considerable interest. Rev. Ritz being called away, brother Sloan and myself arranged to continue the meeting, in the joint interest of the Lutheran and Methodist denominations, for two weeks longer. The result was between thirty-five and forty conversions, and an equal number of accessions to the two churches. It was on Sabbath morning—the day we closed the meeting—that we opened the doors of the church. Brother Sloan insisted upon my taking the lead in the services.

"The house was crowded. We first had an experience meeting of about an hour in length. I then rose and stated that, for those who desired to live a Christian life, it was important that they should connect themselves with some branch of the Christian church. It was, therefore, now the purpose, before closing our series of meetings, to give those present, who were not already members, an opportunity to join either the Lutheran or Methodist Church. There was a railing around the pulpit where penitents bowed and where members of the church knelt to take communion. I said, 'All those who wish to join the Lutheran Church come inside this railing and be seated; and all of you who wish to join the Methodist Church please occupy the seats fronting the altar, while we sing.'

About twenty joined each church. Brother Sloan and myself held two other union meetings during the year—one at Haysville and one at Rowesburg—the one at Haysville resulting about the same as the one at Ashland. At Rowesburg more united with the Lutherans than with the Methodists."

Shortly after Elizabeth's marriage we moved into the old rickety parsonage, and spent in it a very uncomfortable winter. In the spring we got a new parsonage, up on the hill, northwest of the academy, where we were surrounded by excellent neighbors, among them the families of Squire Graham, Mrs. Robbins, and Charles Deming.

Altogether, we had a very pleasant year, attended with considerable success in the Church, small revivals occurring at several points."

It was during this first year at Ashland that father was made a Mason. In company with Squire Stowe, who recommended him, he went to Mansfield and was intitiated an Entered Apprentice, in Mansfield Lodge, No. 35, F. and A. M., February 1, 1843. On July 5, following, he was made a Fellow Craft, and, on the same date, was raised to the sublime degree of a Master Mason.

## Conference Year, 1844.

In the fall of 1843, Conference met at Mount Vernon,* and father was returned to Ashland Circuit, with Jesse Warner as his colleague. Elmore Yocum was still the Presiding Elder of the district. Father says, "This was a year of great excitement. It had been predicted that the end of the world would come this year. It was also a year of great success in the Church. We had large revivals at almost every point on the circuit, the increase in membership numbering over five hundred." Although there is nothing incomprehensible in father's foregoing statement, it will elucidate matters some to call attention to the fact that in the early part of 1843 a great comet appeared—the largest one of modern times. It was of great splendor and fiery appearance. This phenomena in the heavens, shortly preceding the time for the fulfillment of Miller's

---

*This Conference was first assigned to Bishop Roberts, and was to have convened September 6, but in consequence of his death, in March previous, the time was changed to August 30, and his place was supplied by Bishop Soule.

prediction that the world would be destroyed that year, caused more consternation than did the prediction itself. There were persons who, without regarding it, like the Millerites, as foretokening the speedy destruction of the world, still could not gaze upon it untroubled by a nameless feeling of doubt and fear. The excitement in regard to Miller's prediction extended into father's second year at Ashland. To better understand this, it must be remembered that father is referring to his Conference year 1844, which included several months of the calendar year 1843. Furthermore, the author of the prediction claims his language concerning it to have been, "About the year 1843," meaning the Jewish year, which extended the period for the fulfillment of his prophecy to March 21, 1844. This was after all the revivals which father speaks of had transpired.

At Ashland, sister Laura Amanda was born January 17, 1844. She was named for Mrs. Laura Amanda Robbins, a neighbor and friend of the family. Mrs. Robbins was a lady of fine presence and culture, and was highly esteemed in the community. Sister Laura Amanda died at Ashland, July 13, 1844, and was buried in the village churchyard there, of which mention has been made. We get the following obituary notice, relative to her death, from a clipping preserved by our sister Mary Jane Stubbs, from a paper published at that time:

Laura Amanda, seventh daughter and eleventh child of David and Naomi Gray, departed this life July 13, 1844, aged five months and twenty-six days.

Alas, thou art gone from those who loved thee;
  Hast breathed thy last and long farewell,
Thy gentle spirit, freed from suff'ring,
  Hast gone with heaven's High King to dwell.

Bright angels watched around thy death-couch,
  To waft thee home, when ceased thy breath;
With Jesus' lamp of love they led thee
  And chased away the gloom of death.

Not there, the raging storms of sorrow
  Nor clouds of darkness, fear and woe,
Will dim thy brightened skies of beauty—
  Up into heaven they ne'er can go.

But one eternal day of gladness,
  One everlasting song of love,
Will be thy happy lot in glory—
  The sweet employ of those above.    D. GRAY.

In February, 1860, her remains were transferred to the Stubbs' family burial lot, in Ashland Cemetery.*

In thinking of Ashland, we are reminded of the lines—

> "How dear to this heart are the scenes of my childhood,
> When fond recollection presents them to view."

It may be thought by some that the sentiments expressed in "The Old Oaken Bucket" do not meet with much sympathetic response from the offspring of itinerants, when memory carries them back to the days of their youth. It may seem a natural conclusion that the frequent changes they make from one locality to another are calculated to diffuse their feelings, and to weaken that fondness in memory for early scenes and associations which is so common to mankind.

However this may be, we speak for one in expressing the belief that the places where we lived in boyhood, the remembrances of our youthful companions, and the sports and incidents of our early associations are as fondly impressed upon our memory and as deeply rooted in our affections as though we had dwelt all our life in one homestead. And this, despite the fact that, childlike, we were always pleased with the novelty which attended our moving to a new place.

We have had desires to revisit the towns we lived in when a boy, as strong as we ever heard expressed by others in regard to returning to places in which their lives knew no change from infancy to manhood.

We have longed to look again on old parsonage homes, to view once more the localities of our early pastimes and pleasures, and have contemplated the whole panorama of our youth with as much sensibility of feeling, and as many endearing reflections, as could have been engendered by long associations and the impress of many years. Indeed we believe the senti-

---

* In referring to the burial of our sister, Laura, there comes to mind a custom which prevailed in those days, on funeral occasions, different from what we see at the present time. The hearse was not then in use, at least not in villages and in small towns, and the body was carried to the grave on a bier. This was a frame of wood, painted black, with trestle supports at each end so that, when set down, the coffin would be raised to a convenient hight from the ground. We think the bier was usually draped along the sides with some kind of black cloth, hanging low enough to hide the opening underneath. The funeral cortege always moved on foot, in line, along the sidewalk. The pall-bearers at our sister's funeral were twelve young ladies, all dressed in white, making a peculiarly solemn and impressive scene.

ment is stronger in the former than in the latter case, from natural causes. Upon one whose home is fixed the changes of time steal so gradually that he scarcely observes them, and in the kaleidoscopic movement of progress his mind becomes more definitely associated with the last view. Our feelings in mature years are not so tender, nor our memories so capable of lasting impressions, as in youth. After we become men and women, we remember early scenes and events, while we forget those of comparatively recent date. It is only during youth— the period being comparatively short with every one—that upon the mind is made those imperishable engravings of places and things which long afterward become the subject of a peculiarly fond remembrance. It would thus seem that those who leave their homes early in life would have the most tender regard for them in age, and would feel most strikingly the changes wrought by time should they return to them in after years.

It has not been our fortune to review many of the places where we lived in boyhood, but our theory is supported by the fact that we have revisited them all in our dreams. In some cases they have been thus presented to us as having grown into magnificent cities, and we have seemed a wanderer in them, seeking for the companions of other days, but not finding them, and looking for our old habitations, only to learn that they were gone. Being only sixteen months old when the family left Danville, we do not realize that we ever saw our native place. Of Dalton, where we attained the age of three years and past, one imperfectly outlined and shadowy picture of the parsonage home is the only retrospect we have. Of Wooster we have a number of recollections, which, though dim, nevertheless have a good spectrum, and attest that our mental development was then keeping pace with our growth in years. Our remembrances of Norwalk are still more enlivened and varied than those of Wooster, and among them are the first reminiscences of our youth that are now dwelt upon with tender regard. This is interesting to us as a trace of our mind's gradually increasing strength from infancy to the time when it became capable of retaining distinct and ineffaceable impressions of its associations, impressions from which now spring our many happy retrospections. We became seven years old at Ashland, in the spring, following the family removal from Norwalk in the fall of 1842. It was therefore in the rosy period of youth, when life is bright, the heart light and joyous, and the imagination buoyant, that we reached this now fondly remembered boyhood home. Whether owing to natural causes, the peculiarities of age and development, or to special congenialities of place and associations, our mind now goes back to it with more affectionate regard than to any other home of our early life. At that time Ashland was environed with a number of pleasant groves, wooded ravines, and other localities that were entrancing to the roving spirit of boys of our age, and which became the theatres of many of our youthful pleasures and exploits. Wandering with companions along the banks of the village brook, playing in the groves, and sitting in the quiet retreats and shaded nooks of the forest glens, through the idle summer days, are among the scenes and incidents which now fill our mind with golden visions of the place. But the happy pictures of childhood days never again become realities, and the pleasures expected from visits to old homesteads in after years are never realized. Such visits nearly always occasion sadness and regret, instead of the joys that are naturally anticipated from them. Such was our experience in a recent visit to Ashland. Nearly all the old familiar haunts were gone, or changed by the march of progress, and a strangeness brooded o'er the scene. New faces met us on every hand, and only one companion of all that we once knew there was left to recount with us the joys of other days. We drove around to see the parsonage home, which is still standing, although not now a parsonage. While the carriage stopped a moment for us to view the place, one of the present occupants, a lady, came to the door and gave us an inquiring look, as if to say, "Who are you?" Little did she suppose that it was one who, at that moment, was feeling that he had almost as good a right there as she. The situation forcibly reminded us of Maud Meredith's poem, entitled:

## THE RETURN.

I wander down familiar ways,
  I look for old-time faces,
While memory paints again the days,
And strongly with her touch essays,
  To find the old-time places.

I see the house where first I knew
  The summer's golden splendor;
Here first my happy fancies grew,
And dreamed that fairy land was true,
  And life was sweet and tender.

Strange faces meet me at the door,
  And stranger voices telling,
And so my dream of home is o'er,
And I shall find it never more,
  In stranger countries dwelling.

Ashland is now a city of four thousand inhabitants, and contains many handsome residences, adorned with beautiful lawns and gardens. All the old-time edifices which we have described, except the Graham mansion, have passed away. Shorn of its once extensive ground attachments, and standing in a neglected condition, it, at this time, attracts but little notice. It represents the decline and financial misfortune of a family, who, when we knew them, were living there in high life, surrounded by friends, the courted exponents of wealth and fashion. Several instances of other families, who were in prosperous circumstances at the same time, but who are now in poverty, came to our mind. These changes, exemplifying the truth that "Riches have wings," made a stronger impression upon us than the mere destruction of our boyhood haunts and the appearance of many strangers in the places of well-known friends. They portrayed to us more fully the shifting scenes and shadows of life, than did the altered landscapes and the melancholy of our own thoughts in contemplating the vanished pleasures of youth.

# CONGRESS.

### Conference Year, 1845.

In September, 1844, at the close of father's second year at Ashland, the Conference met at Canal Dover, Bishop Waugh presiding. Elmore Yocum's term as the Presiding Elder of the Wooster District also expired at this Conference. His duties as Presiding Elder, however, did not terminate until the Conference there adjourned, and it devolved upon him to recommend to the Bishop the changes and appointments which he deemed advisable to be made on the Wooster District for the ensuing year. Father was thus nominated by Yocum for Congress Circuit, and was appointed to it by the Bishop. Why, under the circumstances, he was nominated by the Elder for Congress Circuit he does not particularly know. There was a faction in the church, on that charge, much opposed to secret societies, which had sent to the Bishop and his cabinet, at Canal Dover, a petition, praying them not to send them a preacher who was a Mason or a member of any secret order.

It is evident that the Bishop and his council did not think it best to comply with the request, and it is presumed that Yocum suggested father as the one he thought best suited to send there under the condition of affairs at the time. This seems plausible for the reason that Congress Circuit was a small two weeks' circuit, different from the kind of appointments father had been receiving. As there was a warm friendship between the Elder and father, it could not have been for any other than a politic cause that the appointment was made.

Congress was a little village in the northwestern part of Wayne County. The parsonage—a small, plain, two-story log house—was located in this village, on a street next to, and west of, Main. The church—a plain, white, frame structure—was situated on the same street as the parsonage—on the same side of the street—and only a short distance south of it. Father says: "Soon after getting settled at Congress, we held our first quarterly meeting at Canaan Bend Church. The official meeting took place in the afternoon of Saturday. James McGinley, the leader of the anti-Mason faction, was present. He was a licensed exhorter. After completing the business of the meeting, I went with a brother to supper, and McGinley went with us. After supper he asked me to take a walk with him, which I did. We had not proceeded far in our walk when McGinley asked me this question, 'Are you a Mason?' I answered, 'I am.' He then said, 'Are you an adhering Mason?' I answered, 'I am.' He then said, 'I can not hear you preach.' I said, 'I am very sorry, Brother McGinley.' All this conversation seemed to be friendly, and other subjects were considered. I was to preach that night in the Canaan Bend Church. Brother McGinley came to the church, but did not enter, and whether he heard me or not I can not say. He was a tailor, and lived in a small village called Jackson, another of the Congress circuit stations, a few miles from Canaan Bend. The steward of the church and the class-leader at Jackson also belonged to the anti-Mason faction. Some time after the meeting at Canaan Bend, I went to Jackson to make my pastoral visits. In these visits I made no distinction between my anti-Mason brethren and the other members of the church. I called at Brother McGinley's just before noon, and they kindly invited me to stay for dinner. After dinner I asked McGinley if he had any objection to my having prayer with the family. He replied slowly and somewhat hesitatingly, 'I guess not, although I have no idea that the Lord will hear your prayer.' To this I answered, 'That is a matter between the Lord and myself.' I then prayed with them and went away. Later in the fall, I gave notice that in four weeks we would begin a series of meetings at Jackson, with a view to having a revival. But about midway between my announcement and the time that the meetings were to begin, McGinley, the steward, and the Jackson class-leader determined to hold a series of prayer-meetings in advance of those I had announced. The intention of this, evidently, was to forestall my efforts, and, by having their meetings precede mine, to make ready to claim any good resulting from the latter as the outgrowth of the former. They held their first meeting on Thursday evening—the regular prayer-meeting night—with but few persons in attendance. Among the number was a man of very dissipated habits. On Friday evening the second meeting was held, and the dissipated man appeared again. After this meeting was over, McGinley, the steward, and the class-leader remained in the church for conversation. Brother McGinley remarked, 'Did you notice that Mr. B—— has attended the meetings both last night and to-night? I believe he is under conviction.' 'Pshaw!' said the class-leader; 'you might better believe the Devil under conviction.' Brother McGinley then said reprovingly to the class-leader, 'If we expect to have any revival at these meetings we must have faith.' The class-leader then charged McGinley with having too much faith, and the result was a hot quarrel between the two brethren, which the steward failed to quell. It also put an end to the meetings. Soon after this occurrence, Brother McGinley met me at Canaan Bend Church with an extended list of charges and specifications against the class-leader. Next, when I went to Jackson to begin my revival meeting there, the class-leader presented me with a number of charges and specifications against Brother McGinley. Under these unfavorable circumstances we had but little success at Jackson. After the meetings closed there, I talked with McGinley and the class-leader in regard to an investigation of the charges they had preferred against each other. It was agreed that a committee, consisting of five persons, should constitute a court of trial. It being my duty to nominate the members of the committee, I did so to the best of my judgment and to the expressed satisfaction of the two men. Notice of the day and hour was given when the committee should meet in the church at Jackson, to hold the investigation. On the day appointed the two brothers were arraigned before the committee, and in the presence of a church full of hearers. The two cases were heard in the order of the time in which the charges were presented—the class leader being tried first and McGinley second. In such trials the preacher in charge is *ex officio*, the presiding officer of the court. The verdict was guilty in each case. After the committee had rendered their decision, it came next in order for the president of the investigation to read to the condemned the law respecting the penalty in such cases. The law reads as follows:

"'If the crime of which the accused is found guilty is positively forbidden by the word of God, and sufficient to exclude a man from the kingdom of grace and glory, let the preacher in charge expel him.' I thus had the right and opportunity to expel them both from the Church. Not wishing, however, to show a spirit of retaliation, and thinking that mild measures might have a better influence upon them than the infliction of the strict letter of the law, I advised that they be not harshly dealt with. It was suggested that they, by making confession and asking forgiveness, might be continued as members by a vote of the class. In this suggestion I was governed by a comment which I had noticed as coming from Bishop Baker. The two brothers seemed glad to avail themselves of this means of escaping expulsion, and a day was set for the class to assemble to hear their confessions. At the stated time the confessions were duly made and the class voted to continue them as members of the Church. Nevertheless they continued obstinate in their anti-Mason feelings and in opposition to my Church efforts.

"But we found many good, kind people on Congress Circuit, and had revival meetings at several points on the charge that year. Rolla H. Chubb succeeded me there. He, also, was a Mason and, probably, profiting by my failure to pacify the anti-Mason element in the Church by mild measures, when they pressed the matter too far he expelled about forty of them. L. Nathan Raymond was the Presiding Elder of the district while I was on Congress Circuit, and, though not a preacher of large experience, he was a good man. Being desirous of having me returned to the charge, at the close of the year he approached me on the subject of Masonry. He suggested that I renounce it, or make some sort of confession concerning it, to the anti-Mason church members of the circuit that would satisfy or quiet them. That, I told him, I could not do, as I had found nothing in Masonry contrary to the teachings of Christianity. Also, that I did not wish to be returned to Congress, as my work for the year had been paralyzed and that it would please me to have a new charge."

In many things our personal recollections of Congress are

quite distinct. The place, as has been stated in father's notes, was small. In length it extended north and south, and its width compassed only two streets—Main, and the little one west of it, on which the M. E. Church and parsonage were situated. Main street ran the entire length of the town; the other, we think, did not. The town is situated between two ridge-like elevations of land, its center being in the hollow, or lowest intermediate point. The surface of Main street was a curved line, gradually sloping upward on either side, north or south, from the center of the village. The street on which we lived, although running parallel with it, was different from Main in this particular. It did not slope gradually down the hillsides and across the ravine between, but from the point where the parsonage was situated, which was near the middle of the town, it went abruptly down a steep hill, toward the low center of the place. The parsonage, we think, was the last house on the west side of this street, south of the ravine, and stood on the corner of an alley that ran east to Main street. We have a remembrance of seeing father, on his way to an appointment, ride down this steep hill, the horse kicking up all the way down, making the saddlebags rattle and nearly throwing him off.

There are several other incidents that we never fail to think of in connection with the old parsonage and our life at Congress. On one occasion a quarterly meeting was being held there, and some preachers from adjoining circuits were assisting father in his work. Among them was Myron T. Ward, who had been father's colleague, the previous year, on the Ashland charge. He had been stopping at our house during the meeting. It was Sunday night, and all the family, together with Ward, we supposed, had gone to church, excepting sisters Emily, Eleanor, and Linda, who had been left at home with us to keep house. We were parching corn and having a good time, and feeling no danger, when suddenly we heard a chair move on the floor upstairs, and somebody cough. Being sure that it could be no one but some evil disposed person, we were greatly frightened, and hurried off to the house of a neighbor named Stickle and gave the alarm. Stickle gathered some additional force, and preparing for an encounter, accompanied us back home. Arriving there, one of the party took a candle, and taking the lead, the procession, with all sorts of weapons, marched up stairs. Father's studio was just at the head of the stairs, and was not shut off from the stairway by any partition or door. When the party got far enough up the stairway to see into the room, instead of a robber or murderous villain, they discovered Brother Ward peaceably seated at father's desk writing a letter. The scene was ludicrous. Everything was soon explained, and all enjoyed a hearty laugh. Ward had determined to leave for home the next morning, and having some letters of importance to write beforehand, he had concluded to remain at home from church that evening and write them. Our not having been informed of this by anybody was the cause of the big scare.

The following is a peculiarly pleasant reminiscence of Congress. Our younger brothers and sisters will undoubtedly remember a low rocking chair painted in imitation of curly maple, that was so long in use in the family, and so great a favorite of mother's. That chair was a present that mother received while living at Congress. There was a Mr. Knisley (a chairmaker) and his wife, who were members of the church there. They lived in sight of our house, looking northwest, a little out of town, on a road running east and west through the center of the village. Father and mother were invited there one afternoon for tea, and just before coming home Mr. Knisley gave mother that chair. It was a friendly offering, and could its donor have known afterwards the good service it rendered, and mother's appreciation of it, he would certainly have realized that "It is more blessed to give than to receive."

The school house at Congress was an old weather-beaten frame of one room, and stood on the north side of the center cross road of the town, a little east of Main street. On the south side of the road, fronting the school-house, was Pancoast's grove, in which, at recess and other school intermissions, we nearly always played ball. The ball game then most in vogue was called corner-ball, bull-pen, or mush-pot. To play this required eight persons—four on each side. A piece of ground would be laid off in a square, the distance between the corners being about fifty feet. One side would occupy the corners and the other side would go into the pen, or mush-pot, formed by the four lines of the square. The corner men would then pass the ball around and across to each other, watching for the best opportunity to throw it at one of the inside party. In the meantime it would be a point with those in the pen to watch and keep as far distant from the ball as possible. When the ball was thrown, a miss put the thrower out, and *vice versa*; a hit put one of the center men out, provided as follows: If a man on a corner hit one of those in the pen, all the corner men had to run, and if one of them was in turn hit with the ball by a pen man, it reversed the result, and the corner man would be put out. Whichever side was put out first, under these conditions, lost the game. Two other games of ball, sometimes played in those days, were called, respectively, one-old-cat and two-old-cat. The first of these was identical with base-ball of the present day, but was not played so scientifically, nor was it so strictly regulated by rules and umpires.

Two-old-cat required only four persons to play it—two batsmen and two catchers. The batsmen would stand from 75 to 100 feet apart, with a catcher behind each one, the ball being thrown backward and forward by the two catchers. Whenever a batsman was caught out he changed places with the catcher behind him.

We remember it was at Congress that we first saw two men fight. We had been sent by mother on an errand to the north end of town, on Main street. On our way, in passing a blacksmith shop, we heard a quarrel going on between some man from the country and the owner of the shop. The smith was a large, heavy-shouldered, muscular man, and seemed rather disposed not to have any trouble. The other man was tall, but of lighter build, and appeared irritable and aggressive, and kept urging the quarrel. We do not remember what was said, but at length the countryman said something particularly aggravating. At this, the blacksmith, who was shoeing a horse, laid down his hammer, put down the horse's foot, and pulling off his apron, walked out of the shop. The two men immediately clinched. In the struggle the blacksmith got his left arm around the other man's neck, pulled his head down against his breast, and with his right hand dealt him terrible blows in the pit of the stomach, which soon made him cry, "enough." We remember well to-day the sympathy that it awakened in our mind for the man who got whipped, and yet, young as we were, we appreciated that he was to blame, and merited the punishment.

Among those we knew in Congress we recall to mind most distinctly the Somertons, Pancoasts, and Stickles. Every village seems to have one or two families who, on account of possessing more wealth than the others, are styled the aristocrats of the place. Such were the Somertons, of Congress. Pancoast was a merchant in good circumstances, and an influential member of the M. E. Church. Stickles, also a member of father's church, was a tailor, and a near neighbor of ours.

Father has said that his year on Congress Circuit was the most unpleasant of his ministerial life.

COL. SAMUEL FRAZER GRAY

# MILLERSBURG.

### CONFERENCE YEAR, 1846.

On the 13th day of August, 1845, Conference convened at Marion, Ohio, Bishop Hamline presiding. At this session father was assigned to Millersburg Circuit, Holmes County, Ohio. The circumstances which led to his transfer to another charge, after one year's stay on Congress Circuit, have been detailed in the preceding chapter. Congress and Millersburg were both in the same district, but a change of Elders on the district, which had also taken place while the Conference was in session at Marion, requires mention to make clear some events that afterward transpired at Millersburg.

As has been stated, L. Nathan Raymond was the Presiding Elder of Wooster District while father traveled Congress Circuit. It was Raymond's first year on the District, he having received the appointment at the Canal Dover Conference Session in the fall of 1844. At the same time Dr. Hiram Shaffer was the Presiding Elder of the Tiffin or of the Sandusky District. The term for a Presiding Elder was four years, usually served out on one district. But, for some unknown reason, at the Marion Conference, in 1845, the two Elders changed appointments, Shaffer being sent to the Wooster District, and Raymond to the Tiffin or to the Sandusky District. Father was very cordially received at Millersburg. His colleague, whose name has been forgotten, was a young man from near Ashland, Ohio, who had joined the Conference that fall. He did not prove acceptable to the members of the church at Millersburg, and, being treated coldly by them, he became discouraged, and in a few weeks went home. The Elder filled his place with a young man named Elliott, a local preacher, who lived on the circuit. The Methodist Church was strong in Millersburg, nearly all the leading citizens of the place being members of that denomination. Among them may be mentioned William R. Sapp, a prominent attorney, who was a very active official of the church, and an excellent person to attend to its finances. Another prominent lawyer, named Tannyhill, and the Sheriff of the county, were also influential members of the M. E. Church, and members of its official board. With respect to Masonry, the condition of affairs in the church there was just the opposite to that found at Congress. A large number of the best citizens outside of the church, and the strongest members in the church, were Masons. Father says the lodge-meetings there were very much like Methodist class-meetings, and the most fraternal of any he ever experienced. The parsonage at Millersburg was quite pleasant. One peculiarity connected with it was a bee-hive and a swarm of bees, to make honey for the preacher's family.

The schools of Millersburg were excellent. Besides the regular district or town school, there was a sort of seminary, or select school, for young ladies, which was taught by a Mrs. O'Fling, assisted by her eldest daughter. At the same time, Frank O'Fling, her son, kept a select school for boys. He was a very painstaking and agreeable instructor. The benefit accruing from these schools was manifest among the young ladies and gentlemen of the place, who, in their scholastic acquirements, compared favorably with those of other and more pretentious places in which we lived.

Rev. Mr. O'Fling, the father, was, as we recollect, a superannuated Methodist minister, formerly a resident of the State of New York. The family, altogether, was genteel, well-bred, and gifted. Mrs. O'Fling had in her school what might be considered a superior collection of girls between the ages of fifteen and twenty. Our sister Sarah attended this school, and we remember hearing her say that Mrs. O'Fling's daughter Louise was frequently called upon to lead in prayer in the devotional exercises of the school. Also, it was commonly remarked that Miss Louise was very bright and scholarly, and specially gifted. She was quite plain in form and feature. Our brother, Col. S. F. Gray, relates the following incident as to his meeting this young lady in after years, and which pertains to her subsequent history:

"A few years since, during a revival meeting held at the Meridian Street Church, in Indianapolis, a lady rose up to relate her experience. Her remarks created something of a sensation. Her words were choice, her thoughts clear, and her zeal and earnestness turned all eyes toward her. She appeared to be a stranger. After the services were over, quite a number of the members of the church approached her, myself and wife being among the number. Hearing my name spoken, she told me that she had known a methodist minister by the name of Gray in Millersburg, and asked me if I was any relation to him. She proved to be Louise O'Fling. She had been married, in New Albany, I think, while teaching school there, and had four very bright boys. Her husband had become an invalid, and had experienced great difficulty in supporting his family. His health had, at that time, failed entirely, and the support of the family devolved on the wife and mother. She had resided at Indianapolis but a short time before her talent for religious work was observed and recognized. She soon became connected with the W. C. T. U. work, and was employed by that organization at a small salary. Her local labors in that work were very successful. She visited different towns and cities throughout the State and came rapidly into notice. Subsequently, her talents brought her into the evangelistic field. She is now the Mrs. L. O. Robinson who has become famous as an evangelist. In truth, she is a great Gospel teacher, never failing to arouse deep religious interest wherever her services have been given. I think her father and mother are both deceased, and the brother Frank, whose school I attended, is a a Methodist minister in Iowa, as is also another brother by the name of Isaac."

In his account of Millersburg Circuit, father says: "We had some revivals that year and some additions to the Church, but I do not remember how large was the increase. Altogether, we had a very pleasant and profitable year. At our last quarterly meeting there, which was held at a country appointment, about five miles distant from Millersburg, Dr. Shaffer was present. The war between the United States and Mexico was then in progress. Shaffer was a strong Whig, and the people of Millersburg and Holmes County were, and are yet, by a large majority, Democrats. He preached very much against the war and the cause thereof, and his sermon gave great offense to the congregation, and especially to the members of the church present from Millersburg. It was supposed if he had come there after the quarterly meeting that the people would have egged him, so intense was their indignation. Shortly after this quarterly meeting, to fix up the business of the closing Conference year, I called a meeting of the Official Board. Among the matters presented for consideration was a deficiency of quarterage that then existed. When we reached that subject, Brother Tannyhill made a speech in which he said: 'Brother Gray, you shall have every cent coming to you, but Dr. Shaffer shall not have another penny.' This sentiment was approved by the Official Board. There was a person at the meeting who heard this speech and the denouncement of the Presiding Elder. It appears that this person lived at Wooster, and upon his return there he told Dr. Shaffer what had been said at the Official Board meeting in reference to him. After this, Dr. Shaffer wrote me a letter advising me to prefer charges against the brethren who had spoken evil of him. He expected the charges to be based on that clause in the Discipline which forbids members of the church speaking evil of magistrates or ministers. In answer to Dr. Shaffer, I told him I could not consent to take the step he advised. I gave as a reason for not complying with this request, that the most influential members of the church were Democrats, and should I get a committee to try them, who would return a verdict of guilty, the accused would appeal to the Quarterly Conference and have the verdict overruled. The members of the Quarterly Conference were mostly Democrats. I thus showed to the Presiding Elder that, by following his advice, I would only get myself into trouble and accomplish nothing. He saw the force of my reasoning, and did not insist upon my carrying out his request. However, he promised me the best appointment on his district if I would not feel hurt at his advising my removal from Millersburg at the end of the year. This explains why I stayed only one year there. Dr. Shaffer recommended my appointment to Canal Dover Station, which was one of the best paying stations in the Conference. For Millersburg Circuit he recommended two preachers who were Democrats—John Michael and young Brother Kennedy. It was not my wish, nor the desire of the Church membership on Millersburg Circuit, that I should not stay with them another year."

The country around Millersburg is mostly hilly. Westward, however, there is a valley of rich bottom land, which, if we remember right, is about six miles wide. The west side of the town borders on a ridge overlooking this lowland, and a few hundred yards off, looking from the eminence, you can see the Killbuck, running southward through the valley. Killbuck! In that name there is a charm which we feel, but can not describe. The stories that we have heard and read, when a boy, of old Killbuck, the Indian chief, gives it a touch of romance, and we think partly accounts for the pleasure of its sound, but we feel that the charm in the name is due chiefly to its association with our boyhood life—the remembrances of its old swimming hole. To reach this we descended the hill at the west end of Main street, and a little further on crossed the bridge over Killbuck. The place was located a short distance above the bridge, on the west bank of the stream, under a wide spreading tree. "The Old Swimmin' Hole," by James Whitcomb Riley, is so accurately descriptive in our own case that we quote the following appropriate lines:

"Oh! the old swimmin' hole! In the long lazy days,
When the hum-drum of school made so many runaways,
How pleasant was the journey down the old dusty lane,
Whare the tracks of our bare feet was all printed so plain
You could tell by the dent of the heel and the sole
They was lots o' fun on hands at the old swimmin' hole.

"Oh! the old swimmin' hole! When I last saw the place,
The scenes was all changed, like the change in my face;
The bridge of the railroad now crosses the spot
Whare the old divin'-log lies sunk and fergot.
And I stray down the banks whare the trees ust to be—
But never again will their shade shelter me;
And I wish in my sorrow I could strip to the soul,
And dive off in my grave like the old swimmin' hole."

But while Killbuck creek is to us the subject of so many happy recollections, the outcome of our associations with it can not be dwelt upon with much felicity of thought. For nearly two years afterward we were an invalid and so much afflicted in mind as to cause the family great alarm. The doctor said it was the result of our going a-swimming too often in the waters of Killbuck.

The location of the M. E. Church at Millersburg was peculiar, appropriate, and we might almost say, sacredly inspiring. It was an old-fashioned frame, without spire or belfry, had two doors of entrance, and stood, isolated from other buildings, on the top of a rather high hill. The hill in front of the church was a half circle in shape, and nearly as smooth and regular on its surface as a mound. One side of it reached around to the east, facing a street which run north and south, and the other extending round to the south, sloped down into a gully. The church, we think, did not stand square with the four points of the compass, but faced slightly southwest toward the central part of the hill. The rising sun reflected its rays full on the front of the old church, and on bright Sabbath mornings, to see the people wending their way, in the sunlight, up the hill, to the house of God, was a happy, peaceful, and a religiously sacred and poetic scene.

The parsonage was situated in another part of the town, east of the church, on a hill-side, near the bottom. It stood on the corner of two streets. The one that went up the hill run east and west. The one that went along the hillside, and in front of the parsonage, run north and south, intersecting Main street on the south. From the nature of the ground on which the parsonage stood, the front door and parlor were about six feet above the street, and were reached by a flight of steps. There was also a little balcony, or railing, along that side of the house, at the same distance above the street, extending out from the house, on a level with the parlor floor. At Millersburg we had neighbors representing nearly every condition in life. The hill, near the foot of which the parsonage stood, was very long and high. The street up the hill, past the parsonage, did not go entirely to the top of it, but stopped at the intersection of another street one square above where we lived.

At that point there lived an Irish family by the name of Mourn. The father and mother were in the habit of getting drunk and having a fight every few days. Above us, also, but not so far off, and on the opposite side of the street running up the hill, there lived a poor washerwoman by the name of Skelly. The sad part of her history was that she was cursed with a drunken, worthless husband. Next door south of us, on the other street, our neighbor was a Mrs. Leadbetter, a very respectable and pious lady. Our recollection is that her financial circumstances were very good. West of us, and on the corner of the square below, was the residence of Lawyer W. R. Sapp. He was well off, a good lawyer, and an influential citizen. He had two daughters, Laura and Amanda, young ladies, with whom we were quite intimate. After the Sapp family moved from Millersburg to Mt. Vernon, Ohio, we paid them a long visit. At one time it was arranged for our brother, D. S. Gray, to study law with Mr. Sapp, but the engagement was never consummated. We have many cherished recollections of Millersburg. It was one of the pleasantest homes the family ever enjoyed.

## CANAL DOVER.

### Conference Year, 1847.

The Conference, which ended the family's stay at Millersburg, convened at Ashland, Ohio, August 12, 1846. Bishop Morris presided. At this Conference, by the recommendation of Elder Shaffer, as has been previously noted, father was appointed to Canal Dover station. The charge had one outside appointment, about five miles in the country, called Oldtown.

Canal Dover is in Tuscarawas County, Ohio, on the west bank of the Tuscarawas River, and at the mouth of Sugar Creek. The Ohio and Erie Canal also extends north and south between the river and the village. The place is regularly and handsomely laid out, and was settled mostly by people from Baltimore and the State of Pennsylvania. It is situated on a high plateau, overlooking the Tuscarawas valley on the east, and Sugar Creek bottom on the south. The ground, which was originally the bank of the river, but is now the bank of the canal, on the Dover side, is high, we might say almost a bluff. In passing the village, the canal runs close in under the bluff, leaving a strip of the original shore between it and the river. Spanning both river and canal is a bridge three hundred and forty-six feet long. The east side of the town verges on a street running along the top of the high bank above the canal. There are no houses on this street, on the side next to the canal, and from it, looking eastward, the spires of the churches and other public buildings of New Philadelphia, the county seat of Tuscarawas County, can be seen, about two miles away. Main street extends east and west along, or near, the southern boundary of the high ground overlooking Sugar Creek bottom and the canal basin. There were some manufacturing establishments, and there may have been a few scattered dwellings, south of Main street, but in general, at that time, it was the south border-line of the place. Its eastern terminal intersected the south end of the street we have described as running along the high bank of the canal, and the two formed one angle of the square which comprised the town plot. Main street, however, was built up on both sides, except opposite the basin of the canal.

The population of Canal Dover at that time was, we think, about twelve hundred. Its corporate expanse suggested a greater number of inhabitants, but the town was not closely built up. The Deardoffs, Slingluffs, Sterlings, Weltys, and Hilts were among the principal families there. Dr. Slingluff was our family physician; John Sterling was a prominent dry-goods merchant, and Welty was the proprietor of one of the large flouring mills. The Deardoffs, according to our remembrance, were quite wealthy, and lived west of us, on the outskirts of the village. Their large, red barn was a very prominent object westward from the parsonage.

There were three organized church societies in the place then—the Presbyterian, the English Lutheran or Moravian, and the Methodist Episcopal. The Methodist was the largest and strongest of the three. The schools at Canal Dover were very fair. Professor Ross was the Principal. He was very tall—considerably over six feet—and spare in his build. We remember the boys used to call him "Crotch Almighty, and legs to eternity." George Warner, a kind of "king's fool," or jester, among the boys and girls, was the author of the appellation. The Moravian preacher also taught a school. We have forgotten his name, but we remember two points of his reputation; one was that he was very severe, and the other was that he was the most beautiful penman in all that country. His, however, was a select school. The Union Graded School system had not then been instituted, and town, as well as country schools, were operated on the old district plan. The regular school building was one peculiar to towns in those times, where, as distinct from the country school-house, it took several rooms to accommodate the children. It was a two story building, with hall in the center, and a room on each side, both up-stairs and down. Its position, common with the school houses of other towns, was broadside to the street, front and back hall doors, with play-ground principally in the rear. The town was then, and we believe is yet, a place of considerable business importance. It was a larger and much more stirring place than New Philadelphia, the county seat. It contained several very large mills, one or more tanneries, a foundry, and one rather rare business interest for a town of its size—a snuff factory. The flouring mills sustained a great many cooper shops, that turned out barrels for the flour that was made. The flour was nearly all for shipment, and the barrels required head linings to keep the heads from falling out in case of rough handling. The flour barrels then were all bound with split ash hoops. We have no remembrance of seeing a hickory hoop used in those days. A head lining was a little stick about twelve inches long, a half-inch wide, and about one-eighth or three-sixteenths of an inch thick. Two of these were tacked inside the chime on the outside of the head of each barrel. The boys of the town were paid thirty-five cents per thousand for making them. The coopers would give the boys the cuttings from their shops for the purpose. This was the first opportunity we ever struck to make a little spending money— a luxury which father's means never allowed us—and we enjoyed it.

The outside appointment, called Oldtown, took its name from an Indian camp, not far from the M. E. Church there, and where some other denomination had a mission. Among the members of the Church at Oldtown was a Mr. Fribley, father of Rev. James Fribley and Jacob Fribley, now living in Marion, Ohio. Another was a Mr. Heller, who had a son that was a local preacher. Father preached in Canal Dover every Sabbath, and in the afternoon at Oldtown every other Sabbath. When the people of Canal Dover heard of father's appointment there, they inquired as to how much of a family he had. This was an inquiry very common with Church Stewards in such cases in those days. They were told by some one in reply that he had seventeen children. They then said they could not see how they were to furnish bread for such a family as that. When the family arrived, however, and they found the number diminished to six, they were much relieved. Father says: "When I first went to Canal Dover, there was but one man in the community with whom I had any acquaintance. He was a Brother Burris, a local preacher. He had some relatives living on Danville Circuit when I was there, through whom we had become acquainted. Brother Burris was also a canal-boat agent at Canal Dover. Not long after commencing my work there I found trouble in the Church, occasioned by members desecrating the Sabbath. An old man, an Irish drayman, who had been quite dissipated, had been converted, and had joined the Church. He was quite faithful in his attendance at public worship and at class, but would on Sundays, if requested to do so, harness his horse to the dray and haul goods from the canal-dock to the stores or to other places. Another member kept a grocery at one of the canal-locks close to town, and would stay at home on Sundays to sell goods and liquor to the boatmen as they passed through the lock. There was also a large flouring-mill, owned by two men, one a member of the Church. This mill was run on Sunday. A young man, while working in the mill one Sabbath morning, fell from the third story to the lower floor, and was killed. The accident caused great excitement among the people who had respect for the Sabbath. Many members of the Church made complaint to me. They thought I ought to visit the recreant members and admonish them, and if admonition did no good, to have them dealt with according to the rules of the discipline. Feeling in my conscience that such a course would be right, I went to see the brother who had a grocery at the lock. After stating to him what had been reported to me respecting his conduct, he confessed that it was all true. I asked him, then, if he thought it consistent for a professing Christian to break the Sabbath. He said he did not, but that he was doing no worse than Brother Burris, who was a local preacher, and kept his office open on Sundays for the transaction of business with the same persons. I did not answer his argument except to say that both were doing wrong. I then went to the old drayman and talked with him. He, too, said he did not think his conduct was proper, but he likewise took shelter behind Brother Burris. After this I went to see Brother Burris, and related to him what the two members— the drayman and the groceryman—had said. Burris excused himself on the ground that the law allowed the boats to run on Sundays, and that consequently some one had to be in the office. He claimed that he had to keep the office open or give up his position and his means of making a living. He had previously applied for admission into the Conference, but was not accepted because he was regarded by that body as a Sabbath-breaker. Brother Burris and myself were good friends. I advised him to resign his commission in the canal office until Conference met, assuring him that I would lay his recommendation before it, and do all I could to have him admitted. Furthermore, he was assured that Dr. Shaffer, the Presiding Elder, would do the same, if he would only give up his office beforehand. But this he steadily refused to do, saying that he would not give up a certainty for an uncertainty, and I could do nothing with him. I then wrote Bishop Morris, stating to him the case of Brother Burris and the cases of the other members, who were excusing themselves by pointing me to him. The Bishop's reply instructed me to take the disciplinary course, prefer charges, and have them tried before a committee for Sabbath-breaking. I gave the Bishop's letter to Burris to read. He then became offended at me, but I told him that I felt it my duty to follow the Bishop's advice. With the consent of the Elder, however, we let him evade expulsion by a withdrawal from the Church. This conscientious discharge of duty cost me sixty dollars. For years previous the station had never failed to make up its allowance for the minister, but the withdrawal of Burris and the loss of support from his friends reduced my pay to that extent.

"At the close of the year I meditated upon the advisability of my return to the charge. When the Quarterly Conference met, there was a full attendance, more than twenty members being present. While it was in session, I arranged with the Presiding Elder that I should retire, and that, during my absence, he should lay before the members the matter of my coming back, and take a vote on it. The result was that all, without an exception, justified my action and thought I did right, but only a majority of three were in favor of my return, the others thinking it impolitic.

"At the close of this year, 1847, the Annual Conference met at Sidney, Ohio, August 11, Edmund S. Janes being the presiding Bishop. When he became acquainted with what had transpired, he said I must go back. I was thus reappointed to

Canal Dover station for the Conference year 1848. My second year there was a prosperous one. The mill which had run on Sundays was shut up on those days. Brother Burris withdrew from the Church. Of the other Sabbath breakers, some changed their course, and those who did not were expelled. We had a good revival during the year, at which there were over forty conversions and accessions to the Church. There was an increase in the subscriptions for the Advocate and other denominational literature. All the quarterage for that year was made up, and thirty dollars of the deficiency for the year previous, and the Church reached a peaceful and prosperous condition."

The church building at Canal Dover stood on the southwest corner of one of the middle streets, running north from Main, and a street running west from the street bordering on the canal. It was a two story frame with a basement and a public-service room above. The public-service room was reached by a flight of steps on the outside as wide in extent as the whole front of the building. It was customary at that day to have Sunday-school exhibitions after the same style of the secular school entertainments. We remember distinctly the part that brother Sam and ourself took in one of these exhibitions at Canal Dover. A stage was built entirely across the pulpit end of the church, far enough forward to take in the amen corners. Draw-curtains were arranged in front. Brother Sam spoke a piece describing Oliver Cromwell at one of the important battles at which he fought. It was from a sermon by the Rev. G. G. Cookman, of the Baltimore Conference. We recollect the following part of it:

"He stood, he looked at his watch, he looked at the field, he looked upward toward heaven, and implored help from the great arbiter of battles. It was an awful moment. Minute succeeded minute, his heart earned laurels for the honor of his country and the destiny of England hung trembling in the balance. At length the cry burst on his listening ears, "The enemy is coming!" He starts from his knees, he flings away his watch and cries, "All is well! The day is ours!"" Sam had a little dumb watch provided for the occasion which at the proper time he pulled out and when he arrived at the part which says, "He starts from his knees, he flings away his watch," Sam flung the little dumb watch over among the audience.

We spoke the Sailor Boy, which commences, "In slumbers of midnight the sailor boy lay." There was some fear in the family about our getting through with it successfully, as we were an invalid then and liable to be queer. But we passed the ordeal triumphantly and won many encomiums. The parsonage at Canal Dover, a nice frame cottage, was almost new, not more than three or four years old. It stood on the same cross-street as the church, one square west of it, and on the northeast corner of the cross-street and another north and south street. It was in this parsonage, in the early part of the year 1847, that we heard father read the first newspaper account of the battle of Buena Vista, which took place in the war then going on between Mexico and the United States. We remember it was after supper and he read by candle light. There was a pleased look in his face during the reading, and we recollect that he smiled when he read Taylor's famous words to Captain Bragg at that battle,—"Give them a little more grape, Captain Bragg." George Francis Train, in reply to a toast delivered before an assemblage of Americans in Liverpool, England, on a fourth of July occasion, a number of years ago, put forth this sentiment,—"Our country's right is our first thought, but right or wrong, our country." We think it must have been some such feeling as is expressed in Train's words, that animated father then, for we believe he did not think that the war with Mexico was just on the part of the United States.

While we lived in Canal Dover, brother William's apprenticeship with Christian Rissor, at Ashland, expired, and he came home. After reaching home he worked but a short time at his trade, as he soon engaged as a clerk in a dry goods store in Dover, owned by John and Jacob Sterling with whom he remained until the family moved away. Among our friends, neighbors, and acquaintances in Canal Dover, besides those already mentioned, were the Tingleys, Harmounts, Winnels, Fraziers, Waltons, Prichards, Brenards, and Shawlters. Brother Frazier was a class leader there. Brother Shawlter's family were specially warm friends of ours, and for their marked kindness to us we will always remember them with deep gratitude.

## ASHLAND CIRCUIT—(Second Time).

#### Conference Year, 1849.

From the time father joined the Conference, at Springfield, in 1835, to the close of his appointment to Canal Dover, in the fall of 1848, he had never had any illness severe enough to interfere with his ministerial labors. In fact, he has no recollection of ever having been seriously sick before or since. But his good fortune in this particular was about to undergo a change, and the family, were on the eve of a trying ordeal.

The Conference that year met at Mansfield, Ohio, Bishop Hamline presiding. Our own mental and bodily affliction during the time the family were at Dover, has been previously intimated. In consequence of this affliction, and not thinking of being taken sick himself, father had gone to Conference with the request that he be sent again to Ashland Circuit. Ashland, at that time, was a kind of common home, or family headquarters. Sister Mary Stubbs lived there, brother David was in business there, and it was felt that under the circumstances it would be a comfort and support to be with them. Besides, we had many warm friends and acquaintances there whom we had left behind us four years before. Father's request was granted, but he returned from Conference much out of health. Arriving home, he just had time to pack the household goods and start them, with five of the children—Sarah, Sam, Emily, Eleanor, and Melinda—for Ashland, before he was taken down with typhoid fever. We stayed with mother and father at Dover. The parsonage had to be vacated for the new preacher, and in the exigency of the case, we three found a home in the family of Brother Shawlters. At his house father lay sick for about six weeks, in a condition which made it unsafe for him to be moved. The people were very kind. Brother Shawlters refused any remuneration for the trouble and expense we were to them, and the physician, Dr. Slingluff, charged nothing for his services. Before this sickness of father's, his weight had been about one hundred and sixty-five pounds. Just after he got over it he weighed but little more than one hundred pounds. Within the next year, however, his weight increased to two hundred and twenty-five pounds, which weight he has maintained, with but little variation, ever since.

While father lay sick at Canal Dover, sister Eleanor, who had gone on to Ashland, took down with the same disease there. Both she and father sank very low, and while we in Dover were daily expecting to hear of her death, the family in Ashland were in constant expectation of like news respecting father. When father had so far convalesced that he was considered out of danger, mother and ourself left Dover for Ashland. Brother William took us in a buggy. A month or two after our arrival at Ashland we were also taken down with the fever, but it was a great blessing to us. Dr. Clark then said if we ever recovered, it would take away from us all our former trouble, and it did. We remember that it broke up in a case of measles, during which the following incident occurred: The doctor had forbidden the folks letting us eat any hickory-nuts or walnuts. A supply had been gathered in the fall, and we knew where they were hidden, under the hay in the barn. We saw the other children eating them and wished some very much. It was on Saturday, and all the family but sister Sarah were out of the house. She was preparing things for Sunday. The snow on the ground was a foot deep. Watching for the opportunity when her attention was away from us, we leaped out of bed and ran, bare-footed and undressed, to the barn. She called to us, saying she would let us have some nuts if we would come back; but we preferred not to trust to promises, and thus accomplished our object. Despite the doctor's injunctions and the fears of the family, no evil results followed.

When father was so far recovered that he could travel, brother William started with him for Ashland.

On their way, a little past Wooster, they met brother David coming from Ashland after him, and William returned to

Dover. A few days after Father's arrival home, David was taken sick with the typhoid fever, and lingered in a low state for a number of weeks. Although mentioned third, our own was the last of the four cases of typhoid fever, that happened in the family during that trying period of our history. William did not remain long at Canal Dover after the family left there. Feeling lonesome, he came home to Ashland, and after a little visit there, left for Norwalk, Ohio, where he engaged as clerk in the postoffice. How long he occupied this position we can not exactly tell, but we are quite sure it was not longer than a year. From Norwalk he went to Sandusky City as book-keeper for the firm of "Belden & Graham." Dr. Shaffer's term as Presiding Elder expired with the Conference session at Mansfield, and father does not recollect who the new Elder was while he was on Ashland Circuit the second time. Neither does he recollect who his colleague was that year, but his old friend Jesse Warner filled his place while he was sick at Dover.

When at last the family were through with their troubles from sickness, and father had again entered fully upon his ministerial labors, matters went on smoothly and prosperously. The building of a new church was put under way, and it was about half done when, at the close of the year, father was unexpectedly transferred to another charge.

The change of father from Ashland Circuit at that time—he having been there but one year and the new church which he had started being yet unfinished—occurred, it is supposed, through the exercise of an unchristian spirit on the part of the Presiding Elder, and grew out of the following circumstances: There was a deficiency in the amount of money required to pay the Presiding Elder and the preachers. Under this state of affairs, the Elder suggested that he should be paid his full allowance, and that the deficiency should be borne by the circuit preachers. Father would not consent to this and therefore, in a retaliatory way, he was transferred to another charge.

## BUCYRUS CIRCUIT.

### Conference Year—1850.

August 1, 1849, Conference sat at Findlay, Ohio, Bishop Waugh presiding. Friday, August 3, following, was observed by the Conference as a day of fasting and prayer for the deliverance of the country from the ravages of cholera, which had been raging for several months. On this occasion Adam Poe preached in the Presbyterian Church at Findlay, from the text,— Numbers, 16th chapter, 48th verse,— "And he stood between the dead and the living, and the plague was stayed." Rev. Ward had died at Sandusky City, and Rev. Cooper had died at Carey, Ohio, just before Conference met. Both died from cholera, and both were members of that Conference. From this session father was sent to Bucyrus Circuit, Edward Williams being his colleague, and Thomas Barkdull the Presiding Elder.

Bucyrus is located on the Sandusky river, and is the county seat of Crawford County, Ohio. The town is laid out regularly, the streets running north and south, east and west. It has a public square, and a town pump, the water from which is sulphurous. The main street of the place runs north and south. At Bucyrus, we found a very comfortable brick parsonage, and a low brick church situated on the same lot with the parsonage. The church was too small for the congregation. Both church and parsonage stood east of the public square, facing south on the main cross-street of the town. The district school-house was almost in the rear of the parsonage lot.

Just across the alley from the parsonage stable was a grove bordered on the far side by the Sandusky river. It was while we were living at Bucyrus that the right of way for the P., Ft. W. & C. R. W. was blazed through this grove. We used to go through its woods back of the stable, to the river, to swim and fish. On one occasion father was away, and not expecting him home before a certain time we slipped off to the river to fish without leaving any wood cut. We caught a big sucker and was on our way back, when we saw father through the trees coming after us. The sight of him meant a whipping unless we could in some way turn his wrath. Knowing he was very fond of fish we held up our sucker prominently so that he could see it while yet quite a distance away, and hoped that in the thought of eating him he might forgive us. But our stratagem availed nothing, for he gave us a good whipping and seemed to take no notice of the fish.

We have the following recollection of the family's moving to Bucyrus. It was a bright sunshiny day in August when we left Ashland, and our course lay in a general westward direction, through Mansfield and Galion. The household goods were loaded in two wagons. A farmer named King, we think, furnished one of the teams. Who furnished the other we do not remember. How the other members of the family reached Bucyrus, we have forgotten, but we rode behind the wagons on father's riding animal, a handsome bay mare of the breed called "Bull-of-the-Woods." The trip occupied one day. A little after dusk we arrived at the home of Col. Stephen Rouse, whose farm lay just outside of Bucyrus on the Galion road. There we stopped over night, but the wagons went on to the parsonage. It seems to us now, that at Rouse's we found father and mother, and probably one or two other members of the family, who had arrived there ahead of us. But Sarah, Emily, and Linda stayed at 'Squire Stowe's. They were taken there in a carriage by the 'Squire's son, Robert. This was the same 'Squire Stowe that had lived in Ashland when we did, five years before, and to whom we have referred as going to Mansfield with father when he went there to be made a Mason.

Mrs. Stowe was the 'Squire's second wife, and an old friend of father's and mother's from the State of Delaware. In Bucyrus Mr. Stowe was a Justice of the Peace, and the proprietor of a nursery. His family lived at the top of the hill, on the west side, at the extreme south end of Main street.

Colonel Rouse was a wealthy and leading member of the M. E. Church at Bucyrus. His family lived in style and elegance.

Their mansion house was a large brick that stood back some distance from the road, with a grassy plot in front. A walk led from a handsome farm gate up through the lawn to the house, the front door of which was reached by a flight of steps ascending to a veranda, a distance of six or eight feet from the ground. We can remember that we were strangely, but perhaps not unnaturally, impressed with the comfort and splendor of our surroundings at this home of wealth. The house was brilliantly lighted, and the handsomely furnished rooms and sumptuous table, with its decorations of silver, were rather bewildering to a boy of thirteen accustomed mostly to the common furniture and plain family fare of a Methodist preacher. The Rouse family comprised six or seven children, but only three of them were unmarried or living at home at that time. These were two grown daughters—Lydia and Adeline (commonly called Puss)—and Henry, the youngest, a boy about sixteen years old. We saw them frequently afterward, but we can now bring them distinctly to mind only in the scenes of that evening. Lydia was a tall brunette, with hair and eyes jet black and complexion somewhat sallow. Puss was not so tall or slim as Lydia, and just the opposite of her sister in complexion—a blonde.

Bucyrus Circuit was a strong one, comprising wealthy members at nearly all its different points. Three of its principal appointments, at that time, were Annapolis (a little village five miles northeast of Bucyrus), Galion, twelve miles southeast, and the neighborhood of the Monnett's about five or six miles directly south. Annapolis had a very pleasant little white frame church and a good society. Horace Rouse, the eldest son of Col. Stephen Rouse, of Bucyrus, kept store there. He was a leader in the Church and his house was one of father's frequent stopping places.

Galion was then a little village, the population of which did not exceed two hundred. In 1880 its census showed seven thousand. On our way to Ashland recently we passed through Galion. With our mind fixed on scenes that met our eye there when visiting the place with father one Sabbath afternoon, thirty-eight years before, we took a good glance at the place, endeavoring to spy out the little church and the farm house where we stopped, at the edge of the village, but these, with nearly all other traces of the village itself, had disappeared.

The Monnett neighborhood embraced a number of families of that name, among whom were Uncle Jerry Monnett, a good old local preacher; Abram Monnett, commonly known as "Mud Run" Abram, because he lived near a small stream called Mud Run; Abram Monnett, junior, son of Uncle Jerry Monnett; and William Monnett. These people were all in good circumstances and father remembers them as among the truest friends and happiest acquaintances of his whole life. Uncle Jerry Morris also lived there, whom we recollect as a member of that congregation, and as the owner of a large farm. He once gave the family a flock of fine chickens—six large yellow pullets and a rooster. The hens were all of one size and so feathered that you could not tell one from the other. The rooster mated the hens.

On one occasion we attended Quarterly meeting with father and mother at the Monnett meeting house. To reach it one had to go directly south about five miles, and then on a cross road to the left directly east; a few hundred yards from the main road stood the meeting house. A mile or so further on past the church you came to the home of William Monnett, with whom we stopped at that time. We already had some acquaintance with the children of the family. Two daughters and a son had previously attended the high school with us at Bucyrus. The following, which occurred while we were there, has never been told before: It is a common thing for a farmer boy to have a colt that he calls his own, and on which he always rides to church, to town, or to see his girl. William Monnett's son had a sorrel colt that he thought was superior to any other in the neighborhood. On Sunday morning father and mother went to service with the older members of the Monnett family. Finding an extra saddle and bridle for our horse, the Bull-of-the-Woods mare, we rode to church horseback, in company with young Monnett and several other farmer boys. It was decided before we got back that the preacher's horse was the fastest nag in the lot.

Mud Run Abram Monnett was a wealthy stock raiser. He had four children, two sons and two daughters. The father, Elizabeth (the elder sister), and the two boys all died of typhoid fever within a few weeks of each other. Mary, the other daughter, and her mother, then moved to Delaware,

Ohio. There, soon afterward, her mother died, and Mary was left an heiress to eighty thousand dollars. She gave an endowment fund to the University at Delaware. How much the subscription was we do not know, but Monnett Hall there is named for her. Such was her friendship for father and mother that she proposed sending two of their children to Delaware to school. It was in acceptance of this proposition that Emily and Linda attended school there, we think during the years 1859 and 1860. Subsequently she was married at Marion, Ohio, to John Bain. After living a few years in Marion they moved East. Mrs. Bain, we understand, is now dead.

The church at Bucyrus being old and dilapidated, as well as too small, the erection of a new and larger one was soon proposed after father arrived there. Everybody seemed to favor the proposition, and early in the year a sufficient amount of money had been subscribed to justify undertaking the work. The old house, however, was not abandoned until after the first winter following the family arrival at Bucyrus. This fact is impressed upon our mind, for, to earn a little extra money, we filled the office of sexton for the church that winter. It was a hard job to keep the old building clean and warm enough to be comfortable. The old structure was torn down in the spring of 1850, and the new one was so far finished by the same time in the following year that services could be held in its basement. In the meantime the Sunday-school and church services were held in the English Lutheran Church, which stood but a short distance away, on the opposite side of the street. We remember that while the English Lutheran Church was being thus occupied by the Methodists, they held a Sunday-school exhibition there, in which the stage was arranged as we have described in our account of Canal Dover for a like occasion there. One part of the exercises was a dialogue by a number of young girls representing a missionary society. The time set in the play was a hot day in August, the thermometer 100° in the shade, and they were making flannel jackets for the heathen in Africa. One girl, very enthusiastic in the cause, exclaimed, "Oh! dear! the poor little heathen! How I wish they had their flannel jackets now!"

The following incident as related by father occurred in connection with his ministerial labors at Bucyrus, before the old church was torn down. "During my first winter there, while the little old church was yet standing, one Sabbath evening near the holidays, I was preaching to a full house. Soon after commencement of the services I saw a stranger enter and seat himself near the door. At the close of the meeting, after the benediction had been pronounced, this stranger rose hastily and came up the aisle about half way to the pulpit. He, then, in a voice that could be heard all over the house said, 'there will be a ball at the Tuttle House, in Benton, on New Year's night, on which occasion there will be some music and a good deal of dancing.' I said to the congregation 'I hope you will not respect that man for making that announcement here.' He turned, and looking at me replied, saucily, 'Help yourself if you can,' and then hurriedly left the church. Upon inquiry I found his name to be Tuttle, a notorious infidel who kept the Tuttle House at Benton, a little place only a few miles from Bucyrus; also, that he had been in the habit of disturbing congregations all about his neighborhood. A consultation over the matter resulted in a decision to try to put a stop to such conduct. A complaint was entered, alleging the charge of disturbing public worship, and a warrant was issued for his arrest. Lawyer Josiah Scott volunteered his services in the prosecution of the case. Tuttle was defended by a young lawyer of ability named Plants. The suit was before Squire Stowe. Tuttle was convicted as charged in the warrant, and was fined the highest amount authorized by the statute and the costs of action. I never heard of his again disturbing a congregation, but he never forgave me, and tried to abuse me as a Minister of the Gospel for several years after." Brother Sam, who was standing near Tuttle at the time he intruded his announcement in the church, says the following were his exact words: "I desire to give notice of a meeting to be held at my house in Benton, on Christmas Eve, to celebrate the return of the prodigal son to his father's house. There will be considerable music and some dancing on the occasion." In the trial, we remember, it was shown that Tuttle had attracted the attention of several persons near him in the congregation previous to his bold act at the close. He took part in singing the closing hymn substituting, for himself, words different from those in the book. The last line of the last verse, he sung, "And send them all to hell." Lawyer Scott, who prosecuted this case, afterward became Chief Justice of the Supreme Court of Ohio.

We find that memory operates very singularly. A little thing will fasten itself in the mind and stick there when whole pages of intervening life and experiences will be entirely forgotten. We do not recollect Elder Barkdull distinctly except in connection with the following incident: He arrived at our house one morning about eight or nine o'clock to attend quarterly meeting. He came in a gig, and driving a tall, chestnut horse with clean limbs, thin mane, and full, round eye. While the horse, splashed with mud, was standing in the stable picking his hay, and drying, father and the Elder were talking over his merits. In the general conversation, to show how good his horse was, the Elder said, "I drove him seventeen miles this morning at the rate of twelve miles an hour."

We notice that the cyclopedia mentions Bucyrus as the place where, in the year 1848, the bones of a mastodon were found, in a good state of preservation. This was about a year before we moved there, and we remember that the discovery was still much talked of at that time. Near the south border line of the town there is a ridge of land, running east and west, technically termed a watershed. North of it all streams flow toward the lakes, and those south of it flow toward the Gulf. It was in the neighborhood of the watershed that the bones of the mastodon were found.

It was in Bucyrus that we first attended Quaker meeting. There was a little white church, not far from the parsonage, in which some members of that denomination were holding service. We were playing in the street, and it was merely accidental that we went into the church. The following is our recollection of the meeting: The church had two doors of entrance, the pulpit being located in the front part of the room, between the doors, and the seats being gradually elevated one after another as they extended back from the pulpit. There were two preachers, and, as we sat in a seat by the door, we could look into the pulpit and see their whole forms. We sat, and sat, and sat; nobody moved; and nobody spoke. Finally, when it seemed as though the silence never would break, one of the preachers rose and said, "Bless God." He stood several minutes without saying another word. He then spoke a longer sentence than he did the first time. Then paused again, but not quite so long as before; and thus he kept on, making his pauses shorter and his talks longer, until he got to going with all the rapidity and noise his tongue and voice would afford.

One of the scenes familiar to us in connection with our residence at Bucyrus was the daily arrival of the old-time stage, or mail coach, from the south by the Galion route. The stage-coach in that day was the only general, public means there was for the conveyance of passengers and the carrying of the U. S. mails. It was then customary for the government to contract with different individuals and companies to carry the mails on certain lines. The latter, known as stage companies, furnished their own offices, agents, horses, drivers, and coaches, and over the more important routes and between main points, where the travel would justify it, they would run a line of stages, to transport passengers, to secure from them a revenue additional to what they received from the government for carrying the mails. On the minor routes the mails were transported separately, by boys on horse-back, commonly styled post-boys. The old-time stage-coach bore no resemblance to the omnibus, hotel cab, or any other vehicle of the present day, that we know of. It was less cumbersome than the modern omnibus, and far more comfortable to ride in, though not so light, stylish; or elegant in finish, as the hack that now waits for passengers at the doors of our city hotels. It was, however, much better adapted to its purpose than either one of the others would have been. The body of the stage-coach was a covered and enclosed box, set low between the wheels, and suspended on thick leather springs. The bottom on the under side was curved, being lowest in the center and rounding upward toward the front and back. Within, it was capable of seating from eight to twelve passengers. Entrance was made by doors at either side. Outside of the box it had what was called a front and hind boot. These were rack extensions with leather coverings, which, when buckled down, made a tight enclosure, having the shape of a common road scraper. In the front boot, under the driver's seat, was carried the mail, and in the hind boot was carried the baggage of the passengers. The top of the coach had a tight deck roof with a railing around it about six inches high, on which parcels and extra baggage could be stowed, and on which passengers sometimes rode when the inside of the coach was full. When under way the body of the coach would teeter backward and forward like a rocking chair in motion. When newly painted or clean its appearance was quite attractive. Usually four to six horses were attached; never less than four. The driver, whose seat was high in front, always carried a bugle horn, with which he signaled the coming of the stage just as it reached the suburbs of the town. After bugling its approach he would next crack his whip, and, reining up his horses, put them under a full gallop through the main street of the place to the postoffice, making almost as much rattle and noise as a train of cars, and attracting everybody's attention. This was the custom on all the principal mail routes, though we believe it was generally regarded as adopted by the drivers as an opportunity to show off. In these displays they sometimes upset the stage. But such accidents scarcely ever occurred except when the drivers were under the influence of liquor. A case of this kind happened at Bucyrus while we were there. The picture of the old stage, lying on its side in front of the postoffice, where it turned over, is clear in our mind yet. Nearly every boy in town went to look at it, and we distinctly recollect that the accident was attributed to the driver's being drunk.

Another clear recollection we have, associated with Bucyrus, was the frequent sight of boys and girls going to the brewery for yeast. Baking powder was unknown, and our warm biscuits were then made with saleratus. If too much was used, or the mixing poorly done, little yellow spots would appear in them. In such cases we have heard mother say, "I put too much saleratus in my biscuit." But to make light bread, nearly everybody in town used brewer's yeast. This was a light, frothy substance that oozed from the bung-holes of the beer barrels when the beer was first put into them after brewing, and while it was still working. The barrels, or kegs, would be filled from a large tub, or vat, and then set in a trough which would catch the yeast and run it into another tub made for the purpose, and from which it would be served out to those coming for it. We think it was two days in each week that the brewery sold yeast. Quite soon after breakfast, on those days, boys and girls, representing nearly every family in the place, would be seen filing along the road to the brewery for yeast, some with tin cups, some with tin buckets, and some with pitchers or other vessels. On a bright morning the long line of tin cups and buckets glinting in the sunlight made a pretty scene. The brewery was located northward, out of town. To reach it we crossed the covered bridge over the Sandusky River at the north end of Main street, and, after going straight on about a quarter of a mile, turned to the right on the road to Annapolis. A short distance farther, and at the top of a hill, was the brewery. On arriving there, every one was served in turn.

During our first year at Bucyrus we attended school in the old district school-house, just back of the parsonage. The teacher's name, we think, was Philo Martin. We can recall a picture of the play-ground, and can remember that the school which we attended was in the lower north room of the building, and that, upon dismissal, the boys and girls would make a general rush for the old town pump to get a drink of sulphur water; but only one special incident of the school appears vivid in our mind. One day the teacher was standing at his desk on the little platform near the entrance door of the room, mending a quill pen for one of the pupils. He had another quill stuck between his head and ear. While standing thus a large boy named Gus. Hetich, who sat in a row of seats almost in line with the door, said, "Please to let me go out?" The teacher replied, "No, sir." A few moments later the boy again said, "Please to let me go out?" The teacher again replied, this time very emphatically, "No, sir." The boy then got up and started for the door. Just as he was putting his hand upon the knob, the teacher quickly stepped from the platform behind him, and grasping him by the collar of his coat, back of his neck, jerked him backward and laid him full length on the floor. He then gave him a whipping and sent him to his seat.

Father was returned to Bucyrus Circuit for another year, from the Conference which sat at Medina, Ohio, August 7, 1850, Bishop Janes presiding. This year Jesse Durbin was father's colleague. Father says of him: "I found Jesse Durbin to be a very pious and talented young man. In our relations with each other he treated me as a father and I treated him as a son, and we had a very pleasant year together. This special mutual regard was preserved for years after separation. His health failing, at last he quit preaching." Our own recollection of Jesse Durbin is quite distinct. He made our house his home, and, as we were stable boy at that time, we remember that he owned and rode a nice iron-grey horse called Selim, in honor, we suppose, of Alexander-the-Great's famous horse of that name.

Bucyrus was the first place in our travels that we lived in after Union schools had begun to take the place of District schools in towns. They were introduced there in the fall of 1850, about the beginning of our second year at that place. Professor Booth was the first Principal. We were far enough advanced then to be a member of the High School. A room had to be provided for it in the start, and until a Union school-house could be built, the authorities engaged the Odd Fellows' Hall. It was a nice room, in the third story of a business house on Main street. It was handsomely carpeted, and had platforms at each end. The pupils sat on chairs and on benches. There were no desks. Adjoining the hall were several side rooms which were always kept locked, and which caused much speculation among the pupils as to what they contained. We recollect that at the close of the first year, Prof. Booth gave the High School a treat consisting of an abundance of candy and a two-bushel basketful of large, red apples. After the school was finally dismissed, a number of the boys and girls noticing that quite a large amount of candy and apples was left, agreed to come back that night and have a time. The arrangement was carried out, and we often think of the pleasures of that evening. We ate all the apples and candy that had been left from the treat during the day, and amused ourselves with a number of plays until after ten o'clock. One of the most popular of the plays in which we engaged was something as follows: All the boys and girls would stand to one side except two to start the play. These two would join hands and circle around singing:

> "We are marching down toward Quebec,
> Where the drums are loudly beating,
> The Americans have gained the day,
> And the British are retreating.

> "The wars are all o'er, and we'll turn back—
> Turn back from whence we started—
> We'll open the ring, and choose another in
> To relieve the broken-hearted."

When the singers came to the words, "We'll open the ring," they would loose their hands, and one of the outside party would be taken into the circle. The play would continue in this way until all were joined in the circle. The whole party would then marry off in couples, by kissing each other and going through some sham ceremony. There was much kissing in the play, which was probably the cause of its popularity. The kissing, or marrying off, was sometimes called "sugaring off."

The teacher of the high school was a pretty, sweet-mannered, black-eyed lady, named Dian Taylor, from Syracuse, N. Y. Later she married a Mr. Kenyon, from the same place. She was highly esteemed by all the pupils. Professor Booth was also much liked by the school. He was a dark-haired, angular-featured, genial hearted seven-footer. He married Julia Brown, a teacher in one of the intermediate schools. In one of his talks before the high school, we remember hearing him say, "I was seventeen years old before I went to school, or had any educational advantages. At that age I was about as tall as I am now, but not being prepared to go with the older and larger pupils, I had to take my place in a class of small ones. I naturally felt embarrassed, standing in line with pupils whose heads reached but little above my knees. But when I missed a word, to have one of them catch it out of my mouth, spell it quickly, and go above me, was more than I could endure. Instead, however, of discouraging me, it fired my ambition, and aroused in me a determination to study and succeed; and chiefly to such circumstances I owe to-day what knowledge I possess, and what success I have achieved."

During father's itinerancy he lost two horses and had two runaways. The first of the runaways occurred at Bucyrus, with the bay mare that we have several times referred to. The circumstances under which he got this mare are as follows: At Ashland he had owned another bay mare that stumbled a great deal. One day while on his way to Orange, she fell down with him, and he determined at once to get rid of her. On his arrival at Orange he traded her for a tall, white-legged, bald-faced, bay horse that had been run to a stage. He was lame, as was supposed, in the shoulder, but father thought he would get over it. In this he was mistaken, and becoming tired of riding a lame horse, he traded him to uncle George for the "Bull-of-the Woods" mare. The horses of this breed were classed among the best saddle animals in the country, but it was said they could not be broken to harness. However, father tested the matter with her, and had driven her considerably, and we think if she had not unfortunately got away from him, in time she would have become quite gentle. In the forenoon of the day the runaway occurred, he had hitched the mare up and had taken mother to Mrs. Stowe's to spend the day, intending to call for her again in the evening. It was while he had gone to bring her home that the accident took place. While standing in front of Mrs. Stowe's, waiting for mother to come and get into the buggy, the mare took fright at something and broke away. Father was dragged some distance, besides being run over by the buggy. He had his face skinned and was hurt otherwise to some extent, but not seriously.

Another incident connected with the family, and involving a runaway, occurred while we lived at Bucyrus. There was a blacksmith shop on the other side of the street opposite the parsonage. The blacksmith's name was Shock. Some man in town had sent one of a span of high-spirited, bob-tailed, bay horses to the shop to be shod, with instructions to the smith to send him back to the stable when the shoeing was done. There were several boys about the shop when the horse was ready to be returned, but all were afraid to ride him except brother Sam. We were on the other side of the street from the shop and saw the whole occurrence. Shock lifted Sam upon the horse and before he had time to gather up the reins the horse started off. The animal was for a time unmanageable and ran some distance down the street, colliding with an old man who was just crossing toward the court-house. The old gentleman was knocked down and seriously hurt. There was some excitement over the matter and we remember that one fellow claimed that he saw brother Sam direct the horse against the man.

Our friends and acquaintances on the Bucyrus charge were

too numerous to be fully recounted, but among the families that lived at Bucyrus while we were there, besides those already mentioned, we recall to mind the Scroggs, Henthorns, Bowmans, Shocks, Howensteins, Failors, Converses, Merrimans, Douglases, Hoffers, Forbeses, Cramers, Gormleys, and Warners. The first four were specially intimate and warm friends of the family. The family of Dr. Douglas were next door neighbors west of us, their lot adjoining that of the parsonage. The family of Henry Converse—a dry-goods merchant—were next door neighbors east of us, just across the alley from the church, which stood between their house and ours. Mrs. Converse we remember as a handsome, fine-looking woman. She would often employ us to cut wood for her. Elizabeth Cramer we recollect as a sewing girl, a zealous member of father's congregation, and a warm friend of the family. Warner was the proprietor of the American Hotel. His girls were great singers. Gormley, we believe, was a capitalist, at least we do not remember that he carried on any special business. His son, James B. Gormley, who was one of our playmates, is now President of the First National Bank there. We are indebted to him for some kind favors in compiling these notes.

But though many circumstances conspired to make our home at Bucyrus an exceedingly pleasant one, yet while there the family were called upon to endure the saddest event in its history. In our last account of Ashland, it is stated that brother William left us there to take a position as clerk in the Post-office, at Norwalk, whence he went to Sandusky City, as clerk and book-keeper for the firm of "Belden & Graham." The following letter written by him to sister Mary, a short time before he left Norwalk, helps us to approximate the time he made the change, and gives us some insight into the state of his feelings over the matter, and the reasons which induced the step that led to his awful death.

NORWALK, July 21, 1850.

DEAR SISTER:

I am aware that I have manifested great negligence in not writing you ere this, but it has not been owing to a want of brotherly love. I have, and always have had, as much affection for you as for any one of the family. I hear from you almost daily and I would have been to see you before this had it not been for my confinement in the postoffice. It is very healthful here at present, and the citizens generally, do not expect much cholera this year. Brewster's family are all well and appear to be prospering. I have had the "blues" this week, or rather all last week, and I can scarcely account for their origin. I have been in poor health for some time past, and I think that is one cause. I am unsettled in my mind as regards business, which I think is another. I do not believe that I could ever do much at my trade, and I desire to obtain a livelihood by a mode a little more independent than by clerking in a postoffice. I think very strongly of going to Sandusky City to live. I have an offer of a situation as clerk and book-keeper there in one of the best houses in the city. I am somewhat fearful that the place will again be visited by the "pestilence that walketh in darkness." Yet if they will give me the salary I think I ought to have, I shall be inclined to go. I will be able to decide next week. Now Mary, a word in your ear,—I have had serious thoughts on the subject of matrimony. I am acquainted with a lady whom I believe to be exactly suited to my mind;—virtuous, intellectual, and affectionate,—but she is not in possession of that quality which renders a woman truly lovely in the eyes of an aristocratic community,—namely, wealth. But to me this makes no difference, and if I were differently situated, I should not let this opportunity of securing a partner for life, go unimproved. However, I have almost come to the conclusion to let the work begun in good faith, end in a flirtation. I can not think of slipping my neck in the halter, while there is a probability of placing myself in embarrassing circumstances by so doing. This is my view of the subject. I would not have you think that I have obligated myself in a marriage contract,—not by any means. I have given no encouragement except by my frequent visits, for you may rest assured that when I once put my head in the halter, I will buckle the throat-latch. This is all I have to say on this subject and I wish you to keep it to yourself. Give my love to mother Stubbs, and the rest of the family. Write when convenient.

I remain your brother,

WM. M. GRAY.

As indicated in the foregoing letter it must have been about the first of August, 1850, that William went to Sandusky City where he lost his life on the morning of the 26th of February, 1851, by the burning of the store in which he was clerking. The following are the circumstances of his death: He and his room-mate, a young man by the name of Allen, were sleeping in a bed-room at the head of the stairs in the third story of the building. They had had the company of two young men in the store room the evening of the 25th until about 10 o'clock P. M., when they retired. About 2 o'clock in the morning William and Allen were awakened by the heat and smoke in the room. William forced his way out of the bed-room. His companion could not tell whether he went down stairs or to the front of the building, to escape. Allen was driven back by the heat and flames and threw himself out of a rear window to the ground back of the store. The fall nearly killed him, but he was able to crawl around nearly a square of buildings to the front of the store and cry, "Fire!" He died during the afternoon of the same day, not from injuries received in the fall, but from having breathed the flames to such an extent that his lungs were crisped. It was from Allen's statements before his death that we learn the circumstances of their being waked up, and the information as to where he had last seen William. We remember hearing the statement made, that the physicians, in hope of saving Allen's life, would not permit him to be questioned, otherwise we might have learned more particulars of the painful occurrence. Brother William and sister Sarah were more intimate at this time than any other two members of the family, and for almost a week prior to his death she had had horrible dreams with regard to him. While she was having these dreams she expressed a fear that something was to befall him. The evening of the 25th was spent by mother and father at the home of John Bowman, in Bucyrus. After supper father went into the country to preach, but mother remained all the evening at Bowman's. When she went home she found Sarah in a state of uneasiness. She said to her mother:—"Well. mother you have come at last! This has been the most unhappy evening I ever spent. I can not tell why, but it is so, I have had a young lady caller, but I did not enjoy her visit, and was glad when she left, for I could not entertain her." This same night Sarah dreamed that William had been murdered and that friends were searching for his body amid smoke and ruins. At Bucyrus there were no telegraphic facilities and no railroads, and of a necessity the sad news did not reach us until two days after the fire. We received it about noon on the 28th. Jesse Durbin was standing on the sidewalk in front of the parsonage, when the newsboy rode up. Sister Sarah was in the front room of the house, up stairs. Hearing voices she stepped to the window and distinguishing the words "Sandusky City," and " Mr. Gray's son," she immediately grasped the truth, and rushing down stairs, said to mother, " William is dead." Father was down town at the time, but reached home shortly afterwards. Sisters Emily and Ellen were just returning from school and were met by a little girl who said to them, " Your brother is burned up." The boy told Mr. Durbin that William had been lost and that citizens were hunting for his body when he left Sandusky City.

The next morning father started on horseback for Republic

where he expected to take a train for Sandusky City, but upon arriving at Republic he received a telegram stating that the body had been found, and taken to Norwalk for burial. Knowing that he could not get to Norwalk to attend the funeral, he returned to Bucyrus. On the following Monday he went to Norwalk after the funeral had taken place. Joseph and Mary Stubbs, William and Elizabeth Brewster, and brother David S. Gray were all the members of the family present at the burial. That brother William's death was a murder there is no moral reason to dispute, though perhaps not intended by those who perpetrated it. He also seems to have been borne to his fate by some silent, unavoidable, and impelling influence that would not permit him to escape. The evening before his death he had just returned from a visit to Norwalk, and the following facts were made known by our sister Elizabeth at the time that the circumstances of the fire were exciting inquiry. "Belden & Graham," proprietors of the store in which William was employed, sent him and young Allen away or at least intimated to them, without any solicitation from the young men themselves, that they could visit their homes or friends if they wished to. It is supposed that the proprietors burned the house for the insurance money, and it was their intention not to have any of the employes in the store at the time. The young men left but returned unexpectedly to the firm and went to their room in the store without the proprietor's knowledge. It was also said that one of the firm,—Belden, we believe,—was at work in the cellar of the building all the afternoon before the fire.

William usually had a fine flow of spirits, was lively, social, and witty, but like all such natures, had his periods of depression. During his visit at Norwalk he seemed more thoughtful and low spirited than ever. Elizabeth desired him to extend his visit beyond the time he had set to return to Sandusky. The nearest point to a railroad was Monroeville, five miles from Norwalk. The journey was made by stage. William was undecided what he should do,—stay or go—and at last decided to go. But on the way he hesitated again, and told the driver of the stage that he had determined to settle the matter in his mind in this way: If the train was at the depot when he arrived at Monroeville, or on time, he would go on, but if at all behind time he would return with him to Norwalk. The train was on time and thus his doom was fixed. The following lines by some unknown friend were published in a Norwalk paper a short time subsequent to his death.

MARCH 11, 1851.

## A TRIBUTE OF RESPECT TO THE MEMORY OF WILLIAM M. GRAY.

So soon hast thou passed from earth away,
    To realms of light this darksome vale beyond;
Though bright and joyous was thy earthly stay,
    Yet thou hast gained a far happier home.

Thou art not lost, but only gone before,
    Released from all earth's weary toils and pain;
And should we wish thee back to suffer o'er,
    That dying strife—those agonies again?

Ah, no! though friends thy absence may deplore,
    And bitter tears in heart-felt sorrow flow,
Though thou with joyous smiles wilt cheer no more,
    That lovely circle in thy home below.

Though thy sad friends, deep stricken now and lone,
    For thy fond coming look and hope in vain,
List for the music of thy gentle tone,
    As oft 'twas heard in sympathetic strain.

They little thought a change would come so soon,
    O'er the fond picture of thy young heart's dream;
That hope so fair in promise, full in bloom
    Should perish thus shrouded by death's dark gloom.

The grave is now thy resting place,—thy home;
    Thy loving friends will soon thy glories share,
And till that coming resurrection morn,
    Unconscious still thou'lt sweetly slumber there.

Loved one! farewell! Around thy lowly bed
    Fond footsteps often-times will linger near;
And o'er thy ashes long in sorrow shed
    The sweet mementoes of affection's tear.

# REPUBLIC.

### Conference Year, 1852.

July 31, 1851, Conference sat at Bellefontaine, Ohio, Bishop Morris presiding. At this Conference father was appointed to Republic Circuit, with John A. Mudge junior preacher. William B. Disbro, who had been father's colleague on Norwalk Circuit, nine years before, was Presiding Elder. Republic is in Seneca County, Ohio, ten miles east of Tiffin, and twenty-two miles north of Bucyrus. It is located on the original line of the old Mad River & Lake Erie Railroad, then extending from Springfield to Sandusky City, the principal intermediate points being Urbana, Bellefontaine, Kenton, Tiffin, Republic, and Bellevue. While we were still living at Republic the route of the road was partly changed, by the railroad company's building a new road branching off from the old one at Tiffin, and running thence to Sandusky City, north of Republic and Bellevue, by way of Clyde, Ohio. This change destroyed the importance of the road through Republic, although, we believe, it was operated by the company for a while afterward, on a small scale, as a branch line.

Republic then contained about one thousand inhabitants, and was the first place we had lived in that was situated on a railroad. The road itself, we think, was the first one built in Ohio, and was a very rough and imperfect affair compared with the railroads of late years. Notwithstanding, at one time it was the only rail line in the State for the transportation of freight and passengers between the West and South and the Lakes, and in this particular did a large business. It was supplanted, however, in its extensive through traffic, when the new railroad was built,—connecting with the Little Miami road at Xenia,—through Columbus to Cleveland. This rival line which, from Columbus to Cleveland, was called the Cleveland, Columbus & Cincinnati Railroad, was finished about the year 1850, and was the one with which our brother, D. S. Gray, first became connected in his railroad career.

The box freight cars of the road through Republic were painted a brownish or dingy red, and were of two sizes,—one with four wheels, the other with eight. Those of four wheels had one truck, those of eight had two. The former were about thirteen feet in length,—just half the size of the latter,—and had a capacity of eight thousand pounds. They were intended exclusively for the transportation of grain from the elevators along the road, to Sandusky City.

The track bore but little resemblance to the smooth, well ballasted railroads of to-day. It was constructed with three-cornered, split, oak ties, laid on the flat sides, with the sharp edges up, no ballast between them. The ends of the ties were all notched in line, and stringers,—long pieces of timber five or six inches square,—were inserted in the notches to hold the ties together and to form a surface on which to lay the rail. The rail was a flat, iron bar, which, instead of causing the wheel to stand up well and clear of the track, let it down so that the inside of the timber, on which the bar rested, formed a part of the bearing for the flange of the wheel, to hold it on the track. At Republic we first saw a locomotive, but it was before we moved there and while we were living at Bucyrus. The church members at Bucyrus were getting up a supper and wished to have oysters; so we were sent in company with young Henry Rouse to Republic to get them. While there we saw an engine on the track. It was painted green, had brass mountings, well burnished, and looked fresh and clean, as if recently out of the shop. We thought it about the handsomest thing we had ever seen. But we returned to Bucyrus disappointed in our trip as there were no oysters in town.

All the preaching appointments of Republic Circuit were within Seneca County, and all except three,—Republic, Attica and Lodi,—were located in the country in prosperous farming neighborhoods. The church at Republic was a counterpart of the one at Canal Dover,—a white frame, with a basement and a broad flight of steps in front leading to the main audience-room above.

The parsonage, also a white frame, was a very comfortable dwelling, with three rooms up stairs, three down, and a summer kitchen attached. It stood on a lot adjoining the church. Both the church and the parsonage fronted east on one of the principal streets of the town, which extended north in a direct line with the road from Bucyrus, which led into the place from the south. The railroad crossed this street about a hundred yards north of the parsonage.

Republic had excellent schools, under the supervision of Professor Aaron Schuyler. Just what organization the schools had there, at that time, we can not now define. Whether Union, District, or in part select, we can not say. The school building was a large, three story brick, that had, evidently, been originally intended for an academy. It stood alone, on the eastern border of the village, on a site comprising several acres of unenclosed ground. The gables pointed north and south, and its side front faced west to the next street east of the one on which the parsonage and the M. E. Church were located. The third story had a hall running through its center the entire length of the building, with little rooms, about ten feet square, partitioned off on both sides of it. The whole number of these rooms was probably sixteen or eighteen. They were for the benefit of students from abroad, who used them for lodging simply, or as rooms in which they might lodge and board themselves. The school had quite a number of students of this class attending it while we lived there. They were mostly the sons of farmers who lived within a distance of eight or ten miles around. When school began in the fall we frequently observed them moving in with their cooking utensils and bedding, and moving out again at the close of school in the spring. We think there were only three schools in the building at that time,—one in the north room on the second floor, and two in the north and south rooms below. The south room on the second floor contained the school apparatus, and was used for recitation and experiment. Professor Schuyler had a State reputation as a mathematician, and frequently lectured on the subject at different places. Amanda Purse, whom he married while we were there, taught in the lower north room. Mary

Scroggs, a friend of our family, from Bucyrus, also taught one department in a little school-house south of the Universalist Church. After Schuyler and Miss Purse were married, they went to keeping house on a little farm contiguous to the school grounds on the east, which they bought from a widow Paddock, whose husband was a relative of the Paddock that used to issue Paddock's Detector, in Cincinnati, in the days of Statebank and wild-cat money. Mrs. Schuyler then quit teaching, but her husband continued to be Superintendent of the school. We remember that one Saturday, in the fall, after moving on the farm, Schuyler made a corn-husking, and invited all the students to attend. In return for the work of the huskers he set out a big supper. It was a shrewd move, for the farmerboy students did not hesitate at the labor, and having been boarding themselves awhile, were in good condition to enjoy a square meal.

There were three different churches in Republic,—the Universalist, the Presbyterian, and the Methodist. The Universalist had no pastor, and the pulpit was not occupied more than three or four times during our stay in the place. Both the Presbyterian and Methodist had strong congregations. The membership of the M. E. Church was largely comprised of women whose husbands were leading men in the town, but not members of any church. We also remember three widows,—Mrs. Baldwin, Mrs. Lambkins, and Mrs. Burrows,—who belonged to the M. E. Church there, and who were very active members.

The town contained two stores,—Ogden's and Simmons's—a large flouring mill owned by a Mr. Russell, a small foundry owned by David Ogden, and two or three large grain warehouses, or elevators. It was a good shipping point for flour and grain. Russell's flouring mill, we think, burned down while we lived there.

## Conference Year, 1853.

August 25, 1852, Conference met at Delaware, Ohio, Bishop Simpson, presiding. From this Conference father was re-appointed to Republic Circuit with James Fribley for his colleague. James Fribley was the son of the Mr. Fribley whom we have before mentioned as living at Oldtown, the one outside appointment that was attached to Canal Dover Station. Father's two years at Republic were quiet, peaceful ones,—no jarrings or contentions in the church. They were not marked by any very large revivals, yet there was a steady, continual increase of membership.

It was while we were living at Republic that we prevented an accident that might have resulted in the death of our mother and a lady friend of the family,—Mrs. Baldwin. At the time brother William lost his life he owned a little black mare that he had bought from Mr. Brewster. The mare was sent to father, and it was the desire of the family for him to keep her. To gratify this wish he sold his other horse, and as the mare was considered too small to do all his work, he bought a mate for her. When he went to his appointments in the buggy he usually drove them double, and when he rode horseback he used them turn about. The mare that had been owned by William was accustomed to the shafts, and though spirited, ambitious, and quite speedy, was yet gentle enough for a woman to drive. One day, mother and Mrs. Baldwin drove her about two miles out in the country to visit the family of a Mr. Church. They reached Mr. Church's home safely and spent the day there. On their return they had arrived just opposite the Universalist Church, within about one hundred yards of our house, when a big dog jumped out of a wagon and ran barking at the mare's heels. This frightened her so that she started to run. We were standing at the parsonage watching for their return when this occurred, and running out into the street we flaunted our hat in the mare's face, causing her to turn down the alley, without striking the fence, to the parsonage stable, where she stopped. Mother afterwards said, she never saw our old straw hat with more pleasure than at that time.

It was while we were at Republic that father had his second runaway. A horse dealer had bought the two black mares, and father was then owning a rough coated white horse, that he did not much admire. Having had a new buggy made at Tiffin, he went to get it. While there he fell in with a young man who had a nice looking sorrel mare, and father traded the white horse for her. In driving her home to the new buggy, he discovered that she was afraid of the top. On coming to a steep hill he, therefore, concluded to get out and lead the mare down. In doing so, and in holding her back, the mare's head was pulled around so that she saw the buggy top, and taking fright, ran away, and broke the buggy almost to pieces. It is likely that in this case extreme caution caused the accident, and that if he had staid in the buggy the runaway would not have happened.

In the winter of 1852-3, while living at Republic, and when we were between sixteen and seventeen years of age, we taught school in Erie County, Ohio, at a salary of sixteen dollars per month, and board. We were employed through the recommendation of Mrs. Amsden, a friend of ours, and a member of father's Church. As Republic had good schools, it was not uncommon then for school Directors from the country around to come there for teachers. Acquaintances of Mrs. Amsden had written her to send them some one whom she thought competent to teach their school. She apprised us of the fact and gave us a letter of recommendation to her friends. Professor Schuyler likewise gave us a letter of recommendation for a license, to the district examiner, who was Superintendent of public schools at Sandusky City. The school district in which we taught was seven miles from Sandusky City, and from the school house in which we taught we could see the Sandusky Bay. We remember that one of the Director's sons went with us to Sandusky to get our license. It was about 1 o'clock P. M. when we reached the public school building in the city. School had not yet taken up for the afternoon, and the boys and girls were yet playing outside. At that time we did not think that we looked green, but something about our appearance or that of our companion indicated to them that we were from the country, and the boys and girls hooted at us as we passed through the grounds into the building. It was while teaching school there that we first attended a ball, on Christmas Eve, and took our initiatory steps in dancing. While there, also, we probably had one of the most varied experiences that ever fell to the lot of a country school teacher in the matter of boarding round. One of the Directors, whose name was Robinson, had his mother living with him. She was quite an old lady and had a cancer in one eye. There were only two rooms in the house down stairs, one in which to sit, and one in which to eat. For one whole week, during the mornings and evenings, we were compelled to stay in the sitting-room with this old lady and go to the table with the sight of her in our mind. At another place where we boarded, the husband could not read, and the wife was ruler of the family. She could swear like a sailor and was as uncouth as a savage. Here we had to sleep in the loft of the log cabin, in one bed with her three boys. To reach the sleeping apartment we had to climb up a ladder to a hole through the loft floor. At another place we had a proposal of marriage from the daughter of one of the Directors. As an inducement on her part she said she had three hundred dollars in money and a span of bay colts. She was much older than we were, was cross-eyed, and very homely. The offer was mildly rejected. But after all, we passed through the ordeal with credit as a teacher, and arrived safe at home again in the spring.

On the 4th of July, 1852 or 1853, we recollect going to Tiffin, and hearing Gen. William H. Gibson deliver an oration. We still think it the best we ever heard. He was then a rising young lawyer, probably near thirty years of age.

On Republic Circuit we found a Mr. and Mrs. Hatton, whom father had married when he was on Dalton Circuit. She was a very pretty woman. They were members of the M. E. Church, and lived on a farm near one of the interior points of the circuit. At Republic we also met a family named Iler, that had lived in Wooster at the same time we did. They were poor when we knew them in Republic, and Mr. Iler teamed about the place with a pair of old, white, "crow-bait" horses. The family were not good looking. The children were freckle-faced, cross-eyed, and had red hair. We learn from father, however, that three or four of the boys now live in Omaha, and that they are very wealthy and among the leading citizens of the place. Father, who has since met them, says, " These red-headed, freckle-faced, cross-eyed children have made very fine looking men. Julia Iler is now a widow in Omaha, and is a very pretty woman."

While at Republic, during the summer school vacations, we engaged in several kinds of employment to make a little money for our own support. At one time we worked in the harvest field, at father Church's, raking and binding wheat. We took the ague there while in the field, and had to lie down in a fence corner until we got well enough to start home. On another occasion during harvest we worked on a farm adjoining the town. We were healthy and strong then, and instead of merely raking and binding wheat, we recollect swinging a cradle all of one day. Our hands, however, were terribly blistered in consequence. The reaping machine was then unknown. At other times we plowed corn for Mr. Simmons, the store-keeper, who kept a team of horses and tilled several acres of ground which he owned near the village. We also hauled wood for him at times with his team, and stayed in his store during noon hours, while he was gone to dinner. The last money-making employment we had while at Republic was clerking in a grocery store. The family were well received at Republic and had quite a pleasant stay there.

EMILY McCULLY GRAY RUTHRAUFF.

# FINDLAY.

### Conference Year, 1854.

The family moved from Republic to Findlay in the fall of 1853. The Conference that year convened at Mt. Vernon, Ohio, August 24, Bishop Ames presiding. Findlay was the second Conference Station to which father was appointed during his ministry; the second place in which we lived that was on a line of railroad; and the first place in all our changes to which the family and household goods were transferred by the cars.

Findlay is the county seat of Hancock County, in the northwestern part of Ohio, and is located on Blanchard River, a branch, we think, of either the Auglaize or Portage River. In railroad facilities it was then the terminal point only of a branch of the Mad River & Lake Erie R. R., running sixteen miles, from Carey, on the main line, to Findlay. Now, however, it is reached by two other railroads—the Lake Erie & Western and the Toledo, Columbus & Southern. It was then a place of about two thousand inhabitants, and was a good mart for country trade and produce, and for shipments of grain and stock. The fact that the railroad company built a branch line to reach it is a good indication of its importance. At that time the charge had two little country appointments attached to it. One of these, when we first went there, was at Switzer's School-House, but before the year closed it was changed to Thomas's School-House, about three miles up the Blanchard. The other appointment was about two miles west of Findlay, at Burkehead's School-House. Father preached at Findlay twice every Sunday, and at each of the country appointments every other Sunday in the afternoon, which made three sermons for him to prepare every week. The membership of the M. E. Church at Findlay was quite large, comprising seven classes; besides, there was a class at each of the country appointments. Judge Corey, Hugh Newell, J. J. Baldwin, and George Biggs are remembered among the class leaders of the town. A 'Squire Philips was the class leader at Burkehead's School-House, and a Brother Grable at Thomas's School-House. Parlee Carlin, whose eldest daughter married General Robinson, now Secretary of State in Ohio, was then one of the stewards, probably the most influential one of the M. E. Church in Findlay. The Sunday-school comprised nearly, if not quite, three hundred members. A Mr. Hayes was superintendent of the school, and a Mr. Mefford was leader of the singing.

Mr. Mefford also belonged to a quartette that sang frequently in the society circles of Findlay at that time. The quartette comprised Mefford, D. M. Stoughton, and his two sisters, Mrs. Hall and Mrs. Firman. They were all good singers. Stoughton was an excellent tenor, and he and his sister, Mrs. Hall, who was a widow, often sang duets at party gatherings of the young people. At these socials we remember hearing them sing "Lillie Dale," which was then a new song just out.

Rev. James Kellam was made Presiding Elder of the Findlay District by the same Conference that sent father to Findlay. Kellam had been the station preacher at Findlay the year previous, and he and his family were still occupying the parsonage when our folks arrived there. They did not get out for a week or more afterwards, and our family had to divide up and quarter for a short time among the church members. Part of the family stopped at Judge Corey's and part at Parlee Carlin's. At both places our folks were received and treated with much hospitality.

The old parsonage then stood west of Main street, on the corner of South Cross street and an alley running north and south between it and Railroad street. An old frame church that had been abandoned, stood on the same lot with the parsonage, in front of it and facing the street, so that you had to go into the parsonage from the alley. The old church had not been in use as such for a year or so before we went to Findlay. It was then occupied as a school-house by a teacher named Kimber. Sister Eleanor remembers going to school to him. A new, plain, brick church, which had been built to take the place of the old frame, stood west of Main, on Railroad, now called Crawford street. It had a basement, with audience-room above, which was reached by inside stairways from the front of the basement below. The church was without bell or belfry, was a poor job, and was always considered unsafe. In time it was pulled down and a new church was built in its place on the same site, but instead of fronting north on Railroad street, it was built on the south end of the lot and made to front on Sandusky street.

Our recollection of the schools of Findlay is not very bright for the reason that we were not much connected with them, but our idea is that they were very deficient at that time for a town of its size. A Mr. and Mrs. Spear kept a select school in a little, yellow-washed, brick house of two rooms—one upstairs and one down—which stood just west of Dr. Baldwin's on Sandusky street. This school we attended in the fall of 1853 only. All the other schools in the place were nothing but common District schools. There was a school institute held at Findlay while we were there, gotten up by Mr. Spear, and, we think, under his supervision. To this school meeting *Professor Aaron Schuyler, of Republic, came to lecture on

---

We had lost all trace of Prof. Schuyler until, after finishing our notice of him, we incidentally came across one of his works which was dated at Baldwin University, Berea, Ohio. This is the institution of which our nephew, Rev. J. E. Stubbs, is now President. Subsequent inquiries through him brought the following letter from Mr. Schuyler which adds some information and interest to what we have said in our previous mention of him. He is now living at Salina, Kansas, and belongs to the faculty of the Kansas Wesleyan University, located there. The account Mr. Schuyler gives of himself, in the letter, embraces the whole period, of thirty-six years, which has transpired since we knew him at Republic in 1851, for our first year at Republic was his first year at the head of the school there. His title is A. M., LL. D.

SALINA, KANSAS, June 10, 1887.

PRESIDENT J. E. STUBBS:

*Dear Sir*—I was Principal of Seneca County Academy, at Republic, for twelve years, and then removed to Berea, and filled the chair of Mathematics for seven years, then the chair of Philosophy and Applied Mathematics for five years, and was President for ten years, filling also, at the same time, the chairs of Philosophy and Mathematics.

I have written the following books: Higher Arithmetic, Complete Algebra, Geometry, Trigonometry, Surveying and Navigation, Analytical Geometry, Logic, and Psychology, all of which have been published save the Analytic Geometry, which I am holding for final revision. We are very nicely situated here. We have an elegant home,—much superior to anything of the kind I ever expected to possess. We have one of the best localities in Salina,— a beautiful and flourishing city.

The prospects of K. W. U. are encouraging. My work is duly appreciated, and we have made many and valuable friends. On these accounts, I could not think of leaving Salina, unless the inducements were very strong indeed. With high regards for you personally and with the best wishes for your success I am truly your friend.

A. SCHUYLER.

mathematics: This is the gentleman we have before referred to as superintendent of the schools at Republic while we were there, and who gave us a recommendation to the examiner at Sandusky City for a license to teach our first District school. Of late years he has written several works on mathematics, a treatise on logic, and one on psychology, for the well-known firm of Van Antwerp, Bragg & Co., Cincinnati, Ohio. While writing these works it appears that he was one of the faculty of the Baldwin University at Berea, Ohio, as his prefaces to them bear dates at that place. We remember him as a tall, lithe, light haired man of fair complexion and about thirty years of age; he was smooth faced, and rather boyish in appearance. He always dressed in plain black and wore Byron turned-down collars.

In the winter of 1853 and 1854 we taught school one mile directly north of town. We still have a distinct recollection of our examination for a license to teach, and how we happened to get this school. The County Board of Examiners, according to notice, met one Saturday in one of the little schoolhouses of Findlay to examine applicants for teachers' license. Many Directors were present from surrounding Districts as spectators with the object of selecting teachers for their respective schools. All the applicants sat in line on a long bench in front of the examiners and were examined orally. Each applicant was given a question in turn from the head to the foot of the class. If one missed a question it was passed to the next and so on. While we were at arithmetic, the following problem, or one similar in condition, was given: "A and B can do a piece of work in eight days, B and C can do it in ten days, and A and C can do it in twelve days. How long will it take each one of them to do it separately?" Before the question came to us a number had declined to undertake its solution. The examiner then said, "Can any one in the class do it?" We then stepped forward and worked it on the black-board. When the examination was over two men stepped up to us, and after complimenting us upon having solved the problem when all the others had refused to try it, they said they were Directors looking out for some competent person to teach their school. During the conversation they offered us their school for three months at twenty dollars per month and board. This was large wages then and the offer was at once accepted. The three Directors of the District were a Mr. Martin, a Mr. Cherry and a Dr. Hurd. The two former were the two whom we had met at the examination and who had hired us. Dr. Hurd never seemed very friendly toward us, because, as we were informed, he had not been consulted in the matter of our employment. However he was not ugly, only silently stubborn and morose in his demeanor. He never visited the school or took any interest in it during the three months, but during the week we boarded at his house he treated us very gentlemanly. We had the confidence however of the other two trustees and a strong support from them. The school we had secured was one that had a habit of whipping the teacher and there was some anxiety about how we would succeed in that respect. There was a man in the district named Foster who had a large boy called "Jack." That boy was bad and a leader of the others. To make it worse, his father, who was a rough man and a bully, always took his part. At Jack's first attempt to create a disturbance, although he was a six-footer, we surprised him with an unmerciful whipping and frightened off the other boys who were to help him. This settled the matter, then and there, among the pupils, as to whipping the teacher. The news went home that evening to every house in the District about the master whipping Jack Foster. The two Directors, Mr. Martin and Mr. Cherry, knowing how Foster would be likely to act about the matter, anticipated his coming to the school-house the next morning. Foster came, on his way to Findlay, and as was expected he wanted to enter the school-house but the two Directors would not let him. On this account he got very angry at them and committed some misdemeanor for which they followed him to town and had him fined twenty dollars and costs. A District meeting was subsequently called, the matter investigated, and the teacher exonerated. Every thing went on smoothly afterward to the close of the term. While teaching this school we had the mumps on one side of our face, having had them on the other side when we were a small child.

At Findlay, father and mother came across an old acquaintance in the person of Father Baldwin, whom they had known in Zanesville, when they first came to Ohio. He had lived across the street from them there, and was a little older than father. The old gentleman died at the residence of his son, Dr. Baldwin, on Sandusky street, the year father was stationed at Findlay. All of Father Baldwin's children grew up to be married, and nearly all of them settled in Findlay. They were among the most respectable and well-to-do families there. Mrs. Strather, the eldest daughter, lived on a farm north of the river, near the northwest corner of the corporation line. Strather was her second husband. Another daughter was the wife of a successful merchant named Hyatt, who kept a store on Main street, in Findlay. A third daughter was the wife of Charles O'Neill, a lawyer there. Father says that Dr. Baldwin doctored our family a number of years without charge.

Five children of our family came with father and mother to Findlay,—Sarah, John, Emily, Eleanor, and Linda.

Brother Sam had left home, to learn the watch-making business, while the household were still at Bucyrus. In the fall of 1851 he left Bucyrus and went into the well-known jewelry house of J. Y. Savage, at Columbus, Ohio, to finish his trade. He remained there more than two years. In the spring of 1854, his time with Savage having expired, he rejoined the family at Findlay, where he opened a little jewelry shop and store on his own account. He married Julia A. Druett, at Findlay, July 17, 1856, and continued in business at his trade there until the breaking out of the Civil War.

About the same time that Brother Sam returned home, we got through with our school north of town, and accepted at Findlay, about two months afterward, a position as clerk in the hardware store of Spinning & Stansberry. We remained with them until September of the same year.

Our brother, D. S. Gray, who had been promising father to find a place for us in the railroad office as soon as affairs permitted, then wrote for us to come to Columbus. We recollect an incident connected with our leaving Findlay at that time. We were going to leave on Monday, and had quit the store on Friday, that we might have time to go around and say good-by to friends and acquaintances.

While thus engaged on Saturday we took the ague. It was just after Conference. Most of the goods at the parsonage were packed, and it seems that the family had left, or were out stopping with the neighbors in readiness to go. However, for some reason that we have forgotten, there was one bedstead with bedding yet standing in the house, and we made for it at once. We got into it and covered up before the shake fully came on, and stayed there until it was over and the fever gone. Sunday morning Dr. Rawson gave us a tremendous dose of quinine in a glass of wine, and we have never had the ague since. Findlay was a great place for ague in those days. The druggists would specially advertise their receipts of quinine. At Langworthy's drug store, cor. Main and So. Cross streets, we have seen painted on a board set out in front, this sign, "5,000 grains of quinine received to-day."

We have always had a peculiar sympathy and regard for our sister Sarah. After Mary, Elizabeth, William, and David, one by one, had gone out from among us, she was the leading help and chief assistant manager in the family for sixteen years.

All this period the hard labor and indoor cares of the household devolved mostly upon her. She did the washing, ironing, baking, and cleaning; and, when father and mother were away, always had charge of the house. During much of this time, while we were still quite a boy, she also looked after us, washed and dressed us for Sabbath School, pinned on our collars, and cared for us in many tender ways. We did not always return her kindness as we should have done. An incident occurred while we lived in Findlay that brings this thought to our mind.

It was Saturday, and father and mother were away. Sarah had baked for Sunday a lot of cakes called "jumbles." Brother Sam and ourself would come into the house every now and then, and each slip a cake out of the dish against her remonstrance. Finally, to save them, she locked them up in the lower drawer of the bureau. Shaking the key at us in defiance, she then said, "I guess you will not get any more of them." The bureau was an old one, of which the keys to all the drawers but the under one had been lost. Sam, who was the ringleader in the affair, studied over the matter awhile and then said, "John, I'll tell you how we can get at them. There is no partition between the drawers, and all we have to do is to slip out the one above." We did so, and ate every cake before our sister found out our prank. She then cried bitterly over it. We have many times, through life, thought of the downright meanness of that trick, and wished to ask her forgiveness for it. We record that wish here.

At the close of the Conference year at Findlay, our home with the family terminated. While they bid the place adieu, for father's new location, we left there, as anticipated, to take a position in the railroad office at Columbus, Ohio. Brother Sam remained at Findlay.

# MAUMEE CITY.

### Conference Year, 1855.

August 23, 1854, Conference sat at Tiffin, Ohio, Bishop Simpson presiding. At this Conference father was appointed Presiding Elder of the Maumee District. The territory then comprising this district embraced all the country extending north from the Maumee River to Michigan, and west from Toledo, inclusive, to Indiana. Also, a section south of the river, extending south ten or fifteen miles, and from South Toledo, inclusive, west as far as Indiana. The portion north of the Maumee River took in the cities and towns of Toledo, Maumee City, Waterville, Napoleon, Wasseon, and Bryan. The south part included Perrysburg, South Toledo, Bowling Green, Gilead, Defiance, and some other small towns. In short, we think, the district embraced the six northwest counties of Ohio, named Lucas, Wood, Henry, Fulton, Williams, and Defiance. Maumee City was headquarters, and contained a very comfortable district parsonage. This was occupied when the family arrived there, and father rented another house for a few weeks. The founders of Maumee City expected it to become a large and important place. In visiting home after our folks had moved there, we were surprised at the town's desolate and melancholy appearance. It seemed half deserted. Many buildings that must have cost thousands of dollars, and that would have been valuable property in any live business place, were standing there idle, valueless, and, as it seemed, absolutely abandoned. Maumee City is situated on the Maumee River, about ten miles from its confluence with Lake Erie, and the hopes of its founders were based, we understand, on the idea that it would one day become the head of lake navigation.

Congress had made an appropriation to improve the channel of the river so as to make it navigable for lake boats that distance from its mouth. The town was therefore laid out and started on a scale in accordance with such expectation. Unexpectedly, however, Congress, at a later day, changed the appropriation and gave it to aid in building the Miami and Erie Canal, extending from Cincinnati to Toledo. This action of Congress destroyed all the large business anticipations of the place, drove away many of its inhabitants, left a large number of its houses tenantless, and its streets almost deserted. Toledo sprang up in its stead, and became the important place that was expected of Maumee City.

The location of Maumee City is admirable. It is built on a plateau, which extends back from a high bluff that borders the town on the east and south. The line of the bluff makes nearly a direct turn from the direction of north and south to east and west, and, in this particular, is quite similar to the location of Canal Dover. The Miami and Erie Canal, and the Toledo, Wabash & Western Railroad run almost parallel on the north side of the place. On the west side the country is open. Directly across the river, southward, you see Perrysburg, and the site of old Fort Meigs. On the north bank of the river, not far from the district parsonage, and nearly opposite where the old fort once stood, we were shown a large elm tree, which, it was said, had the following incident connected with its history: During the war of 1812, while the American forces were occupying the fort, and it was besieged by the British and Indians under Col. Proctor, the north bank of the Maumee was picketed with Indian sharp-shooters, who took every opportunity to pick off our soldiers when they came outside the fort for water or any other purpose. On one such occasion an officer had ridden his horse down to the river to let him drink. At the same time a soldier on the ramparts of the fort discovered a redskin in the top of the tree, making ready to shoot the officer. Before he could do so, however, the soldier shot the Indian dead and he fell from the tree.

During the summer of 1854 there was a great deal of cholera throughout the West. Toledo alone reported that season about seven hundred deaths from the disease, and Maumee City and Perrysburg over one hundred each. The two latter places were in mourning when our folks moved to Maumee City, on account of the deaths that had occurred in them that year from cholera. Nearly all the members of the Church wore mourning. The Maumee valley was not considered a healthful country, but the family never enjoyed better health than while they lived at Maumee City. Father says he never missed but one appointment, by reason of sickness, during the four years he traveled that district. April 11, 1855, at Maumee City, our sister Sarah was married to M. L. Higgins, by Rev. Ralph Wilcox, pastor of the M. E. Church there.

### Conference Year, 1856.

September 19, 1855, Conference met at Sandusky City, Bishop Ames presiding. At this session there were three new Presiding Elders appointed, Henry E. Pilcher to the Delaware District, William C. Pierce to the Sandusky District, and Wesley J. Wells to the Findlay District. Father was continued on the Maumee District. It was also the last session of the North Ohio Annual Conference which he attended, and with which he had been so long connected. In May, 1856, at the General Conference of the M. E. Church in the United States, the territory embraced in the North Ohio Annual Conference was divided and a new Conference formed, which was called the Delaware Conference.

### Conference Year, 1857.

The first session of the Delaware Conference convened at Mansfield, Ohio, September 17, 1856, Bishop Ames presiding. At this meeting the name of the Maumee District was changed to Toledo District, the territory remaining the same. At the start the new Conference embraced the following districts and Presiding Elder appointments: Delaware District, H. E. Pilcher, P. E.; Sidney District, John Kalb, P. E.; Lima District, E. C. Gavitt, P. E.; Findlay District, W. J. Wells, P. E.; and Toledo District, David Gray, P. E.

### Conference Year, 1858.

In the fall of 1857 Conference was held at Toledo, Bishop Baker presiding. No change was made in father's work.

## Conference Year, 1859.

In 1858 the Conference met at West Liberty, Ohio. At this session father's term as Presiding Elder of the Toledo District expired. He had previously concluded that, after leaving Maumee City, he would locate the family permanently at Findlay, and therefore asked the Bishop to give him a junior relation. The Bishop complied with this request, and appointed him to Adrian Circuit, just east of Findlay.

THE FAMILY HOME AT FINDLAY, OHIO.

# FINDLAY.

While yet on the Toledo District, father had purchased the present homestead in Findlay from a Dr. Patton, for twelve hundred and seventy-five dollars. This was in fulfillment of his purpose not to move the family about any more after leaving Maumee City, and to secure a comfortable and pleasantly situated home for himself and mother the remainder of their days. Pursuant to this intention, immediately after Conference adjourned in 1858, the family returned to Findlay. Up to this time, since its purchase, the property had been occupied in turn by sister Sarah's and brother Sam's family.

### Conference Years, 1860-61.

At the close of father's year on Adrian Circuit, the Conference sat at Bucyrus, Bishop Janes presiding. Then father was appointed to the Arcadia Circuit, which he traveled two years. This circuit was made up altogether of country appointments, with the exception of Arcadia. In May, 1860, there had been another session of the General Conference of the M. E. Church, at which the name of the Delaware Conference was changed to that of Central Ohio Conference, so that father received his second year appointment to Arcadia Circuit at the first session of the Central Ohio Conference in the fall of 1860.

The first event of any importance in the family after its settlement at Findlay, was the marriage of sister Emily to John Ruthrauff, May 29, 1861. Father performed the ceremony. A short time after this event, brother Sam entered the army. Emily and her husband first went to housekeeping on East Hardin street, but shortly afterward moved into the house next to the old homestead, which is situated on the corner of Liberty and Lincoln streets. In this house their first child, Harry Ruthrauff, was born, July 27, 1862.

### Conference Years, 1862–63.

In the fall of 1861, the second session of the Central Ohio Conference sat at Kenton, Ohio, Bishop Ames presiding. From that Conference father was appointed to McComb Circuit, on which he continued two years.

### Conference Year, 1864.

In September, 1863, the Conference was held at Upper Sandusky, Bishop Simpson presiding. From there father was appointed to Findlay Circuit.

### Conference Year, 1865.

In September, 1864, the Conference sat at Marion, Ohio, Bishop Ames presiding. Father was then appointed supernumerary preacher with Joseph Wykes at Findlay, where, from that time until now, he has continued doing a little work, when able, for the different churches, sometimes in town and sometimes in the country. He took a superannuated relation, at the session of the Central Ohio Conference which sat at Toledo in 1870, under Bishop Clark.

May 19, 1862, sister Linda was married to C. C. Godman, father officiating at the ceremony. After marriage they went to Marion, Ohio, where they rented a small house and went to housekeeping. He engaged there in the business of keeping a book-and-stationery store. In the spring of 1863 Linda visited home, and while there, on the 15th of March, their first child, Gray Godman, was born. At this time brother Sam's family was living in the house next to the homestead, Emily and Ruthrauff having moved into their present residence on Sandusky street. July following, sister Sarah and her husband, who had been living in Findlay almost ever since their marriage, moved to Cincinnati. In 1864, Emily Ruthrauff took her child, Harry, and went to Marion on a visit. Soon after her arrival Harry took sick and died there. His remains were brought home to Findlay and buried in Maple Grove Cemetery.

In 1866, Linda Godman and her husband had returned to Findlay and were living in the house next to father and mother, which had been previously and successively occupied by Ruthrauff's and brother Sam's family. Brother Sam, who had at that time come back from the war, had removed with his family to Indianapolis. In this house Linda Louise, the second child of Linda and C. C. Godman, was born February 17, 1866. Her mother lived only until the 3d of March following. At her death she gave her daughter into the care of her sister, Sarah Higgins, with the request that she should raise her. But troubles seldom come singly. Suddenly, unexpectedly, and without any certain knowledge of the cause, the death of Gray Godman occurred on the 15th of March, two weeks after the death of his mother, at the home of his grandfather and grandmother, where he was born. Linda Louise, his sister, was also destined not to live long. She died at the home of Mrs. Higgins, in Cincinnati, February 5, 1867. The following obituary notices of Mrs. Godman and little Gray Godman are copied from a Findlay paper:

DIED.

"In Findlay, March 3, of pneumonia, Mrs. Linda A. Godman, wife of Charles Carroll Godman, and daughter of Rev. David Gray. Mrs. Godman was born January 9, 1841, and was early taught to fear God. She was beautiful in person, amiable in disposition, pleasant and lovely in her manners, and was loved and respected by all who became acquainted with her. She was also a Christian, having experienced a change of heart and made an open profession of faith in Christ in the year 1860, while attending the Female College in Delaware. As a wife and mother she was ardently devoted, a helpmate indeed to her now sadly bereaved and sorrow-stricken husband. But she has gone home and is now

> "Far from a world of grief and sin
> With God eternally shut in."

In connection with the above we have to tell the sad story of the death of Jas. Gray Godman, son of Mr. C. C. and Mrs. M. A. Godman, a double bereavement having fallen upon the heart of our brother and fellow citizen. This little boy, though only about three years of age, exhibited rare qualities of both body and mind. Physically well developed, and having good health, he was a happy and playful child. His mental and moral nature were precocious, giving promise of unusual powers of mind and heart. He had a very retentive memory, learning readily the Sunday-School hymns, and, having great musical powers, would sing them with accuracy, to the delight of his friends. But this beautiful flower has been cut down and withered.

On the evening of his death he ate supper cheerfully with his father, and afterward sang two or three hymns, and retired to bed. But soon the last struggle commenced, and the language, "Oh, dear me, I can not stand this," alarmed his friends. Medical help was called but this bright, beautiful, and loving child soon slept in death, and winged his flight to his mother in a better land."

For three or four years before mother's death she was a great sufferer, and, during that time, father did not attend any of the Conference sessions, as she was unwilling for him to be absent. But the time was rapidly approaching when, after fifty-six years of earthly joys and sorrows, pleasures and hardships, hopes and disappointments, rest and toil together, they were to be separated. On Saturday morning, April 1, 1876, she was suddenly taken worse, and seemed to be impressed with the thought that the time of her departure was at hand. She said to father, "The Lord has spared us to live together many years, but I think the time has now come when we are to be parted." On Sunday evening, Rev. Winter, the Presiding Elder, said to her, "Sister Gray, do you feel that Jesus is precious?" She answered, "I feel very calm." These were almost her last words, and the next morning, Monday, April 3d, she passed away. We were not present at the closing scene of her life, but well remember the sad day that we took leave of her dear form and it was laid to rest in the quiet grave. The funeral services were held in the M. E. Church and were conducted by Rev. Wm. Jones, the regular pastor, at that time, of Findlay charge.

Although mother's death was naturally a sorrowful and painful event to all the family, father's deep emotion and manifest inward struggle, on the occasion, to bear up under the affliction, invoked special sympathy. He walked to and fro, forward and back, almost incessantly, scarcely knowing what to do or which way to go. The whole panorama of his and mother's associations, experiences, and life together, must have been passing and repassing in review before him. Indeed, in all its bearings, the trial to him was one which, ordinarily, few men are called upon to undergo. The woman whom he had wooed and wed when she was young and beautiful, who had left home, friends, and native soil, to go with him and her children to a new country and among strangers, was gone, and was soon to be hid away from his sight and presence, in this world, forever. She had shared with him, for more than half a century, privations and toils that are known only to the poor, had traveled with him from place to place for many years, economizing, struggling, and shifting to make the meager allowance for his services supply the wants of his family; and amid all the varied experiences and changing scenes of a long and eventful life, had been his counselor, support, and loving companion. No wonder that his usually tranquil and fortified Christian spirit betrayed the deep sorrow of his heart, and that his sturdy frame was restless under its strong but suppressed emotions. The following memoir and notice of mother's death are taken from the minutes of the Central Ohio Conference held at Defiance, Ohio, in September, 1876:

"Naomi H. Gray, wife of Rev. David Gray, of the Central Ohio Conference, departed this life April 3, 1876. The deceased was born in the State of Delaware, September 9, 1799. Her maiden name was Lofland. She was united in wedlock to her now bereaved husband, September 14, 1820, and came with him to Ohio in 1829, and settled in Dresden, Muskingum County.

In 1835, brother Gray joined the Ohio Conference, and for nearly thirty years she shared the trials and labors of her husband in his efforts to carry the gospel to all classes of our people. She was of a retiring disposition, and never conspicuous as a public worker; yet she met her responsibilities as a Christian wife and mother, cared for the family in the absence of her husband on his large circuits or extensive districts, trained them for Jesus, and had the satisfaction of seeing them grow up to maturity, and take respectable positions in the business, social, and religious departments of life. For three years preceding her death she suffered severely from periodical attacks of epilepsy and was, much of the time, confined to her bed. When the hour of dissolution came she was ready. Her sun went down in a cloudless sky, her chamber was a place of triumph, and the sorrows of death were broken by the shouts of praise and the voice of Christian song.

WM. JONES."

Mother died at the residence of Mr. and Mrs. Ruthrauff, on Sandusky Street. Previous to her death she and father and sister Eleanor were keeping house alone together at the old homestead. On Thursday morning, March 30, they shut up the house and went to Ruthrauff's, the old folks intending to remain there for a few days, while Eleanor made a short visit to Indianapolis. Thus it happened that mother was at Emily's when she died. On Saturday morning, April 1, she was taken down with a spasm, and when it was over, she seemed to be so fully convinced that she was going to die, that telegrams were immediately sent out, to all members of the family, notifying them of her alarming sickness and probable death. A number of the children reached Findlay in time to see her still alive and to bid her farewell, but some did not. All, however, arrived in time to attend the funeral and to witness the burial rites which took place on Wednesday, April 5. Her remains were deposited in Maple Grove Cemetery. In the evening, after the funeral was over, all the children and relatives present gathered at the old home for supper, and to listen to a short talk from father upon the subject of their soul's salvation. It was an event of much interest. When father was through with his talk he invited an expression from the others, of their thoughts and purposes, in the same direction. A number of them responded, and while the occasion was one of sadness and deep solemnity, it was, we think, one of much profit and satisfaction to all.

For about three years subsequent to mother's death, father and sister Eleanor continued to keep house at the old homestead, after which they broke up house-keeping and went to Ruthrauff's to live. Almost immediately, however, after father became a widower, he formed the plan of making a round of visits, once a year, to the families of his children. We remember two of these visits at our house, but it was not many years until the infirmities of age and the fatigues of travel caused him to discontinue them. The following, by an old associate of father's, in the ministry, is an account of the first of these visits to sister Mary's at Ashland, Ohio, in May, 1876:

### A PLEASANT INTERVIEW.

After the lapse of twenty years, it afforded me great pleasure to meet my highly esteemed friend and brother, Rev. David Gray, of the Central Ohio Conference. When I entered the ministry, in 1839, brother Gray was in the prime and vigor of his manhood. It is a matter worthy of notice that religion has kept him youthful in appearance and sweet and amiable in spirit even down to old age. Many precious memories were called up by our interview. After the death of sister Gray, he conceived the idea of a large circuit, having five appointments, which he intended to fill once a year. These were Columbus, Ohio; Ashland, Ohio; Indianapolis, Ind.; Cambridge City, Ind.; and Cincinnati, Ohio. He is here filling his appointment, and the occasion is one of rare pleasure and profit. He is a beautiful specimen of a sweet old age. His most ardent desire is the salvation of all his posterity. The Lord has blessed him with eleven children, thirty five grandchildren, and twelve great-grandchildren. In this heritage he feels he has one of earth's richest blessings. He tells me, that every day of his life, he remembers them, by name, in prayer to God. Oh, what a blessing that this aged servant of the Lord is spared to pray for his children's children, down to the third and fourth generation! These lives are spared in answer to his prayers, and we hope their souls may be saved because he prays for them. And if he could only know that they were all saved, through the blood of the Lamb, he would then offer the prayer of Simeon, saying, "Now, Lord, lettest thou Thy servant depart in peace, for mine eyes have seen Thy salvation." Brother Gray preached in the M. E. Church, on Sabbath morning, the 3d inst., and as he had been pastor in Ashland in the days gone by, many touching recollections were brought out, and the general class that followed was one of special interest. On Wednesday evening, the 6th inst., it was our privilege to enjoy a delightful interview with brother Gray and some of his old friends, at the house of Col. J. D. Stubbs. It was the occasion of the baptism of three of his great-grandchildren. After the solemn ordinance was performed, Dr. Robinson, of the Presbyterian Church, made some very touching remarks in relation to his long acquaintance with brother Gray, and of his first appointment to Ashland. He alluded to the time when they two first met. It was on the occasion of the funeral of an infant daughter of brother and sister Gray. That precious little form now sleeps in the beautiful cemetery at Ashland. But however widely apart brother Gray's numerous family may be buried; wherever the particles of the dust of their dissolving bodies may be scattered, they all lie within the range of God's knowledge and power, and will come forth at the "Voice of the Arch-angel and the trump of God," to meet their kindred spirits in the skies. In view of that grand and blissful scene above, I can not refrain from offering the prayer to our common Father, to grant that when father and mother Gray stand at God's right hand, they may look around and see all their children there. As the venerable father took those little ones in his hands to consecrate them to God, we thought how beautiful the scene where age and infancy meet; the one just ready to step off from the stage of action, and the other just on the threshold. May the parents and children, consecrated in holy baptism, follow in the footsteps of their venerable grandfather, and be fully prepared to enter upon the glories of another world.

> "O how sweet it will be, in that beautiful land,
> So free from all sorrow and pain,
> With songs on our lips, and with harps in our hands,
> To meet one another again."

ASHLAND, OHIO. S. L. YOURTEE.

His visit to Cambridge City, Ind., which followed that to Ashland, was a very interesting one both to himself and our family. While at Cambridge City he met Rev. Westlake, an old acquaintance whom he had not seen for many years. Their meeting was joyful and affecting. On Sunday, June 5, he preached in the M. E. Church. We remember that when he was invited, by the pastor, to preach, we endeavored to dissuade him, fearing that he might not do well enough to satisfy public expectation. We told him that he was a stranger to nearly every one in the place, that the people would likely expect too much from him, and that if he did not fully meet their anticipations, they would hardly consider that he had long since passed the prime of life. He hesitated, but finally accepted the invitation. Appreciating our fears, he selected a text, made special preparation for the occasion, and preached a sermon that was both interesting and well received. And now comes what seems so singular in connection with the matter. At home, when the services were over, he informed us that he had not used the text at all, which he had, at first, selected; that after he had arrived at the church his prepared thoughts forsook him and that he chose another text and spoke without premeditation. The incident reminded us of Christ's words to his apostles, "When ye are delivered up take no thought what ye shall speak, for it shall be given you in that same hour what ye shall speak." On Monday, June 6, we had a little gathering at our house, and on the occasion, father baptized another of his grandchildren, our youngest child, John Ruthrauff Gray.

We have often contemplated the great happiness and consolation father must derive from the glory of a well-spent life; from thoughts of the good which he has accomplished in the world, through the grace and power of the Holy Spirit; and from the testimonies which he has received from those who, through his instrumentality, have been saved from spiritual death. The following is one of many such testimonies:

OLNEY ILL., July 18, 1886.

MRS. MARY J. STUBBS:

*Dear Madam*—I have a deep interest in your father's welfare. In looking over some old letters, I came across one, which I received from you in 1879, and it brought to my mind many remembrances of him. Although fifty years have passed since I heard him preach, the influence which his sermon had upon me then still lingers. It was his preaching that caused me to seek the pardon of my sins, and I now feel glad that I hearkened to his words and made an early start for a better country. In all the time that has since passed, I have never once regretted the step I then took, and I believe that it will finally bring me to a home above. I often bless the day that I heard your father preach. I frequently ask myself the question, "Shall I know him in heaven?" I believe that I shall, and that I will be the cause of adding one star to his crown of rejoicing. I would be glad to receive a letter from you telling me all about your father's family as I have not seen nor heard from any of them since you wrote me in 1879. It may be that your father has gone to his reward, but if so, I have not heard of it. A great many of my friends have passed through the dark valley since then. Three brothers and one sister have died, but I rejoice that all of them were good religious members of the M. E Church. My sister was the wife of Dr. Sapp. No doubt you well remember her, as, I think, she also experienced religion under your father's preaching. Hoping that I may be favored with an answer from you soon, I will close by wishing you and all your father's family well.

Yours truly,           P. SHAW.

In 1886, Mrs. Higgins returned to Findlay, and father and Eleanor went to housekeeping with her in the old homestead again.

---

Father is now far advanced in years and, as Rev. Yourtee has said, is a beautiful specimen of a sweet old age. He is quite strong and erect for one so old. He still attends church regularly every Sabbath, and walks a mile or so to market and back nearly every day. The fatigues of travel, however, prevent him from now venturing upon visits to the homes of any of his children away from Findlay. His whole life is a noble exemplification of the sustaining power of the Christian religion, and of an abiding trust in the promises of God. It has been sixty-eight years since he was converted. He has lived so long a life of piety and religious practice; has been so long accustomed to putting aside every impure thought and desire; to repelling every wicked disposition of his mind and heart; and to cultivating love and charity for all mankind, that his purity of character has become written in his face and features, and from his countenance beams forth the spirit of holiness that is within him. We bear witness too, that we never knew him to exhibit a violence of temper, a malignancy of thought, a dishonesty of purpose, nor to indulge in unchaste and unbecoming conversations. In all our intercourse with the world, whenever we have heard persons malign Christianity, decry the church, and assert that professors of religion are no better than other people, his example has always come up before us as an incontestible and convincing proof that their statements were false and their minds ignorant. Further, father's life corroborates the words of the psalmist David,—"I have been young, and now am old, yet have I not seen the righteous forsaken, nor his seed begging bread." He started out in his religious course with scarcely two coats and, figuratively speaking, almost without staff or scrip for his journey, yet by the blessings of God he has always been provided for and now in the sunset of his life he has a comfortable home and more than enough to meet all his wants for the remainder of his days.

It is a matter worthy of explanation, as to how father and mother obtained a home for themselves in their old age, as it is evident it could not have been purchased by any surplus funds saved by him out of his salaries for preaching. Upon this subject he says,—"During the whole of my active ministerial life, I could and did, truthfully and joyfully sing:—"

> "No foot of land do I possess
> Nor cottage in this wilderness."

"I was a poor wayfaring man and my salaries were so small that it took all that was paid me to support my family, so that I saw no chance for getting any money ahead until the year 1851, when Mary, Elizabeth, and David, met at Norwalk to attend William's funeral. After arranging for the payment of his burial expenses and for a monument for his grave, there were several hundred dollars of his earnings left which legally belonged to his brothers and sisters. But they said in their consultation,—'We will give this to father and mother to be invested in a home for them when they have grown old!' That money and five hundred and seventy-five dollars given to me by David as a Christmas present, were the first expended in buying our home in Findlay. A north wing was afterward put on the house by Samuel, and another amount of five hundred dollars was subsequently given by David to further improve it. Later still, with a part of the money received from your uncle Samuel's estate, the house was again beautified and improved. I also received a yearly donation of four hundred dollars, from David, for several years after I was superannuated and up to the time that I received my portion of my brother Samuel's estate. Thus from the blessings bestowed upon our children and through the unforeseen providences of God, we were provided with a home in which to spend the autumn and winter of our lives, and were freed from the troubles of want and poverty in our declining years."

Father has taken a great interest in our work, and has one

statement, concerning his private life, which he wishes recorded for the benefit of those of his posterity who remain, and who may come after him, when he is gone. He says, "My conversion to Christianity was as clear and satisfactory to me as Saul's, of Tarsus, was to him when on his way to Damascus and while there. Immediately after my conversion I began a life of prayer, and it has been my daily practice, ever since, to retire at morning, noon, and night, for private devotions. In those prayers my first subject was my kindred, then others. After I was married, my wife was one for whom I made special supplication and, as our children were born, each one was added to the list. And so on it has been through life; after our children were married and had offspring who grew up and also became parents, the names of these grandchildren, and great-grandchildren were all included, and each one mentioned, by name, in my daily prayers to God. But in all this period I have never felt greater concern about the welfare of my posterity than I do to-day, while in my eighty-eighth year, and I want these truths, these honest truths, made known to them. These earnest, prayerful desires of my heart for my kindred have been going up to the throne of grace, for more than a half century and, as my course in life is almost run, and I shall soon be called away, I wish through the medium of our family history, to finally commend them to God's care and keeping, hoping that he may bless them abundantly and fill their hearts with the riches of His grace and Holy Spirit."

MARY JANE GRAY STUBBS.

## MARY JANE STUBBS.

Mary Jane Stubbs, our eldest sister, was born at White's Cross Roads, Sussex County, Delaware, August 15, 1821. We have a sincere pride in referring to her as one of earth's noblest women. From childhood she was always good. From youth her mind had a strong moral force and religious tendency, and her whole life has been one of meekness and purity before God and the world. Her daily walk has exemplified an earnest Christian faith, and her every day practice a spirit possessed of charity and a heart that expresses itself in good words and works. A devoted wife, and tender, watchful, praying mother, the honorable positions which her children fill, and the marked success which some of them have achieved, are largely the fruits of her training and her influence over them. As much as we could say of her home career, up to the date of her marriage, is already contained and foreshadowed in her contributions to our notes of the family to that period. She was married to Joseph D. Stubbs at Wooster, Wayne County, Ohio, November 5, 1840, and left there the same day with her husband for his and his mother's home at Loudonville, a small village in the same county. Mr. Stubbs was then engaged in business at Loudonville as a cabinet-maker. We recollect living with our sister there a little while, some time between the years 1840 and 1843. Just in what year it was, how old we were at the time, and how long we remained, are matters that have escaped our memory. We remember, however, that the house occupied by the family was an unpainted, weather-beaten, two-story frame, the upper part of which was reached by an out-door flight of steps on the rear side of the building. The residence was in the rooms below and the shop in those above. Besides this, one scene we witnessed there has never been forgotten. It was the burning of a barn in the village during a thunder storm. The barn was struck by lightning and set on fire. It was early in the evening, but quite dark, and from one of the upper story windows the hay on fire in the mow could be seen through the open haymow door, making a brilliant appearance and a deeply interesting sight to us. In 1843 Mr. Stubbs moved his family to Ashland, then in Richland County, Ohio, where he continued in the furniture trade until 1852. After having suffered severely for some time with felons on his fingers, caused, as was supposed, by bruises received in running the turning lathe, he concluded to engage in some other business. Consequent to this decision, he became a partner with Joseph Wasson in a shoe store, but without relinquishing his furniture trade, which he still carried on under the direction of a foreman. He continued in the shoe store until 1860, when he again turned his attention to the furniture business exclusively.

In March, 1860, grandmother Stubbs died, after a short illness. Our sister Mary thus speaks of her: "This was a great bereavement to us all. Her home had been with us ever since our marriage. We had lived pleasantly and harmoniously together for nineteen years. Up to the time of her death my life had been equally divided between my two mothers, having lived nineteen years with each. She was a very kind, unselfish, tender mother to both Joseph and myself, and an untiring, indulgent grandmother to our children. She was my counselor and adviser at all times. It became the habit of my life to consult her in almost everything I did, and consequently upon her death I greatly missed her in many ways. In 1861, just one year after her death, the war broke out. Then began the days that tried not only the souls of men but women, too. All was commotion and excitement throughout the country. In July of that year my husband received the appointment of Regimental Quarter-Master in the 42d Ohio Volunteer Infantry, of which General Garfield, afterward President of the United States, was Colonel. Soon after the completion of the regiment it went into quarters at Camp Chase, near Columbus, O., and I was left to steer my little family bark alone."

Mr. Stubbs continued with the 42d regiment until November, 1862, when he was promoted to the rank of Captain and Assistant-Quartermaster of Volunteers, and stationed at Nashville, Tenn. In 1864 he was ordered to Johnsonville, Tenn. In the spring of 1865 he was ordered to Raleigh, N. C. While on his way from Ashland to Raleigh, President Lincoln was assassinated, and that was the first news that greeted him on arriving at his post. He there assumed the duties of Post Quartermaster and Superintendent of Transportation. In 1866 he was made Chief Quartermaster of the Department of the South, with headquarters at Raleigh. In the spring of 1867 he was relieved as Chief Quartermaster by Major-General Tyler and appointed to duty as Post Quartermaster at Charlestown, S. C. He was mustered out of service in August, 1867, and employed by the Government to superintend the National Cemeterial operations in the Carolinas until 1868. He was then ordered to Atlanta, Ga., to assume the same duties there. His field embraced the States of North and South Carolina, Alabama, Georgia, and Florida. He continued in this service until the spring of 1869, at which time he resigned and came home. A short time after his return to Ashland Mr. Stubbs accepted the position of General Agent for the Ashland Mutual Fire Insurance Company. This position he held until March, 1879. He was then elected President of the company, which place he filled until March, 1883, when he resigned it to assume more active duties as Secretary of the company, which office he now holds.

The children of Joseph and Mary Stubbs number seven— four sons and three daughters. Their names, in the order of birth, are Elizabeth Ellen, Florence Hortense, David Deyarmon, John Christian Spayd, Joseph Edward, Mary Naomi, and William Morris.

Elizabeth Ellen Stubbs was born in Loudonville, Wayne county, Ohio, August 19, 1841. She was married to Jacob J. Dorland, at Ashland, Ohio, April 10, 18 5, and after a few months' residence there, they removed to Lee Summit, Jack county, Mo., where her husband engaged in farming, although his regular occupation is that of a marble cutter. After remaining a few years in Missouri, Mrs. Dorland's health became so poor that they sold their farm and returned to Ashland, where they are now living, and where Mr. Dorland is again carrying on business at his trade.

Florence Hortense Stubbs was born at Loudonville, Wayne

County, Ohio, January 20, 1843, but died in infancy at Ashland, Ohio, September 28, 1844.

David Deyarmon Stubbs was born in Ashland, Ashland County, Ohio, April 6, 1845. He was only sixteen years of age when the war broke out but was employed by his father as a clerk in the Quartermaster's office most of the time while the war lasted. At its close, Mayor General Tyler, who had been assigned to duty as Chief Quartermaster at Louisville, Ky., selected David to go into the office with him there as his chief clerk. It was not long afterward that General Tyler was ordered to San Francisco, Cal., and he took David with him. General Tyler died while filling the office of Quartermaster at San Francisco, and David got employment on the Central Pacific Railroad. Subsequently he accepted the Secretaryship of the Occidental and Oriental Steam Ship Co. of San Francisco, which office he still retains. He was married to Wilhelmina Winning, November 27, 1873.

John Christian Spayd Stubbs was born in Ashland, Ashland County, Ohio, May 31, 1847. He was also with his father in the Quartermaster's office during the war and after its close, but came home for awhile, intermediately, and went to school. He afterward returned to his father in the South. He again came home in 1868 and clerked for T. C. Bushnel, who had some office in the court-house at Ashland.

During the winter following his last return home, there was a revival in the M. E. Church at Ashland, and also at the rooms of the Y. M. C. A. there, and John was converted and joined the church. In the spring of 1869 he went to Columbus, Ohio, and took a clerkship in the General Freight Office of the C., C. & I. C. R. R. Co., under Mr. C. W. Smith. He was there one year. In the meantime, however, Mr. Smith had severed his connection with the C., C. & I. C. R. R. Co. and had accepted the position of General Freight Agent for the Central Pacific R. R. in Sacramento, Cal. In the fall of 1870 he sent for John to come and be his chief clerk, which offer he accepted. Within two years afterward Mr. Smith resigned his office and came East again, and John was appointed Assistant General Freight Agent, but performed under that title all the duties of the General Freight Agent. This he did until 1873 when his title was changed to that of General Freight Agent. August 14,

1871, at Sacramento, he married Mary R. Patterson. Sometime after 1873 the general offices of the railroad company were removed to San Francisco, and he and his family became residents of that city. In 1881 he was appointed to the high position of General Traffic Manager, of the Central Pacific R. R. and its leased lines, which position he now occupies.

Joseph Edward Stubbs was born in Ashland, Ashland County, Ohio, March 19, 1850. When his father and brothers went to the war, he was left at home with his mother, and proved a great help to her in their absence. At the same time he attended the public schools of Ashland, and there acquired the knowledge necessary to fit him for college. We understand he always had a disposition for earnest study and an inclination to follow some literary pursuit. He entered the Ohio Wesleyan University in September, 1869, and graduated therefrom, with the degree of Bachelor of Arts in June, 1873. He was married to Ella A. Sprengle July 10, 1873, about a month after he graduated. He was so proficient in his course that he was elected tutor of Latin and Greek in the University, a year before he graduated. This position he held until his health failed in 1875 being a term of three years. Subsequent to his marriage he spent a short time at Drew, but on account of poor health he was again compelled to give up and come home. Not long afterward he went to California and spent a few months there trying to recuperate. On his return from California, in 1876, he became editor and proprietor of the Ashland Times, and continued in that capacity until 1880. He then accepted the office of Professor of Greek language and literature in Ashland College. This place he filled until 1882 when he became Superintendent of the public schools of Ashland. In 1886 he resigned this position to accept the Presidency of Baldwin University at Berea, Ohio.

Mary Naomi Stubbs was born in Ashland, Ashland County, Ohio, December 19, 1853. She received a common school education in her native place and graduated at the Ohio Wesleyan Female College, at Delaware, Ohio, in June, 1874. Soon afterward she became a teacher in the public schools of Ashland, where,—excepting an interval of about three years,—she taught until the close of the school year 1886. She then retired from the position to take a course in German, French, and music in Baldwin University, Berea, Ohio.

William Morris Stubbs was born at Ashland, Ohio, July 28, 1856. When about five years of age he fell into a cistern at his home there, and came very near being drowned. He was rescued, in an unconscious state, by his mother, and was resuscitated. His mother thus relates the circumstances of the event: "The cistern had no pump in it, but was covered with a heavy board two inches in thickness. We had been exceedingly particular about keeping the cistern top closed, never allowing it to be open a moment after use. On this day I had sent John to get me a bucket of water, and I feel certain that he put the cover back over the cistern after he was through. I am equally sure, however, that he did not get the board clear over the opening, but left one end of it just inside the curb. The board was longer than it was wide, Willie sat down on the cover and it tipped into the cistern with him. A little boy named George Hootman was with Willie at the time, and his mother was in the house with me talking. George came in where we were and began to strike and teaze his mother to go home, and his mother noticing him, said, 'Why, George, how did you get so wet?' I was washing dishes, and also said, 'George, where is Willie?' At the same time I stepped to the door to look for him, and seeing the cistern open ran to shut it, when to my horror I saw my precious child floating on the water, apparently dead. The thought at once darted into my mind that he had come up for the last time, and if I did not get him then I never could until he was past hope of resuscitation. I called Mrs. Hootman and got down and leaned as far as I could into the cistern, and tried to reach him but could not. In my desperation I gave myself another pitch forward and went into the opening far enough to grab hold of him. When I tried to get out I found myself fast. I said to Mrs. Hootman, 'Oh, help me!' She thought I said, 'Hold me,' and caught me by my feet. I succeeded in getting loose, and brought out with me my dripping drowned child. As I lifted him out I threw him over my shoulder. The water gushed out of him, and he gave a cry. I told Mrs. Hootman to get me a blanket, quick, and I proceeded to strip off his clothes. By this time the neighbors began coming in, and Mrs. Hootman had beckoned to Dr. Clark's people, who lived across the street, to come over. Before we got him in the blanket, he showed signs of going into a spasm, but timely remedies prevented it, and in a few hours he was running around again. After the danger was over I went out to shut the cistern and found the cover swimming on the water. Two things saved him, the cistern being nearly full and the cover. He was floating on the cover when I discovered him, and supposed he had come up for the last time. He must have caught the board as he slid in. It makes me shudder to think of it. For days afterward when I looked at him I felt as if I had gotten him from the grave. Alas, it holds him now in an unyielding grasp, and I am a grief-stricken mother."

William passed his boyhood days in Ashland, and after receiving what education was afforded by the schools of that place he spent two years in the University at Delaware, but did not graduate. He then went into the office of the Ashland Times and learned printing. He married Jessie Fremont Sprengle March 10, 1880. Upon the retirement of his brother Joseph from the management of the "Times," which occurred that same year, he and a partner bought the office, and William became editor of the paper. He continued in that business until a short time after his wife's death, which took place June 25, 1883. This affliction caused him to sell his interest in the "Times" and to go to California. At Sacramento he was engaged to fill a responsible position with the Standard Oil Company, and was with them up to the time of his death, November 29, 1886. Our nephew William Stubbs was a most worthy young man, and died at an age when life is most enjoyable, attractive, and full of promise. He wished to live, but did not fear death, and bravely said at the last, "If my Maker wills it, I am ready." His remains were brought home and buried beside those of his wife and babe in Ashland Cemetery. The funeral took place December 9, 1886. We can not here give a detail of the solemn services, the many condolences received by the family, and the numerous and handsome tributes paid to his memory. They will probably be taken notice of more fully, at a future day, in a more direct history than this, by his own people.

Our sister Mary and her husband are now well advanced in years. Their career together has been marked by general good fortune, fair prosperity, and many blessings. All their children that are living are grown up, married, and have families, and all are honorably and comfortably situated in life. For forty-three years previous to the demise of their son William, death had not entered their home to make a break in the family circle. It is, therefore, not strange that after so long a period, one such reverse should have befallen them. And now, at most, only a few short years can transpire until in the common course of events, the home circle will be again thus invaded. In considering this, the natural end of all earthly existence, they have consolation in the hope of eternal life and family reunion beyond the grave.

DAVID SIMPSON GRAY.

## DAVID SIMPSON GRAY.

The fruits of a worthy ambition; the results of a steady purpose and an honorable, diligent, and systematic course in life; the manifestation of a filial love and respect for parents,—so frequently lacking in children; the spirit and energy to cope with difficulties and to educate and fit one's self for society and business without fortune and high-school advantages to start with; the possession of an unselfish, benevolent, and philanthropic disposition; and the virtue and strong, common sense judgment so essential to success, are all so marked and demonstrated in the character and history of our brother David, that we think him entitled to special mention in our family record.

The wealth he has acquired and the position and influence which he has attained, in society and the business world, mainly, if not altogether, by his own mind-force and strict integrity, are not only a credit to himself and to his parentage, but a source of pride and gratification to those connected with him by family and other kindred ties.

Moreover there are events and incidents of his life which, it is believed, will be a matter of special interest to his own offspring, and, perhaps, inspire them and other family posterity with a determination to emulate his merits.

It is much more an evidence of individual worth for a person to reach a high standing in the world, over natural obstacles and by his own powers, than it is to have gained it by inheritance. To be poor is not a discredit, but respectability of birth is always inquired after, as bad parentage usually entails bad blood, and experience shows that few children of such origin ever rise to prominence and respectability. It is this fact that makes so many biographies of self-made men and women begin with the words, "Born of poor but respectable parents." That his parents were poor but eminently respectable has already appeared in our general notice of the family.

David Simpson Gray was born in Broad-Kiln-Neck, Sussex County, Delaware, February 8, 1829, and was a babe when his parents emigrated to Ohio. He was always a puny child, not to say unhealthy, but delicate, and in this particular, unlike the other children of the family. He is yet spare in build, having never manifested the natural tendency of the other children to increase in flesh after maturity and as they advance in age.

He early displayed an activity of mind, and a desire to be doing something to earn money. At the same time he showed a self sacrificing spirit in its use. He was not selfish in spending his earnings upon himself or for his own pleasure—a practice so common with boys—but was very liberal in buying for his sisters the many little articles of dress they so often needed or desired. Whenever there was a celebration, sight-seeing, or other entertainment, to which his brother William wished to go, and both could not, David preferred staying at home, and if he had any money, and it was necessary, he would give it to his brother to help him off. Contributing to the pleasure and happiness of his brothers and sisters seemed a greater natural enjoyment to him than the gratification of his own desires and temptations.

Based upon the frailty of his constitution, however, it is evident that his future was never in the least imagined or contemplated by his parents. What he has achieved financially was probably not expected of any of their children, but that he of them all should be the one, and the only one, to amass an independent fortune, and that he should be the strongest support of their old age and the chief counselor and benefactor of the family, was undoubtedly never conceived.

A peculiar incident, pertinent to this point in our sketch, is told as having happened while the family was on its way to Ohio. Uncle George's family and ours, as has been elsewhere stated, both came to Ohio together, and as the conveyance they had was only one wagon and two horses, the members of the household had to do a good deal of walking. Father usually walked at the head of the team, and, being of a contemplative disposition, would once in a while become so absorbed in thought that he would take no heed of how fast the horses were going, and would go on without looking back until he would get out of hearing of those in the rear. On one occasion, when this was the case, mother, who was carrying David in her arms, grew tired, and becoming vexed at not being able to halt the wagon, took the following plan to impress father with a sense of his unthoughtfulness: Laying David down in a safe place at the side of the road, she quickened her steps until she approached near enough for father to hear her. On reaching the wagon, he inquired what she had done with the baby. "Oh!" says mother, "I left him back there at the road side. I got tired of carrying him, and as he is a poor child that will, probably, not live long, or ever be able to do any good, I thought it of no use to bother with him longer." Father hastened back and got the child. In reading this story, those who are acquainted with subsequent events in the private history of the family will scarcely fail to appreciate the applicability here of the words contained in the seventeenth verse of the twentieth chapter of Luke. "What is this, then, that is written? The stone which the builders rejected, the same is become the head of the corner."

As David grew into boyhood, he retained the same delicacy of constitution that belonged to him in infancy, and a circumstance which he relates as having occurred when he was yet a small boy, shows that his parents regarded his deficiency in physical strength as a serious, if not an insuperable obstacle in his future career. He thus speaks of the matter himself: "Though small in body and bone, I was yet perfectly proportioned and had the ambition to be the equal of other boys of stronger build and more helpful surroundings. The exact facts of the occasion I do not now remember, but it was one day, that in a bright and aspiring mood, I was telling mother something I was going to do, or who I was going to be like, when she replied, 'Oh! my dear child, what can you do? You are nothing but a poor delicate boy, and have neither the strength means, nor opportunity to do as you say.'" It may appear from the foregoing that his energy, spirit, and strength of mind were not given due consideration by his parents, in contemplating what he might accomplish in life. But, if so, in this they were not so much in fault as might at first be supposed. They, themselves, were children at a time in this country, when the person who could accomplish the most at manual labor was the greatest hero; at a time when the idea, "Its the mind (alone) that makes the man," did not so extensively prevail; when it was fashionable for boys of the first families to learn a trade; when speculation and large business deals were not so rife, and fortunes were mostly of slow growth, and were made by economy and industry. At such a time, and in such a state of public mind and feeling, health and physical strength were of the first importance.

However, while David felt hurt and was not insensible to his mother's words, and to like expressions which, on different occasions he met from others, their actual effect was only to nerve his spirit and strengthen his resolution to rise superior to every disadvantage under which he labored. As gold is tried by fire, so was his nature tried by these discouragements, and he was benefitted where others of less resolute disposition would have become disheartened.

He further says: "I was old enough to know that what mother said was kindly meant, and prompted in love, but it wounded my feelings and touched my pride. I met with something similar several times in my boyhood or youthful days,—a kind of pitying love, it was, which coming from any one but a mother is only a species of contempt. It always wounded and annoyed me greatly, but I schooled myself to conceal my chagrin, and secretly and firmly resolved that I would quietly win my way in the battle of life, no matter if the odds were against me. Prompted by my pride, I did not tell my grief to any one, and made it a rule for life to keep my own counsel; to work persistently, neglecting no duty committed to me; and to be patient and cheerful, performing every service in which I was engaged to the best of my ability, and letting my work speak for itself. I never made application for increase of salary, or for promotion, or for official position, during my whole business life. Such as I have received came to me without personal solicitation, and on my own merits, as my employers or superior officers rated them, or through the unsought efforts of kind business friends. I have met with some kicks and back-sets in business and official life, but I have never complained about them. I have kept quiet and patiently bided my time for things to come around right, and, in doing so I have never been disappointed."

At this distance of time, from the period when he was a boy, these facts and circumstances bring to view the inherent worth of character possessed by our brother then unperceived, and uncalculated upon by his parents.

David's earliest recollections of his life date back to the year 1833, when he was four years old and the family lived at East Union. He remembers the famous shower of stars that occurred all over the United States on the 13th of November of that year, a celestial phenomenon, which was, probably, viewed with more intense admiration by one class of community, and with greater dread and alarm by another, than any other that has ever happened in this country since its settlement. Being nearly seven years of age before the family left East Union, he remembers blowing the bellows there for father while he was still working at his trade. The first money he ever earned was gained by labor in a harvest field, near Dalton, father's second charge in the ministry. He also went into the country, while at Dalton, to stay over winter, but took sick and had to come home. At Wooster he went to school to a Col. Taylor in what was called the "West school-house." He has a strong recollection of the VanBuren and Harrison presidential campaign of 1840. William Allen, Wilson Shannon, and Richard Johnson held a big meeting at Wooster, on Stibb's Hill. David was a Democrat boy—another feature in which he differed from the rest of the family, but one which he afterward overcame. He wanted to raise a hickory pole, but father objected. He went to the meeting, however, and was coming back, carrying a hickory bush, when he ran across father, who made him drop it and skip for home.

The family next moved from Wooster to Norwalk. Father was imbued with the old time notion that every boy should learn a trade, and the necessity which he felt of reducing the number and expenses of his family only tended to strengthen it. So at Norwalk, when thirteen years of age, David was apprenticed to a man by the name of Carkuff to learn the tailor's trade. One of the conditions of the agreement was that he should have a year's schooling at the Seminary there. This, with probably a few months previous attendance at the Seminary, and what opportunity he had of attending the country district schools up to the time he was eleven years of age, comprise all the educational advantages he ever experienced. He was regarded by his teachers as a bright, alert boy, of a happy, generous disposition, and quick in getting his lessons. He seems to have been quite zealous as a young Democrat, for he speaks of going with a party toward Milan, in 1844, to meet Lewis Cass, who was coming to Norwalk to hold a meeting.

David was apprenticed to Carkuff for six years. There were two reasons that governed father in selecting the tailor's trade for his son. First, because it was a respectable, and, at that time, a fairly lucrative occupation. The sewing machine, though patented, was still crude and imperfect, and was not yet sensibly felt in competition with hand sewing in the business of tailoring. Much less was it anticipated that it would finally impair the standing and importance of the business to such an extent that men of force and ability would no longer find an inducement to learn the trade or to engage in it practically. All gentlemen's clothing was then made by hand, and the tailor who sat cross-legged on the bench and made clothes with his needle, ranked in respectability with the merchant who sold goods, with the doctor who practiced medicine, and the lawyer who settled his neighbor's difficulties for a fee. The second consideration was that the business required but little capital to run it, and this suited father, who was too poor to give his children any money assistance in starting them out in the world to take care of themselves.

In 1846, after having been four years at his trade, David was released from his apprenticeship by Carkuff, who sold out his business and went to California. Our folks were then living at Millersburg, and immediately after his release David came home on a visit. While at home, at Millersburg, an arrangement was about made for him to study law with W. B. Sapp, a prominent attorney of that place, afterward of Mt. Vernon, Knox County, Ohio. Why it was not consummated we are not informed. The practice of law, we have often thought, is a business especially suited to the natural mind, genius, and capabilities of father's and mother's children. She reached conclusions intuitively and he by reason, and their children partaking of the two characteristics are both strongly perceptive and logical. They would have one drawback, however, in this profession, and that is a disposition to put too much faith in human nature, and to be led into trusts contrary to their better judgment. David would undoubtedly have made a first class lawyer, but it is not presumed that he would have been more successful as such than in his chosen pursuit. Leaving home at the end of his visit in the fall of 1846, he went to Wooster, and worked at his trade, with William Smith, for about one year. He then formed a partnership with Smith's nephew and opened a tailor shop in Ashland, where they continued in business until the latter part of 1849. David next went to Wellington, Ohio. There he first clerked a year in the drugstore of Dr. Beach, and in the dry goods store of his friend W. F. Herrick. While holding these positions he had much spare time, which he spent in reading and study and in building up his health, which had suffered from a severe attack of typhoid fever while at Ashland, in the winter of 1848-9. He next clerked another year there, in the office of the Cleveland, Columbus, & Cincinnati railroad.

Wellington was a rather unimportant point on the road, but nevertheless his ability was recognized, and on the opening of the road through to Columbus he was offered a clerkship in the office there. He commenced at Columbus at thirty-five dollars per month, which was in a short time increased to fifty. This was in the fall of 1851. While working there he had a spell of sickness, on account of overwork, which lasted about one month.

In September, 1852, David was appointed Master of Transportation of the Louisville & Frankfort R. R. at a salary of twelve hundred dollars per year. His office was at Louisville, Kentucky, and the position comprised the same duties as that of General Freight and Ticket Agent. While in that city he had his first experience with slavery. He there saw slaves chained in couples for the Southern market, the slave pens and auction blocks where they were sold, and buyers walking around feeling the limbs and muscles of the slaves to find if they were hard and strong. These sights cured him of his Democracy. Not liking the situation with its surroundings, he remained at Louisville only until February, 1853, when he returned to Columbus,

Ohio, to take the local agency of the Central Ohio R. R. there, at an offer, as he understood, of one thousand dollars per year. This road extends from Columbus to Bellaire, a point on the Ohio River opposite Benwood, West Virginia, and four miles below Wheeling. The whole distance is one hundred and thirty-seven miles, but the road was then open and in operation only from Columbus to Zanesville. A few months after he entered upon his duties as agent at Columbus, a collision occurred on the road between a passenger train and a gravel train just outside the city limits. In connection with this affair David's forethought, activity, intelligence, and general capabilities, showed to great advantage. The following is his account of the matter:

"I entered the service of the Central Ohio Railroad Company in February, 1853. The road was then under construction, but the company was running trains from Columbus as far as Zanesville. I was station agent at Columbus, and general representative of the company's work and interest at that end of the line. The construction of the engine house, the yard tracks and the freight depot, and the graveling of the depot grounds there were then in progress. I was acting as overseer of this work. At the same time I was keeping watch over a gravel train that was being run, by the contractor, between Alum Creek and Columbus, to see that it did not interfere with the movements, nor get in the way of regular trains in and out of the station. It was, I think, in June, 1853, that a temperance or some other kind of convention was held in the city of Columbus, and we had brought in from Zanesville and way points a train of six or more coaches well filled with passengers. After the convention adjourned, the train, containing the visitors and delegates, left the depot at about 4 P. M., and had barely got out of sight around the curve, when it came into collision with the gravel train, the engineer of which was trying to run into the station before the time for the passenger train to leave. A frightful wreck of cars and engines was the result, but fortunately no one was killed, though quite a number were hurt and badly bruised. I immediately reported the fact of the collision to headquarters, at Zanesville, by telegraph, using the National Telegraph Company's wire (at that time the road had no telegraph line), and at once set to work energetically to remove the wrecked cars and engines, clear the track, make up a new train, and get the passengers on their way home. Mr. Lough, who was then agent of the Little Miami R. R., at Columbus, was very kind, and rendered me much assistance in the work. By early morning we had the track clear and train ready to leave for Zanesville on regular schedule time. Just as all work was done, President Sullivan arrived on an extra train, and appeared to be much gratified to find the road clear and everything ready for regular service again. He asked me for the particulars of the collision, which I gave him, and also informed him that previous to the accident I had frequently cautioned the contractor in charge of the gravel train not to run in from the gravel pit to Columbus unless he could surely arrive and get out of the way of regular trains ten minutes before they were due to leave. The President complimented me for the promptness manifested in the clearing up of the wreck, for the intelligent account I was able to give him of the whole matter, and for my good management of the company's interests. He then said, 'Is there anything I can do for you? Is everything satisfactory between you and the company?' After a little hesitation I said, 'Yes, except that when Col. Medbury employed me to take the station agency here, I understood that I was to receive one thousand dollars salary per year. I have been paid only at the rate of nine hundred dollars per year.' To this he replied, 'Well, sir, you shall have one thousand dollars salary, and I will give you a check for the difference between what you should have been paid and what you have received.'"

Of this matter it is important only to say further that the care with which David had guarded the company's interests, and the steps he had taken with a view to the safety and protection of its trains and property, afterwards enabled the company to collect from the contractor the damages sustained by them from the collision.

In the following November the road was opened to Bellaire, but was in very bad condition, being scarcely anything more than a mere line of rail. The business of the company was almost constantly interrupted by cars getting off the track, by land slides, by the falling in of tunnels that were yet unarched, and by accidents of various kinds. We were then in the office at Columbus, and remember the Cambridge tunnel, and a place called Section 16, as two points of great annoyance and trouble. Many transfers of passengers and goods had to be made at those places in consequence of obstruction of track. Every effort and precaution possible, with the means at hand, were used to avoid these accidents and difficulties, yet they seemed to continue as if they would never end. The troubles were vexatious and dispiriting to the management, since it was then required by the stockholders that the road should pay its own way, and it took no small portion of the earnings to repair and settle damages caused by the disasters. They were discouraging also, from the fact that a large increase of traffic had just come to the road from its Baltimore & Ohio R. R. connection at the river, and the opportunity thus afforded to meet the requirements of the stockholders was forestalled by the bad luck and a consequent failure to hold and transport the business satisfactorily. Moreover, it is to be presumed that there was some concern among the officers and directors lest the road should become severely crippled for the future with a bad name, and that they themselves would be judged incompetent. The accidents and difficulties referred to were due partly to natural causes, but were mainly the result of a mistaken policy on the part of the company in attempting to operate the road without money, without other necessary facilities and outfit, and before the track was in a settled and safe condition. Also, in railroad enterprises, under these circumstances, it is nearly always the case that the blame, sooner or later, falls upon the Manager or Superintendent, who is made the scapegoat for those higher in authority, whose policy has controlled him, and who are really the ones in fault. The track had been laid through to the river during the very dry summer and autumn of 1853. Side-tracks, water-stations, yard facilities, and almost everything necessary to enable a road to transact business safely, promptly, and economically, were wanting, and there was no money in the treasury to provide them. The locomotives and cars were new and untried, and the breakages and failures at weak points in their construction were frequent. Also, there was an effort to burn coal in the freight engines, which had been built at Baltimore and were called coal burners. The engineers and firemen on the road were not accustomed to coal and were unfavorable to its use as a fuel for locomotives. Besides, the winter of 1853-4 was very cold, and the rains and snows falling on the new, dry banks, cuts, and fills of the unballasted road-bed, played havoc with the track. All these things, together with the employes unpaid, conduced to accidents, delays, losses, complaints, and general dissatisfaction and discomfort to all concerned, and were amply sufficient to wreck any operating management, however able and experienced, where the President and Board of Directors were seeking an excuse for their financial needs and bad economy.

George W. Fulton had been appointed Superintendent, and brother David, Master of Transportation of the Central Ohio R. R. in the fall of 1853, the former a little before, and the latter a little after, the opening of the road through to the river at Bellaire, and both were thus prominently and responsibly connected with its management and operating affairs, during the trying period of which we have spoken. David's salary was $1,500 per year.

In February, 1855 an accident happened to him by which he nearly lost the middle finger of, and otherwise injured, his right hand. The accident, too, was indirectly caused by the crippled and hampered condition of affairs on the road. He was going east on a freight train, and had reached Cambridge, Ohio, when the engine run out of wood. On reaching the wood-pile there was found no wood ready sawed. It was night, the wood-sawyer had gone home, and the train could not proceed until the engine was replenished with fuel. A steam-power saw, which was located there, was put in motion, and David undertook to assist in sawing the wood. Not being physically strong, and at the time much exhausted by his labors, he forgot for a moment, the danger of his position, and dropped his right hand on the saw. The result was a serious wounding of the hand, and the almost entire severance of the large finger, which was left hanging only by the skin or a small part of the flesh. A physician, however, replaced and dressed it, and the finger grew fast again, although in a somewhat disfigured shape. To show the circumstances under which David happened to be with the freight train at the time of the accident, and more clearly to demonstrate the indirect cause of it, we quote the following from his notes;—"On that morning in February, 1855, in a drizzling, half snow and half rain storm, I left Columbus on the 10 A. M. passenger train, for Bellaire. The trains from the east that day were all very late. The road had no telegraph line at that time, and freight trains had to wait indefinitely, at meeting points, for passenger trains. On reaching Zanesville I stopped off, finding three delayed freight and stock trains there, waiting for the passenger train from the east to pass. It was late in the evening when the road became clear for them to proceed. The Master Mechanic wanted the trains abandoned and the engines put in the engine-house until morning. The conductors of the freight trains, also, were rather reluctant to start out and take the chances of getting over Section 16 and through Cambridge Tunnel without further delay and trouble. I insisted, however, on the trains proceeding. One of the conductors said to me, 'It is not a pleasant prospect for those who have the work to do;' or in substance this, 'It is, comparatively, an easy thing for you to give the orders to proceed, but not so easy a matter for us who have to obey the orders.' To this I replied, 'I never ask men to do what I would not be willing, or am afraid, to do myself. I am on my way to Bellaire and will go with you.' So I got on the middle one of the three trains. We got over the heavy grade, at Section 16 and through the Tunnel, and arrived at Cambridge in good time, where occurred the wood sawing, and the accident to my hand."

Near the time that this accident happened, Mr. Fulton resigned the Superintendency of the road. He was popular with the employes, and they arranged to make him a present of a set of silver,—pitcher, goblets, etc. David was selected to make the presentation address, which he composed while lying in bed with his injured hand, at Columbus. The presentation and supper on the occasion took place at the Zane House in Zanesville.

In April or May, following Mr. Fulton's resignation, Mr. Isaac H. Southwick was appointed Superintendent, and George L. Chase, Assistant Superintendent. Mr. Southwick also brought with him, from the East, a Mr. Palmer, who acted as his Secretary and as Purchasing Agent for the road. Southwick and Palmer were from Massachusetts, and Chase from Connecticut. This change of officers in the operating department was, we understand, the result of an effort to obtain for the company financial relief, and Mr. Fulton's retirement was a sort of cover for the former miscalculations of the company as to the road's financial and physical needs. At about the same time that Mr. Fulton resigned, David's salary was cut down from $1,500 to $1,200, brought about by the report of a committee on retrenchment. The change of Superintendents, however, brought only temporary relief. It is true that there were fewer accidents and delays to trains during the favorable period from April to December that Southwick was in charge, yet it was simply because the banks had settled, because the weak points of the cars and locomotives had been developed and strengthened, and because side-tracks, water-stations, and other facilities had been supplied. The operating expenses were increased under his management, and the chronic need of more money was soon as pressing as ever. Fault-findings, criminations and recriminations between the Superintendent's department and the Treasurer, President, and Board of Directors, grew and multiplied. The old and new Superintendent's administrations were frequently compared and criticised to the credit of the former. It was under this state of affairs that Mr. Southwick resigned in the fall of 1855, and returned to the East, with all his importations. All the old men and officers that had remained with the company during his time (but on the back seats, as it were), then came to the front and in favor again, and continued so from that time forward, as long as they remained in the service of the company. David's salary was restored to $1,500 per year, with back pay at the same rate for all the time that had elapsed since it had been reduced, and in a few months thereafter it was advanced to $2,000 per year.

After Southwick resigned, Vice President Deshler (President Sullivan having also resigned) appointed David to act as Superintendent until a new one could be chosen. But David was not a candidate for the Superintendency at any time, and declined to assume the title. He, however, performed the duties of Superintendent together with those of Master of Transportation, until the meeting of the Board of Directors, in the spring of 1856. Then Elias Fassett was elected President, H. J. Jewett, Vice President, and Thatcher Perkins, Superintendent. David's title was changed to that of General

15—HISTORY.

Freight Agent, and in addition, he had charge of all commercial relations with connecting lines. He remained with the Central Ohio R. R. as General Freight and Commercial Agent until January, 1864, when he accepted the position—in the interest of the Pennsylvania R. R.,—of General Superintendent of the "Union Line." Several times previously, between 1855 and 1864, he had received favorable offers of positions from other railroad companies if he would leave the Central Ohio and take service with them. At one time he was offered the General Freight Agency of the C., H. & D. and Old Mad River Line; at another time a similar position with the Michigan Southern R. R.; and later on, the Superintendency of the Little Miami, known in those days as the "Old Reliable." David was much attached to the Central Ohio R. R., and some of its head officials and employes, on account of early experiences and hardships endured together. The main reason, however, for declining these offers was his desire to remain at Columbus. He had many good and helpful friends in that place and on the railroads centering there, who were always ready to recommend him for his ability and to help him forward. Besides, he felt that in the long run, the chances for him to do well would be as good by remaining where he was known, among friends and at moderate wages, than at a higher salary, among strangers, where he would have to build up anew his reputation.

The "Union Line" was incorporated under the name of "The Union R. R. and Transportation Co." It was not a regular railroad company, but what is called a "fast freight line," that does a through transportation business over regular railroad companies' tracks. The "Union Line" was organized in the interest of the Pennsylvania Railroad and its connections, to compete with similar companies on rival routes. In most cases these "fast freight lines" are owned by the regular railroad companies over whose tracks they operate. But the "Union Line" had features in its organization that were different from those of other fast freight lines. It owned its own cars, employed its own officers and agents, and operated under contracts with the railroad companies for the transportation of merchandise by fast freight trains, as Express companies do by passenger trains. The managers of the Pennsylvania R. R., we understand, were not at first favorably disposed toward the institution of a "fast freight line" over their route, but were impelled to it in consequence of the policy of competing lines, and to protect their own business. "The Union Line" was successful from the start, so much so, indeed, that afterward, at a meeting of the managers of the Pennsylvania R. R. and those of the other great trunk lines, it was proposed that if the former would abolish their "Union Line," the latter would abandon the "fast freight lines" of their routes. The proposition, however, was rejected. The selection of David, by the Union R. R. and Transportation Company," to look after the interests of so important an enterprise showed a great confidence in his ability, and the success of his efforts justified the trust imposed in him. David remained General Superintendent of the "Union Line" until February, 1869. He then accepted the position of Second Vice President and General Manager of the P., C. & St. L. R. R. and its leased lines. This position embraced what was to him an enlarged field of labor, and, although in line with his more particular knowledge and experience as a Master and Superintendent of Freight Traffic and of railroad commercial interests, he accepted the position with great reluctance and with the understanding that he should not lose his connection with the Commercial department of the Pennsylvania system. The P., C. & St. L. R. R. Co. is, practically, the western extension of the Pennsylvania R. R. out of Pittsburg into the southwest, and is under its control through ownership of a majority of its stock. Its affairs were then in a formative state, and it was understood that, as soon as its plans were matured, David was to return to the "Union Line." He held the position until the spring of 1870, at which time he resigned as General Manager, but retained the position of Second Vice-President in charge of the commercial relations of the same company.

In 1872 he resigned this position and resumed relations with the "Union Line" as General Western Manager, which position he now holds. David's open title as Western Manager of the "Union Line" only partly covers his field of work; he is really the commercial agent and accredited representative of the great Pennsylvania railroad system in all its through freight traffic relations with other roads—a masked power that advises as to its interests, and is influential in shaping its competitive freight policy. In recent years and since his connection with that company, David has been repeatedly solicited to accept relations offering official titles, higher and more representative of the important duties he actually performs in the railway service, and at salaries which expert knowledge, experience, and influence, such as he possesses, always command. They have all been declined, however, because involving larger direct responsibilities and cares than he was willing to assume, and because they required his removal from Columbus, all of which would interfere with the personal comfort of himself and family, and cause a severance of his almost lifelong associations. Within the past fifteen years he has had several positions offered him at salaries ranging as high as $12,000 per year; in two instances from trunk lines, and in one instance from the road of largest importance west of Chicago. When the Central Traffic Association was formed, about two years ago, he was urged to accept the Commissionership at a salary of $15,000 to $18,000 per year, but declined it because he was unwilling to change his residence to Chicago. This was a very gratifying offer to him, however, as it showed the confidence which the different and conflicting interests embraced in the association had in his fairness and integrity, as well as his competency. We are also credibly informed that he has, even more recently, been urged by the company he is now connected with to go to New York City in a representative capacity, and that if he would do so he might name his terms. The following notice of him is taken from the Columbus (Ohio) Despatch, printed January 4, 1886:

BRIEF RESUME OF THE RAILROAD EXPERIENCES OF D. S. GRAY.

David S. Gray, Western Manager of the Union Line (the through-freight organization of the Pennsylvania system), and Director of the Pittsburgh, Cincinnati, and St. Louis Railway, began his railroad career as clerk and agent of the Bee Line, at Wellington Station, over thirty years ago. Shortly afterward he came to Columbus as cashier of the same road. From that position he went to the old Central Ohio road and became Master of Transportation, and then General Freight Agent. On the organization of the "Union Line," he was made General Superintendent, and took a very active part in the building up of the through-freight-line business, which was then in its infancy, and has since done away with the old mode of transferring and rebilling freight at the terminus of each road.

Mr. Gray was, for a period, Vice-President and General Manager of the "Pan Handle" system, but for the greater part of the past twenty years his energies have been principally devoted to the through-freight traffic of the Pennsylvania system, although his long and varied experience in all branches of service, in the building and operating of railways, and his sound judgment, have made him a general consulting man for nearly all departments.

In the various pooling operations of the past few years, in which the principal roads have participated, Mr. Gray has been a prominent adviser, and his large experience and clear-headed conceptions of the difficulties to be overcome, have aided much in shaping the policies that have been adopted. For the same reasons he has been frequently called upon to arbitrate cases in dispute between roads other than those with which he is officially connected.

Mr. Gray was one of the projectors and builders of the Columbus & Toledo road, and has been connected with a number of other similar enterprises. He has also been prominent in various branches of manufacture that have contributed to the growth of Columbus. His influence and quiet generosity in church, educational, and charitable institutions have also been greatly felt."

From statistics before us, it is estimated that David's public and private gifts and benevolences will aggregate $60,000, probably more, certainly not less. Of this sum about $25,000 have been contributed to father and mother, to brothers and sisters and their children, and to one or two persons outside of his relatives. In a public way, for the last twenty years, he has contributed, not largely, but liberally, to the building of every new church in Columbus, of whatever denomination. His largest donation was to the present "Broad Street M. E. Church," the society of which he has been connected with since July 18, 1875. This church is a Gothic edifice, built of green stone, shipped from near Philadelphia, Penn. It cost in round numbers $70,000, not including the lot on which it stands, and was dedicated July 5, 1885. It is not the largest, but is regarded as the handsomest church in the city, if not in the State. David was the President of the Board of Trustees, and Treasurer of its Building Committee, and paid about $28,000 of its entire cost, including the price of the ground upon which it is built.

David has also manifested considerable interest in educational affairs. For several years past he has been, and we think is now, one of the trustees of the Ohio Wesleyan University at Delaware. He has aided several young men in acquiring an education at this institution, to fit themselves for the ministry and a life of usefulness in the world.

In age our brother is now approaching his fifty-ninth birthday and possesses remarkable energy and mental activity for a man of his years. He has been married twice. We have not referred to his family record here as it has been noticed in the genealogical tables and biographical dictionary connected with this work. He is still living in Columbus, and will probably pass the remainder of his days there. His attachment to the place and his friends there remind us of the words of Ruth to Naomi:—"Entreat me not to leave thee; thy people shall be my people, and thy God, my God. Where thou diest will I die, and there will I be buried."

When his life closes we think it can be said of him that few men have lived to a better purpose, have been prompted by worthier motives, or have left a more honorable inheritance to their offspring.

# THE CLOSING SCENE OF FATHER'S LIFE.

> Rest from thy labor, rest,
> Soul of the just set free!
> Blest be thy memory, and blest
> Thy bright example be!

We had hoped to get this book in print during father's life on earth. We labored to that end, calculated, almost daily, the probabilities and improbabilities of realizing this hope, drew pleasure from the thought that it would gratify him to see the book, and to know that it was done, and had obtained quite a settled confidence that our desire was to be fulfilled.

On the 24th of October we went to Indianapolis to give the manuscript to the printer for publication. This being accomplished, we again took the cars for Cambridge City, feeling more than ever elated with the prospect that the work would be completed before father's death. But, in the providence of God, it was not to be so. On reaching home in the evening we found a message awaiting us which stated that he had died suddenly that day at 1 o'clock P. M. This sorrowful event, thus unexpectedly obliterating our anticipations, naturally calls for a supplementary chapter pertaining to the closing scenes of his long, eventful, important, and beautiful life.

By this dispensation of the Almighty, it almost seems to us as ordered that another leaf should be given to his history, that it was not to be finished until his sun had set, and the precious letters of condolence received by the family, and the fitting words spoken at his funeral service, were added to further attest the glory of his earthly life.

The approaching event of father's death gave the family but little warning. About eight days before it occurred brother David received a telegram from Mrs. Higgins, at Findlay, saying that father was unwell and wished to see him. Having an important business engagement set for the following week, David asked in return if the illness was serious, and receiving a reply that father was better, he did not go. In the meantime, David Stubbs, father's grandson, from California, was visiting his parents at Ashland, and not having seen his grandfather since 1867, he said he would not return to California until he had made him a visit. Consequently, sister Mary and her son, David Stubbs, unexpectedly arrived at Findlay the week preceding father's death, and thus it happened that she was the only one, of his children not living in Findlay, who saw him recently before he passed away. She had left, however, and had scarcely reached home again, when she was summoned to attend his funeral.

Father had complained a little of having a cold, of some difficulty in getting his breath, and of a pain in his breast, shoulders and the back of his head. But his ailing occasioned no alarm, as he was up and about and his voice was strong, indicating no weakness.

On Monday morning, October 24, Sister Sarah, with whom father was living in the old homestead, asked him if he had rested well during the night. He said yes, except that he had had a little pain and at times a difficulty in getting his breath. Yet he arose, dressed himself, and was so strong that he refused to let Sarah help him put on his socks. He sat down to breakfast, ate sparingly of a little oatmeal, drank a cup of coffee, and said that he had no appetite. Near 1 o'clock in the afternoon he was reclining on the lounge in the sitting room, and was talking of getting up. Sarah was standing just within the door leading into the kitchen when she heard a noise like the overturning of a chair. She hastened into the sitting room and found father lying on the floor unable to speak. A gentleman who happened to be passing was called in and requested to go for a physician, but he said it was unnecessary, that nothing could be done. Father breathed a few times and was dead. He must have fallen from a sitting posture, for, were it otherwise, the fall would have made a greater noise.

Father never liked the idea of living so long as to become mentally weak or physically helpless on account of age, and the thought of having to be waited upon or cared for, under such circumstances, was always distasteful to him. But he never became thus enfeebled. His mind continued clear and his body comparatively strong and erect up to the last hour of his life. Also, he was unused to and shrank from physical suffering, and it was ever his wish to die without pain or lingering sickness. God favored him in this special desire, for his passing away was so sudden and painless that death was deprived of its sting, and the grave could claim but little victory.

It is thought by physicians that father died of apoplexy of the heart. At the time of his death he was probably the oldest Methodist minister in Ohio. Had he lived five months and four days longer he would have been eighty-eight years old.

The funeral occurred on Thursday, October 27. The following, of his children and their families, were in attendance:— Mary and Joseph Stubbs, and son Rev. J. E. Stubbs; David S. Gray and wife; Mrs. Sarah C. Higgins, her daughter Mamie, and son Charles; Col. S. F. Gray and son Rev. Wm. D. Gray; John Emory Gray; Emily and John Ruthrauff, their daughters Ella and Linda, and son Fred; Eleanor Gray, and Wm. Morris Brewster, son of sister Elizabeth, who was in too poor health to make the journey from St. Louis. Letters of condolence were received from a number of the grandchildren and friends, who could not come, expressing their love and respect for father, sorrow for his death, sympathy for the family, and regret at the circumstances that prevented their presence on the occasion. Of these letters we present several, from friends and acquaintances outside of the family, because of their special character and value as attestations to father's virtues, and of the good he did in the world, and, for this reason, peculiarly appropriate in the record of the close of his life.

From Rev. E. K. Bell, former pastor of the Lutheran Church at Findlay.

CINCINNATI, OHIO, October 25, 1887.

MRS. JOHN RUTHRAUFF:

*Dear Friend*—I have just learned the sad news, that Father Gray is dead. His death impresses me deeply, for I had learned to love the dear old man during my ministry in Findlay. He was a man of the purest heart, and for one of his age, had a very clear head. Indeed he was one of the rare, true, good men, whom you always feel better for having met. I shall never forget his good influence over me. His prayers were a benediction. God permitted him to live long as a witness for righteousness. His soul was ripe for heaven and he is now at rest with the blessed Christ, Who was his constant joy, and Whom he loved out of a full and trustful heart. Accept my heart-felt sympathy in your bereavement. Convey the same for me to Miss Gray and your dear family, and believe me to be

Sincerely your friend,

322½ LINN ST.                                                         E. K. BELL.

## From Rev. C. S. Ehrenfeld, one of the Professors of Wittenberg College.

SPRINGFIELD, OHIO, October 25, 1887.

MR. AND MRS. RUTHRAUFF:

*Dear Bereaved Friends*—I have just seen the announcement of Father Gray's death, and am prompted to write you a word in the midst of your sorrows. Though I made his acquaintance only recently, and saw him only a few times, yet, I came to regard him highly,—indeed to feel for him an affection that moves me to join you in mourning his loss. Though so very aged that you must have been, for many years, not unprepared for his death, still, none the less, I am sure, are your hearts stricken, especially by his sudden departure. He was to me, both physically and spiritually, a grand man, and I shall carry his memory with me through life.

I pray the God of all consolation to comfort your hearts and keep you ever in his loving care. Give my kind regards to the other members of Father Gray's family, that I met, and also to your daughters.

Believe me ever yours sincerely,

C. S. EHRENFELD.

## From T. M. Roberts, father-in-law to Rev. W. D. Gray, to Colonel S. F. Gray:

CLINTON, MO., Oct. 25, 1887.

MY DEAR FRIEND: The announcement of your sainted father's departure from us was quite a shock to me, as I had anticipated his living some years longer, and had looked forward with great pleasure to a repetition of my recent delightful visit to him. There was something in the association which lifted me on a higher plane of experience while in his presence, and its healthful influence stayed with me, strengthening my faith. Although aged, he seemed to be still doing good for the Master he served so long and faithfully to the end of his grand life. My thoughts are with the mourners to-day. I would like to have looked upon that good face again before it was shut out forever from mortal gaze. I had a strong desire to assist in the last sad rites, the only opportunity left us for manifesting our love. I did not receive soon enough the reply to my telegram asking if I had time to reach there. I desire to extend my sympathy to those who will necessarily feel his loss the most by reason of living so long and constantly under such a noble presence of Christian manhood, with the lamp of faith always burning brightly. "The prayers of the righteous availeth much." Your dear father's prayers seemed to be answered while here. May their influence still prevail in behalf of his kindred and friends! By cherishing his memory, example, and wishes, his children will be keeping his spirit with them as a consolation here—as a ministering spirit, it may the better prevail for them beyond. With many assurances of my deepest sympathy and regard, I beg to subscribe myself, your sincere friend,

T. M. ROBERTS.

From Mrs. Florence Richards, daughter of a Mr. Donnelson, an old acquaintance and friend of father's, who lived at Grand Rapids, Ohio, during the time that he was Presiding Elder of the Maumee District. She subsequently resided in Findlay.

LEIPSIC, OHIO, October 25, 1887.

MY DEAR BEREAVED FRIENDS—Your letter, announcing the sudden death of dear Father Gray, has just been received, and I hasten to reply. I am so sorry for you all in this, your hour of sore affliction and bereavement. You loved him so dearly, and he was such a treasure to you all, that his going from you will leave you quite disconsolate, indeed. I trust that He Whom your father so deeply loved, so sweetly trusted, and so nobly served, may sustain you, and so send the Comforter into your hearts that you may bow submissively to the will of Him "Who doeth all things well." Although you were not permitted to receive his dying blessing, you have been daily blessed by his prayers for you, and his life has been a sweet benediction. I have thought much of him in the last few weeks. So many things that he said, in the counsel he has given me, have been recalled. Last Sunday evening I was talking to the young people in their six-o'clock meeting, and spoke to them of him. I told them some of the many good things he had said to me, and while I was talking and they were listening, with much attention, the Holy Spirit came and took possession of our meeting—carried the words of dear Father Gray right to the hearts of the young men and ladies, and we were all greatly blessed. And now as I learn that he has gone to his home in glory, and while I feel sad that I shall not meet him again in his earthly home, I rejoice that he was permitted to go without suffering, and that to-night he is singing, with those who went before him, the blessed song of the redeemed. Beautiful thought, isn't it?

How glad I should be to be with you and attend the burial services of your dear father. Just now it seems impossible to come, but if I can leave home I will come. I thank you for remembering me in your sad hour. May God cheer you all, and the "Strong to deliver" "uphold you with the right hand of his righteousness," while you are "passing through the waters," is the prayer of your sincere friend,

FLORENCE RICHARDS.

The children, grandchildren, and relatives present, took final leave of father at the house. When all had fondly and sadly viewed his face for the last time, in this world, the affecting scene was closed with prayer by Rev. J. E. Stubbs.

On the lid of the casket containing the remains were laid—one at the head and the other at the foot—two beautiful, white floral offerings, the design of each being that of an anchor and cross. One of these was a kindly remembrance from Mrs. J. R. Ballentine, of Findlay, and the other was from Mr. and Mrs. Walter Higgins, of Chicago. The latter tribute bore the following address, and was deposited with the body in the grave:

DEAR GRANDFATHER:—Knowing that thou hast reached the haven to which thy faith has long been anchored, we send this symbol of safety as an expression of our love and respect for you. "Blessed are the dead which die in the Lord."

Between the two floral decorations mentioned was placed a miniature sheaf of wheat contributed by Mrs. David S. Gray, of Columbus, Ohio.

Eight of the clergy officiated as pall-bearers:—Rev. A. C. Barnes, Rev. J. W. Hill, Rev. S. M. Boggs, and Rev. Peter Biggs, members of the M. E. Central Ohio Conference, to which father belonged, and Rev. W. W. Criley, Rev. J. R. Mitchell, Rev. E. S. Bender, and Rev. S. H. Randabaugh, pastors, respectively, of the English Lutheran, Presbyterian, and United Brethren churches, in Findlay.

The general services were held in the First Methodist Episcopal Church, under the direction of Rev. Lyman E. Prentiss, the regular pastor.

The exercises were opened with singing by the choir:

*Hymn read by Rev. W. W. Criley.*

"How blest the righteous when he dies!
 When sinks a weary soul to rest,
 How mildly beam the closing eyes!
 How gently heaves the expiring breast!

"So fades a summer cloud away;
 So sinks the gale when storms are o'er;
 So gently shuts the eye of day;
 So dies a wave along the shore.

"A holy quiet reigns around,
 A calm which life nor death destroys;
 And naught disturbs that peace profound
 Which his unfettered soul enjoys.

"Life's labor done, as sinks the clay,
 Light from its load the spirit flies,
 While heaven and earth combine to say,
 How blest the righteous when he dies!"

Prayer was then offered by Rev. A. C. Barnes, presiding elder of the Findlay district. The choir then sang:

(Hymn read by Rev. J. R. Mitchell.)

"Asleep in Jesus! Blessed sleep,
   From which none ever wakes to weep!
   A calm and undisturbed repose,
   Unbroken by the last of foes.

"Asleep in Jesus! O, how sweet
   To be for such a slumber meet!
   With holy confidence to sing
   That death hath lost his venomed sting.

"Asleep in Jesus! Peaceful rest,
   Whose waking is supremely blest!
   No fear, no woe shall dim that hour
   That manifests the Savior's power.

"Asleep in Jesus! O, for me
   May such a blissful refuge be!
   Securely shall my ashes lie,
   Waiting the summons from on high.

"Asleep in Jesus! Far from thee
   Thy kindred and their graves may be;
   But thine is still a blessed sleep,
   From which none ever wakes to weep."

Rev. E. D. Whitlock, of St. Paul's Methodist Episcopal Church at Toledo, Ohio, then made the following address:

We stand to-day at the summit of a long and eventful life—a life that runs parallel with very much that is important in our history as a country, and in our labors and triumphs as a Church. To have lived more than four score years at any period of time is to have borne great responsibility; but to have been contemporaneous with some who aided in founding our State, and with others who in this country had to do with the planting of the Church, is to have shared in opportunities calculated to awaken the most latent powers and to inspire the dullest minds. It is no uncommon thought that to be a participator to-day in the great and important movements of the times is an honor worthy to be conferred on the greatest men and the most courageous hearts. Indeed, we are apt to regard it the greater opportunity for prominence and honor to be present when important enterprises are completed and far-reaching plans are consummated. But to be permitted to place in proper and essential positions the foundation stones, and to rear for the support of great concerns strong columns and enduring pillars, is, in my opinion, the better opportunity for distinction. To plant the tree of civil liberty and to lay the foundations of moral and religious progress are, indeed, greater achievements than to have a hand in gathering the fruit of the former or in putting the finishing touches upon the latter.

A life beginning when this man's life began, and ending at the time when it did, can not but have been of some importance to our prosperity and welfare as citizens, and to our enlightenment and happiness as members of our Father's kingdom, especially so if a great purpose has stirred the heart and inspired the life. It is but fact to say that a noble aim accounted for the pure pulsations of this man's soul, and the holy deeds of his long career. When years enough had elapsed to enable him to form proper views of life and its relations, he looked out upon it, not with an idler's gaze, but with the inquiring eye of a mind already illumined with the light of heaven.

Eighty-seven years ago this country was in its infancy, and the Church, to which this father, and our common friend, belonged, was beginning to mark out her noble work and to write her splendid history. It was Father Gray's privilege and honor to watch the early growth of our free institutions, and the first steps of our aggressive denominationalism. He was one of the pioneers of this portion of the then West. He was one of the Church's early messengers, who went up and down this sparsely settled and well nigh unexplored region, shedding moral light upon the cabin home, and carrying glad tidings to the new settlement. He had to do, as a man, as a citizen, and especially as a minister of the "new and better covenant," with the organization of the forces and the direction of the means, which, under the providence of God and through the dauntless courage of our fathers and mothers, have given us this broad inheritance of good that we see all around us. And as we gather here to-day, though in tears and with great sorrow burdening our hearts, it behooves us to ask: "What are the lessons to be learned from this long life, and what are the inspirations breathed into our hearts by this venerable father in the Church and this crowned saint of Heaven?" Certainly these long, full years can not be void of teachings, which, by you and me should be turned to profit.

One of the first lessons that we may learn from the life before us is that of early piety. Born of godly parents, reared at a consecrated fireside, developed under Christian influences in the home, he began, when a boy, to see how important it is to turn life's early steps toward paths of purity and righteousness. Accordingly, he sought, with all his heart, an interest in the religion of the Bible. He was radical in his views of Christian life, and sound in his conversion to God. To take upon himself the sacred and public vows of Christ was no slight or thoughtless matter. It was a holy duty and a solemn consecration. It meant everything to him. It was a deep radical work of divine grace in the heart, in its affections, desires, aspirations, and life purposes. It stirred and penetrated the deep places of his young soul. It meant forgiveness—conscious forgiveness of sin; absolution—thorough absolution from guilt; it meant a divine renovation of the inner man, and a fire—a holy fire—kindled on the spiritual altar.

Piety, with Father Gray, from the outset, was no mere passive submission to God. It was an active and mighty force, absorbing his thoughts and energies. It was a new and heavenly light, sending forth its rays into all the future, and a controlling power, giving direction to plan and purpose. At the age of nineteen, in the flexible period of life, this man of God sought his Savior. Would that we all, especially the young who hear me, might learn and fully master this great lesson of early religion—of remembering our Creator in the days of youth. How much this prolonged life owes to an early acceptance of Christ, I do not know, but I have no hesitation in saying that over all his after years and experiences, this deliberate choice of religious ways exerted a directing hand and a moulding power.

Another lesson taught us by this life is the recognition of the Divine claims, and the acceptance of duty and obligation at any cost and at all hazards. Two reasons, true to the laws and demands of the Christian life, accounted for his acceptance of duty. The first is found in the subjective character of the Christian religion. There is in it, always, as a personal experience, a feeling and purpose to accept obligation as a means of spiritual growth and happiness. He must be dutiful and active who would maintain Christian joy and blessing. None seem to have experienced this feeling more fully and clearly than Father Gray. The other reason is found in what the godly man sees about him to be done for others. Human society, he felt and was assured, needed the reforming power and the regenerating spirit of our holy Christianity. Conditions, essentially opposed to man's best welfare, were about him, and these must be mastered and changed.

It was the part of great courage and the manifestation of a heavenly mind for our forefathers to undertake the establishment of a spiritual kingdom throughout this western country. It was no small task to brave the storms, to plunge into the trackless forest, to ford unexplored rivers, and to face the dangers and circumstances incident to rude and unrefined life, in order to build up the Church. It required heroes—Christian heroes—to undertake the great mission of preaching the Gospel. But our friend and father in the Church acknowledged the Divine claims, accepted the heroic duties of that early day, and went forth to change these rude circumstances into those that refine. In short, to lift up before men, the best standards for business, society, and morals. The forces by which this was to be done were found in the Gospel. Father Gray chose to preach this Gospel and wield these forces. The clearness with which he recognized God's claims, and the promptness with which he chose duty, were all the more manifest because of the meager equipments which that early day afforded the ministers of the Church. The education of that day was practical, rather than theoretic; was more from contact with living things than from books and schools. To learn was to do; to be educated was to master every-day problems. And yet our pioneer preachers were, by no means, unqualified for the stupendous work of building up the Church, and of pushing on our civilization.

The books that constituted the early preacher's library were, chiefly, the Bible, the discipline of the Church, Clarke's Commentary, Watson's Theological Dictionary, Wesley's Sermons, Fletcher's Checks, and later, Watson's Institutes. But these were all studied and familiarized. There were no colleges or theological seminaries in those days. The outfit of the pioneer Methodist preacher, though simple, was capable of certain and large execution.

As a preacher, Father Gray was evangelical and scriptural, seeking always to affect conscience and life with the truth of God; and, in the work of the pastorate, the vows of the Church, and the obligations of the Christian life were first and supreme. In all his varied and self-sacrificing career he allowed nothing of a personal or secular character to come between him and religious duty. Even after he had quit the active service of the ministry, the habits he formed while in the regular work clung to him, rendering him in spirit and manifestation as desirous as ever before to meet the requirements of the great Head of the Church. Dangers, obstacles, deprivations, and oppositions, all these he was willing to encounter for his Master's sake. With him duty was paramount and the Church was first. The spirit of secularism, the attractions of the world, and the difficult path of the early itinerant were all powerless to dissuade him from that service which brings joy when it is performed, and heaven when the labors on earth are done.

A third lesson we should profit by here to-day is that of loyalty. He ever remained true to the cause he had espoused; he never deserted the colors of his victorious Captain. His loyalty was manifest in all the elements of his character as a Christian, and in his relations as a minister of the Lord, Jesus Christ. This trait was evinced in what he conceived to be the true mission of the minister. He bore the stamp of the earliest Methodist preachers, and it was clear and well-marked because of his personal convictions. He believed, and his own course is the best illustration of his belief, that a preacher should proclaim the truths of the gospel. He was always intolerant of anything in the pulpit purely sensational; of any effort, preparation, or mannerisms for the sake of a crowd; of any popularity obtained at the expense of the simple truth and the obvious teachings of the sacred Word. He severely condemned anything like ministerial legerdemain in the sacred desk, and was prepared to show a just indignation when the functions of the pulpit were reduced to a secular plane or to the world's level. It is altogether probable that on account of this marked characteristic, made prominent by self-culture and by the times, that some regarded him as unduly fearful of the influences of the discussion of modern themes by the ministry. But whatever criticisms might be made of the sensitiveness of Father Gray in this respect, he was always tending, in his views and utterances, to the safe side in orthodoxy and in practical religion. He was always loyal to the Methodist Episcopal Church. He was a true and unwavering believer in her policy, in her broad doctrines, in her evangelical mission, and in her adaptability to all peoples and to all times. He was denominational without being sectarian. He did not love other churches less, but his own more. He could sing for his own church first, and for all other churches second.

> "I love thy Church, oh God!
> Her walls before thee stand,
> Dear as the apple of thine eye,
> Engraven on thy hand."

He was the true friend of his pastor, and had a zealous regard and a genuine solicitude for his standing and influence. He was one of the first to welcome, by an early call at the parsonage and by a warm grasp of the hand, the man sent by the Conference as pastor. He was faithful in the exhibition of his personal fealty to the preacher by attending, whenever health and circumstances would permit, the services of the sanctuary. He was slow to criticise, in the minister, what he might deem false in practice or deviations from doctrinal standards, and when he did so it was done in a kindly spirit and with a feeling of charity. Some may not have fully understood him on this point, but so far as I knew him, and so far as others have testified, this was true of the man and minister whose fidelity we hold up to-day as worthy of imitation. I never knew a man whose anxiety for the prosperity of Zion, and whose personal regard for his pastor, were any stronger than the solicitude and attachment of him whose life and example are before us. And I am the more thoroughly convinced of the truth of what I say, because I saw him when his whole character and life, as a servant of God, and a minister of the new and better covenant, were being subjected to the most trying tests. Under it all no unkind word escaped his lips, no vindictive spirit appeared in his manner, and no uncharitable expression or feeling was ever uttered or manifested. There was, under the most convincing evidences of personal injury, a deep undertone of forgiveness and charity. David Gray was a loyal brother, a helpful associate, a Christian of tested virtues and of eminent graces.

We may learn from his life the lesson of a sweet and triumphant old age. It is a beautiful and instructive sight, all these tints and hues and maturities of autumn. The fading, yet fragrant flower, the golden shock, and the ripened fruits are objects calculated to impress us with the beauty and loveliness of normal growths. It is a great thing to live well while one's vigor and life's duties are upon him, but it is equally great to live well when we lay aside the armor and peacefully await the will and call of God. A sweet, happy, restful old age! How beautiful, how suggestive, how instructive! Coming down under the full development of all the powers and faculties, prepared to emit the fragrance of holy deeds and to bless others out of abundant spiritual experiences. Such is the picture I behold to-day. Nothing to complain of, and if there was, no disposition to complain. Nothing to turn life's cup sour, and no desire to drink that cup were there any excuse for acidity of speech or experience. I never knew Father Gray to complain or fret or become cynical. He was content with life's lot and pleased to see others rising. He was glad that others could endure the march and carry aloft the banner of our King, though his own sword had been sheathed and his place was vacant in the new, active ranks. His heart was filled with the grace of heaven, and therefore a sweet old age and a triumphant close. And so I say, as a last word, we may learn the lesson of a victorious and crowned life. His victories have been many. They may be recounted as you pass over the fields he has entered and cultivated as an itinerant Methodist preacher. You may note them when, as a youth, he found the Lord; when he accepted duty and obligation at the hands of the Church, and at the call of God; at a period in the history of our country and of the Church, when dauntless and holy men were needed to start a free Nation and to plant a free Church; when hardships and privations were bravely encountered for the Gospel's sake; and when in a long and varied experience there came bereavement and sorrow and darkness.

We see some of his richest triumphs in the evening of his life. In the gentleness of a firm spirit, in the sweetness of a strong growth, in the breadth of a decided character, and in that abundant grace of God, which enabled him in his last days to enjoy delightful visions of the better land.

He fell asleep at last in the arms of Him, Who, for so many years, had given strength for the day, and by Whom this our father in Israel and your father in the flesh has been received to the mansions of everlasting rest and to a crown of undying lustre!

I stood, the other day, beneath a great oak. I measured with my eye its massive trunk and its spreading branches. There were other smaller trees standing by. These seemed to lean for shelter and protection toward this giant of the forest. You could imagine them saying something like this: "You have been tested; the tempests have sought to uncrown your lofty head; the hurtling storms have striven to shake you in your deep establishments; but you stand fast and firm, and so we look to you for help and shelter and protection. We gather to-day beneath the great strength and broad protection of a long, eventful, and victorious life. This life has watched your coming into being, your passing on in its paths, your growth. To you this life in the strength it has afforded, in the sympathies it has extended, in the prayers it has offered to our Heavenly Father, and in the helpfulness it has so uniformly bestowed, is an inspiration and guide and protection. Accept its proffered blessings; heed its sage teachings and counsels; and, above all, follow the Savior, Whom our friend, brother, father followed, and reap the reward he has reaped—a home in heaven and an undying influence for the good of others.

At the conclusion of Rev. Whitlock's address, Rev. Hollyday, who was pastor of the Presbyterian Church in Findlay when father first went there in 1853, and who had known him quite intimately ever since, then made a few supplementary remarks. He said:

My acquaintance with Brother Gray extends back about thirty years, and had ripened into one of mutual love and confidence. I shall speak briefly of two features in the life of the deceased. First, as to his broad catholic spirit. While, perhaps, no one ever had a deeper regard and a more sincere love for the Church of which he was so long a member and minister, yet few had a greater love toward his brothers in other branches of the Christian Church than he. Often have I heard him speak of his early experience in this regard. His great interest centered in the Methodist Church. He wanted to see it prospering and growing, and the feeling was strong with him then that the best Christians and the most religion were to be found in the Methodist Church. But that feeling, he said, had been greatly changed and modified by the light of advancing years. He had come to love Christians in other denominations as well, and could worship with them as cordially as in his own loved Church. This was an experience in which Brother Gray and myself were in very close sympathy, the only difference being that he was in the Methodist Church and I in the Presbyterian. But we have both been taught, in later years, to love the children of God no matter in what branch of the Church we find them. Again, Brother Gray was a man of prayer. He prayed much and often. The spirit of earnest devotion was in his heart. He prayed for specific objects. He prayed for the Church in its wide and broadening interests. His life illustrates the truth that—

"Prayer is the Christian's vital breath—
The Christian's native air,
His watchword at the gate of death;
He enters Heaven with prayer."

But Brother Gray has passed from among us. "He rests from his labors, and his works do follow him." You will never see him again in that seat now wearing the crape. You will not again hear his voice in words of counsel or in earnest prayer, while leading the devotions of God's people. "The silver cord is loosed" which bound him to kindred and loved ones left behind; and yet, that tie, though loosed, is not broken. It is still true that—

"One family we dwell in Him,
One Church above, beneath,
Though now divided by the stream,
The narrow stream of death.
One army of the living God,
To His command we bow;
Part of the host have crossed the flood,
And part are crossing now."

Brother Gray, while called to his rest in heaven, is not lost to the Church on earth. His example and influence for good will continue and bear rich fruit in coming years. To-day we look for the last time upon that familiar form. The clay tenement from which the immortal spirit has gone is present with the Lord. His life will be cherished with fond remembrance. We shall think of him as amid the joys of heaven. With him the victory is won; to him the crown of glory has been given.

When Rev. Hollyday concluded the choir sang:

(Hymn read by Rev. LYMAN E. PRENTISS.)

"Servant of God, well done!
   Thy glorious warfare's past;
The battle's fought, the race is won,
   And thou art crowned at last.

"Of all thy heart's desire
   Triumphantly possessed,
Lodged by the ministerial choir
   In thy Redeemer's breast.

"In condescending love
   Thy ceaseless prayer He heard,
And bade thee suddenly remove
   To thy complete reward.

"With saints enthroned on high,
   Thou dost thy Lord proclaim,
And still to God salvation cry,
   Salvation to the Lamb!

"Redeemed from earth and pain,
   Ah! when shall we ascend,
And all in Jesus' presence reign
   With our translated friend?"

The closing prayer was offered by Rev. E. D. Whitlock. While the congregation retired the choir sang:

(Hymn read by Rev. G. J. JONES, of the Congregational Church in Findlay.)

"Jesus, while our hearts are bleeding
   O'er the spoils that death has won,
We would, at this solemn meeting,
   Calmly say, 'Thy will be done.'

"Though cast down, we're not forsaken;
   Though afflicted, not alone;
Thou didst give, and Thou hast taken;
   Blessed Lord, 'Thy will be done.'

> "Though to-day we're filled with mourning,
>   Mercy still is on the throne;
> With Thy smiles of love returning,
>   We can sing, 'Thy will be done.'
>
> "By Thy hands the boon was given:
>   Thou has taken but Thine own;
> Lord of earth, and God of heaven,
>   Evermore 'Thy will be done.'"

When the church services were over, father was laid to rest by the side of mother, in Maple Grove Cemetery.

# A TRUE MINISTRY.

### LINES BY REV. W. D. GRAY.

A village blacksmith trained to wield
   The hammer of God's Word,
Whose forge within its breast concealed
   A fire the spirit stirred;
A man whose glowing heart was laid
   On the anvil of the Lord.

The live coals touched his lips and heart
   Soon as the message came;
Humbly he chose the better part
   Whate'er the lot or fame,
To work in union with God's thought
   And honor Jesus' name.

His call, like Abram's, was to leave
   His home and kindred dear,
An unknown heritage receive,
   A Western pioneer,
He went to preach the promised Christ
   To those who gladly hear.

Yet not alone—a faithful wife
   Was partner of his youth,
Whose lovely face in early life
   Inspired him as God's truth,
Who bore the precious mother's name
   Of Orpah and of Ruth.

To them were sons and daughters born;
   While at his humble trade
The husband toiled; then came the morn
   When he a farewell bade
To earthly cares, and on the Lord
   His heavy burdens laid.

His preaching plain, directly spoke,
  It captured sin's retreat,
And all the noble passions woke
  In hearts for Christ made meet;
While ev'ry precept was enforced
  In his example sweet.

And thus he wrought with single eye
  To benefit his race;
And God alone to glorify,
  The ointment of whose grace
The vessel filled—whose perfume yet
  Hangs round the broken vase.

Such was he to the Church he served,
  Such in the eyes of all;
And he was one who never swerved,
  Whatever might befall,
From truth and right and duty's path,
  Who loved his master's call.

His faith, like Abram's was his shield,
  His prayers their own reward
Exceeding great! from him concealed
  No purpose of the Lord;
His faith and works were known of God,
  His life built on His Word.

His household, taught the way of God,
  Were bid that way to keep;
And follow in the steps he trod,
  Who prayed while some would sleep.
O may his angel visit us,
  As o'er his grave we weep.

Though now no more from earth ascends
  The incense of those prayers,
From Heav'n their fragrance still descends;
  Fond memory ever bears
The empty censer—bright with praise
  And hopes that banish tears.

Our father's God! upon whose breast
  Alone we find our place,
O give to us the promised rest,
  The children of Thy grace!
O may the righteous' seed be blest
  And brought to see Thy face!

His peace, who in the sleep of death
  Reflected that repose
His face e'er bore in life—whose breath
  O'er wrath triumphant rose—
Be ours in all the strife of life,
  To conquer thus our foes.

## TIMES AND PLACES OF FAMILY RESIDENCE.

January 1, 1821—White's Cross Roads, Sussex County, Delaware.
January 1, 1822—Cedar Creek Hundred, Sussex County, Delaware.
January 21, 1824—Slaughter-Neck, Sussex County, Delaware.
January 1, 1827—Broad-Kiln-Neck, Sussex County, Delaware.
May 20, 1829—Zanesville, Muskingum County, Ohio.
July —, 1829—Dresden, Muskingum County, Ohio.
July —, 1830—West Carlisle, Coshocton County, Ohio.
July —, 1832—East Union, Coshocton County, Ohio.
September —, 1835—Danville, Knox County, Ohio.
September —, 1836—Scank's Creek, Knox County, Ohio.
September —, 1837—Dalton, Wayne County, Ohio.
September —, 1839—Wooster, Wayne County, Ohio.
September —, 1841—Norwalk, Huron County, Ohio.
September —, 1842—Ashland, Richland County, Ohio.
September —, 1844—Congress, Wayne County, Ohio.
September —, 1845—Millersburg, Holmes County, Ohio.
September —, 1846—Canal Dover, Tuscarawas County, Ohio.
September —, 1848—Ashland, Ashland County, Ohio.
September —, 1849—Bucyrus, Crawford County, Ohio.
September —, 1851—Republic, Seneca County, Ohio.
September —, 1853—Findlay, Hancock County, Ohio.
September —, 1854—Maumee City, Lucas County, Ohio.
September —, 1858—Findlay, Hancock County, Ohio.

# GENEALOGICAL TABLES.

## DAVID GRAY'S GRANDPARENTS.

### WILLIAM AND ELIZABETH GRAY.

#### THEIR CHILDREN.

Joseph—Born in New Jersey.
Elizabeth—Born in New Jersey.
Polly—Born in New Jersey.
**Frazer**—Born in New Jersey, July 26, 1764.

### SAMUEL AND ZIPPORAH LOCKWOOD.

#### THEIR CHILDREN.

Benjamin—Born in Sussex County, Delaware.
William—Born in Sussex County, Delaware.
Samuel—Born in Sussex County, Delaware.
Zippa—Born in Sussex County, Delaware.
**Elizabeth**—Born in Sussex County, Delaware, January 27, 1771.
Rachel—Born in Sussex County, Delaware.
Nancy—Born in Sussex County, Delaware.
Leah—Born in Sussex County, Delaware.

## NAOMI LOFLAND'S GRANDPARENTS.

### LYTTLETON AND GRACE LOFLAND.

#### THEIR CHILDREN.

**Luke**—Born in Sussex County, Delaware, 1770.
Elias—Born in Sussex County, Delaware.
James—Born in Sussex County, Delaware.
Hevelow—Born in Sussex County, Delaware.
William—Born in Sussex County, Delaware.
Jonathan—Born in Sussex County, Delaware.
Grace—Born in Sussex County, Delaware.
Hannah—Born in Sussex County, Delaware.

### WILLIAM AND SOPHIA MORRIS.

#### THEIR CHILDREN.

William—Born in Sussex County, Delaware.
**Elizabeth**—Born in Sussex County, Delaware.
Polly—Born in Sussex County, Delaware.
Bivans—Born in Sussex County, Delaware.

## DAVID GRAY'S PARENTS.

(First Marriage.)

### FRAZER AND MARY HEVELOW GRAY.

#### THEIR CHILDREN.

JAMES—Born in Sussex County, Delaware, December 10, 1785.
WILLIAM—Born in Sussex County, Delaware, January 27, 1788.
NANCY—Born in Sussex County, Delaware, August 31, 1789.
JOHN—Born in Sussex County, Delaware, September 15, 1791.
ELIZABETH—Born in Sussex County, Delaware, December 13, 1793.

(Second Marriage.)

### FRAZER AND ELIZABETH LOCKWOOD GRAY.

#### THEIR CHILDREN.

RACHAEL—Born in Sussex County, Delaware, October 8, 1797.
**David**—Born in Sussex County, Delaware, March 28, 1800.
SAMUEL—Born in Sussex County, Delaware, August 1, 1803.
GEORGE—Born in Sussex County, Delaware, May 18, 1806.
MARY—Born in Sussex County, Delaware, April 10, 1810.

---

## NAOMI LOFLAND'S PARENTS.

(First Marriage.)

### LUKE AND ELIZABETH MORRIS LOFLAND.

#### THEIR CHILDREN.

MORRIS—Born in Sussex County, Delaware.
**Naomi**—Born in Sussex County, Delaware, September 9, 1799.
MARY—Born in Sussex County, Delaware, April 15, 1803.
SOPHIA—Born in Sussex County, Delaware.
LUKE—Born in Sussex County, Delaware.
ELIZABETH—Born in Sussex County, Delaware.
JOHN—Born in Sussex County, Delaware.

(Second Marriage.)

### LUKE AND ELIZABETH EVANS LOFLAND.

#### THEIR CHILD.

LYTTLETON M.—Born in Sussex County, Delaware, September 5, 1820.

# CHILDREN

#### OF

## DAVID AND NAOMI GRAY.

MARY JANE—Born in Sussex County, Delaware, August 25, **1821**.
ELIZABETH—Born in Sussex County, Delaware, April 26, 1824.
WILLIAM MORRIS—Born in Sussex County, Delaware, July 27, 1826.
DAVID SIMPSON—Born in Sussex County, Delaware, February 8, 1829.
SARAH CATHARINE—Born at West Carlisle, Coshocton County, **Ohio, June 24,** 1831.
SAMUEL FRAZER—Born at East Union, Coshocton **County, Ohio, December** 16, 1833.
JOHN EMORY—Born at Danville, Knox County, Ohio, **May 15, 1836**.
EMILY McCULLY—Born at Dalton, Wayne County, Ohio, September 8, 1838.
ELEANOR WOLCOT—Born at Dalton, Wayne County, Ohio, September 8, 1838.
MALINDA ANN—Born at Wooster, Wayne County, Ohio, **January** 9, 1841.
LAURA AMANDA—Born at Ashland, Richland County, Ohio, January 17, 1844.

# GRANDCHILDREN

OF

# DAVID AND NAOMI GRAY.

## CHILDREN OF JOSEPH D. AND MARY JANE GRAY STUBBS.

MARRIED BY REV. ELMORE YOCUM, AT WOOSTER, WAYNE COUNTY, OHIO, NOV. 5, 1840.

ELIZABETH ELLEN—Born at Loudonville, Ohio, August 19, 1841.
FLORENCE HORTENSE—Born at Loudonville, Ohio, January 20, 1843.
DAVID DEYARMON—Born at Ashland, Ohio, April 6, 1845.
JOHN CHRISTIAN SPAYD—Born at Ashland, Ohio, May 31, 1847.
JOSEPH EDWARD—Born at Ashland, Ohio, March 19, 1850.
MARY NAOMI—Born at Ashland, Ohio, December 19, 1853.
WILLIAM MORRIS—Born at Ashland, Ohio, July 28, 1856.

## CHILDREN OF WILLIAM AND ELIZABETH GRAY BREWSTER.

MARRIED BY REV. ELMORE YOCUM, AT ASHLAND, RICHLAND COUNTY, OHIO, IN 1842.

CHARLES E.—Born at Norwalk, Ohio, December 24, 1843.
ELIZABETH—Born at Norwalk, Ohio, January 7, 1845.
WILLIAM MORRIS—Born at Norwalk, Ohio, October 17, 1854.

### CHILDREN OF DAVID SIMPSON AND MARY LOUISE JACKSON GRAY.

MARRIED BY REV. DAVID GRAY, AT BELLEVILLE, RICHLAND COUNTY, OHIO, DECEMBER 27, 1858.

WALTER— Born at Columbus, Franklin County, Ohio, February 29, 1860.
HELEN LOUISE—Born at Columbus, Franklin County, Ohio, February 29, 1860.

### CHILDREN OF DAVID SIMPSON AND EUGENIA DOOLITTLE GRAY.

MARRIED BY REV. DAVID GRAY, AT COLUMBUS, FRANKLIN COUNTY, OHIO, OCTOBER 12, 1865.

INFANT SON— Born at Columbus, Franklin County, Ohio, June 30, 1866.
LOUISE— Born at Columbus, Franklin County, Ohio, August 12, 1869.
DAVID RICHARDS—Born at Columbus, Franklin County, Ohio, January 12, 1872.
MELDRUM—Born at Columbus, Franklin County, Ohio, December 7, 1874.
EUGENE—Born at Columbus, Franklin County, Ohio, September 24, 1876.

### CHILDREN OF MARTIN LUTHER AND SARAH CATHARINE GRAY HIGGINS.

MARRIED BY REV. RALPH WILCOX, AT MAUMEE CITY, LUCAS COUNTY, OHIO, APRIL 11, 1855.

CHARLES C.—Born at Maumee City, Lucas County, Ohio, June 16, 1857.
WALTER G.—Born at Findlay, Hancock County, Ohio, November 14, 1858.
NETTIE A.—Born at Findlay, Hancock County, Ohio, April 15, 1861.
MARY L.—Born at St. Louis, St. Louis County, Missouri, May 14, 1869.

## CHILDREN OF SAMUEL FRAZER AND JULIA A. DRUETT GRAY.

MARRIED BY REV. WILLIAM S. LUNT, AT FINDLAY, HANCOCK COUNTY, OHIO, JULY 17, 1856.

WILLIAM D.—Born at Findlay, Hancock County, Ohio, April 4, 1857.
MARY E.—Born at Findlay, Hancock County, Ohio, January 3, 1860.
LINDA—Born at Indianapolis, Marion County, Indiana, January 13, 1867.
HARRY H.—Born at Indianapolis, Marion County, Indiana, July 26, 1872.

## CHILDREN OF JOHN EMORY AND JANE RAMSEY GRAY.

MARRIED BY REV. JAMES STEVENSON, AT LOVELAND, CLERMONT COUNTY, OHIO, APRIL 30, 1863.

WILLIAM FRAZER—Born at Loveland, Clermont County, Ohio, March 8, 1864.
DAVID RAMSEY—Born at Loveland, Clermont County, Ohio, October 11, 1866.
JESSIE RAMSEY—Born at Cambridge City, Wayne County, Indiana, May 8, 1869.
JOHN RUTHRAUFF—Born at Cambridge City, Wayne County, Indiana, December 13, 1871.

## CHILDREN OF JOHN AND EMILY McCULLY GRAY RUTHRAUFF.

MARRIED BY REV. DAVID GRAY, AT FINDLAY, HANCOCK COUNTY, OHIO, MAY 29, 1861.

HARRY—Born at Findlay, Hancock County, Ohio, July 27, 1862.
MARY ELLEN—Born at Findlay, Hancock County, Ohio, October 15, 1866.
LINDA GRAY—Born at Findlay, Hancock County, Ohio, December 23, 1868.
FREDERICK GRAY—Born at Findlay, Hancock County, Ohio, August 6, 1879.

## CHILDREN OF C. C. AND MALINDA ANN GRAY GODMAN.

MARRIED BY REV. DAVID GRAY, AT FINDLAY, HANCOCK COUNTY, OHIO, MAY 19, 1862.

JAMES GRAY—Born at Findlay, Hancock County, Ohio, March 15, 1863.
LINDA LOUISE—Born at Findlay, Hancock County, Ohio, February 17, 1866.

# BIOGRAPHICAL DICTIONARY.

BARR, MARY JANE—Daughter of William and Mary Barr; born in Sussex County, Delaware, October 29, 1809; married George Gray, son of Frazer and Elizabeth Gray, February 13, 1827; emigrated to Ohio May 20, 1829; died at Scott-Town, Marion County, March 28, 1869, and was buried at Pleasant Hill Cemetery.

BREWSTER, WILLIAM—First husband of Elizabeth, daughter of Rev. David and Naomi Gray. He was born in 1807, and died July 5, 1854. He was a widower at the time of his marriage to Elizabeth Gray, at Ashland, Ohio, in 1842. He had two children by his former wife, named Willie and Platte, who were living at that time. His first wife's name was Benedict. His occupation was that of a carpenter and joiner.

BREWSTER, CHARLES E.—First child of William and Elizabeth Gray Brewster, born at Norwalk, Ohio, December 24, 1843. He was married, by Rev. E. B. Raffensperger, to Caroline Margaret, daughter of James and Mary Anne Lloyd Milligan, at Newark, Ohio, May 29, 1867. She died at Columbia, Ohio, September 16, 1878. He was again married, by Rev. J. E. Stubbs, to Mary E., daughter of John P. and Nancy K. Harrison, near Milford, Clermont County, Ohio, October 5, 1881. Occupation, railroad clerk.

BREWSTER, HELEN E.—First child of Charles E. and Caroline Margaret Brewster, born at Cincinnati, Ohio, January 26, 1869.

BREWSTER, MORRIS B.—Second child of Charles E. and Caroline Margaret Brewster, born at Cincinnati, Ohio, June 25, 1874.

BREWSTER, MARY GRAY—Third child of Charles E. and Caroline Margaret Brewster; born at Columbia, Hamilton County, Ohio, May 8, 1878.

BREWSTER, JOHN P. II.—First child of Charles E. and Nancy K. Brewster; born at Milford, Clermont County, Ohio, January 17, 1884.

BREWSTER, ELIZABETH—Second child of William and Elizabeth Brewster; born at Norwalk, Ohio, January 7, 1845. She was married to H. J. Raffensperger, by Rev. E. B. Raffensperger, D. D., at Toledo, Ohio, June 20, 1866.

BREWSTER, WILLIAM MORRIS—Third child of William and Elizabeth Brewster; born at Norwalk, Ohio, October 17, 1854. He was married by Rev. David Gray, to Lillie May, daughter of William W. and Susan Eichelberger Higbee, at Cincinnati, Ohio, April 30, 1879. Occupation, railroad clerk.

BREWSTER, GEORGE DUNCAN—First child of William Morris and Lillie May Brewster; born at Cincinnati, Ohio, April 23, 1880; died January 15, 1883.

BREWSTER, ALICE BERNICE—Second child of William Morris and Lillie May Brewster; born at St. Louis, Mo., September 8, 1883.

BEARNES, JAMES N.—Son of Ashford and Rebecca Galispie Bearnes, born in Licking County, Ohio, July 1, 1853. He was married to Mary E., daughter of Samuel F. and Jufia A. Druett Gray, at Indianapolis, Ind., October 4, 1882, by Prof. Whitlock, Dean of "Woman's College," Delaware. Occupation, attorney-at-law.

BEARNES, CLARA G.—First child of James N. and Mary E. Bearnes; born at Indianapolis, September 3, 1883.

BEARNES, JULIA—Second child of James N. and Mary E. Bearnes; born at Minneapolis, September 4, 1885.

CREIGHTON, ANNA BELLE—Only child of David Meade Creighton, by his first wife, Belle Grover Creighton, and wife of Charles C. Higgins. She was born at Columbus, Ohio, June 20, 1857, and was married October 16, 1880. She was a teacher of music at the time of her marriage.

CAMERON, R. R.—Son of Elzie and Jane Reed Cameron; born August 2, 1831; married Mary E., daughter of John and Mary Gray Postle, November 19, 1857. He died August 7, 1866, and was buried in the Missionary Graveyard at Upper Sandusky, Ohio.

CAMERON, LORA E.—First child of R. R. and Mary E. Cameron; born October 26, 1858.

CAMERON, CHARLES M.—Second child of R. R. and Mary E. Cameron; was born December 20, 1860; died September 5, 1869.

CAMERON, CARRIE B.—Third child of R. R. and Mary E. Cameron; born October 27, 1863.

DORLAND, JACOB J.—Son of John and Jane Postlewaite Dorland, born in Congress, Wayne County, Ohio, March 9, 1833. He married Elizabeth Ellen, daughter of J. D. and Mary Jane Stubbs, at Ashland, Ohio, April 10, 1865, Rev. C. Hartley officiating. Occupation, marble cutter.

DORLAND, MARY LINDA—First child of Jacob J. and Elizabeth Ellen Dorland, born at Ashland, Ohio, January 21, 1866.

DORLAND, JOSEPHINE CATHERINE—Second child of Jacob J. and Elizabeth Ellen Dorland, born at Lee's Summit, Missouri, January 22, 1873.

DORLAND, BESSIE NAOMI—Third child of Jacob J. and Elizabeth Ellen Dorland, born at Ashland, Ohio, May 9, 1876.

DORLAND, ARTHUR CRANE—Fourth child of Jacob J. and Elizabeth Ellen Dorland, born at Ashland, Ohio, October 14, 1881.

DULEBOHN, HENRY—Son of George and Mary M. Hoffer Dulebohn, born May 17, 1846. He married Mary E. Postle Cameron, widow of R. R. Cameron, March 18, 1871.

DULEBOHN, JOHN A.—Son of Henry and Mary E. Dulebohn, was born October 5, 1872.

DULEBOHN, DAISY—Daughter of Henry and Mary E. Dulebohn, was born May 4, 1874.

DRUETT, JULIA A.—Daughter of James and Elizabeth A. Hughes Druett, born at Piqua, Ohio, May 3, 1838. Was married at Findlay, Ohio, July 17, 1856, by Rev. William S. Lunt, to Samuel F., third son of David and Naomi Gray.

DOOLITTLE, EUGENIA—Fifth daughter and fifth child of Enos and Bathsheba Doolittle, born in Centreville, Montgomery County, Ohio, June 6, 1836. Was married at Columbus, Ohio, October 12, 1865, by Rev. David Gray, to David Simpson, second son of David and Naomi Gray.

GRAY, WILLIAM—David Gray's grandfather; husband of Elizabeth Gray, born in New Jersey. Dates of birth and death unknown.

GRAY, ELIZABETH—David Gray's grandmother; wife of William Gray, born in New Jersey. Name before marriage, and dates of birth and death, unknown.

GRAY, JOSEPH—First child of William and Elizabeth Gray, born in New Jersey. Dates of birth and death unknown. Never married.

GRAY, ELIZABETH—Second child of William and Elizabeth Gray, born in New Jersey. Dates of birth and death unknown. Married William Robbins.

GRAY, POLLY—Third child of William and Elizabeth Gray, born in New Jersey. Dates of birth and death unknown. Never married.

GRAY, FRAZER—David Gray's father; son of William and Elizabeth Gray, born in New Jersey, July 26, 1761. Died October 11, 1849, in Marion County, Ohio. Buried in Union Cemetery, near Scott-Town.

GRAY, JAMES—Son of Frazer and Mary Hevelow Gray, born December 10, 1785. He was murdered about the year 1820, while on his way to New Orleans on a flat-bottomed boat containing a cargo of slaves.

GRAY, WILLIAM—Son of Frazer and Mary Hevelow Gray, husband of Mary Tatman, born January 27, 1788; died April 4, 1838.

GRAY, NANCY—Daughter of Frazer and Mary Hevelow Gray, wife of Philip Wingate, born August 31, 1789; died March 30, 1872.

GRAY, JOHN—Son of Frazer and Mary Hevelow Gray, husband of Mary Ponder, born September 13, 1791. Died ———.

GRAY, ELIZABETH—Daughter of Frazer and Mary Hevelow Gray, wife of James Morris, first, and John Long, second, born December 13, 1793. Died ———.

GRAY, RACHEL—First child of Frazer and Elizabeth Lockwood Gray, born October 8, 1797; died in Sussex County, Delaware, December 11, 1806.

**GRAY, DAVID**—Second child and eldest son of Frazer and Elizabeth Lockwood Gray, born in Sussex County, Delaware, March 28, 1800; married Naomi Lofland, September 14, 1820. Died at Findlay, Ohio, October 24, 1887.

GRAY, SAMUEL—Third child and second son of Frazer and Elizabeth Lockwood Gray, born in Sussex County, Delaware, August 1, 1803; died in Marion County, Ohio, November 22, 1884; buried at Scott-Town.

GRAY, GEORGE—Fourth child and third son of Frazer and Elizabeth Lockwood Gray, was born in Sussex County, Delaware, May 18, 1806; died in Marion County, Ohio, December 29, 1880; buried in Pleasant Hill Cemetery, same county.

GRAY, MARY—Fifth child and second daughter of Frazer and Elizabeth Lockwood Gray, and wife of John Postle, born in Sussex County, Delaware, April 9, 1810.

GRAY, MARY JANE—First child and daughter of David and Naomi Gray, born in Sussex County, Delaware, August 25, 1821; married Joseph D. Stubbs, at Wooster, Ohio, November 5, 1840.

GRAY, ELIZABETH—Second child and daughter of David and Naomi Gray, born in Sussex County, Delaware, April 26, 1824; married Wm. Brewster, first, and Dr. Gibson, second.

GRAY, WM. MORRIS—Third child and first son of David and Naomi Gray, born in Sussex County, Delaware, July 27, 1826. Perished by fire at Sandusky City, February 26, 1851. Buried in Wood Lawn Cemetery, at Norwalk, Huron County, Ohio.

GRAY, DAVID SIMPSON—Fourth child and second son of David and Naomi Gray, born in Sussex County, Delaware, February 8, 1829. Married Mary Louise Jackson, at Belleville, Ohio, December 27, 1858. Married Eugenia Doolittle, at Columbus, Ohio, October 12, 1865.

GRAY, SARAH CATHERINE—Fifth child and third daughter of David and Naomi Gray, born at West Carlisle, Coshocton County, Ohio, June 24, 1831. Married M. L. Higgins, at Maumee City, April 11, 1855.

GRAY, SAMUEL FRAZER—Sixth child and third son of David and Naomi Gray, born at East Union, Coshocton County, Ohio, December 16, 1833. Married Julia A. Druett, at Findlay, Hancock County, Ohio, July 17, 1856.

GRAY, JOHN EMORY—Seventh child and fourth son of David and Naomi Gray, born at Danville, Knox County, Ohio, May 15, 1836. Married Jane Ramsey, at Loveland, Ohio, April 30, 1863.

GRAY, EMILY McCULLY—Twin daughter of David and Naomi Gray, born at Dalton, Wayne County, Ohio, September 8, 1838. Married John Ruthrauff, at Findlay, Ohio, May 29, 1861.

GRAY, ELEANOR WOLCOTT—Twin daughter of David and Naomi Gray, born at Dalton, Wayne County, Ohio, September 8, 1838.

17—History.

GRAY, MALINDA ANN—Tenth child and sixth daughter of David and Naomi Gray, born at Wooster, Wayne County, Ohio, January 9, 1841. Married C. C. Godman, at Findlay, Ohio, May 19, 1862. Died there March 3, 1866. Buried at Findlay.

GRAY, LAURA AMANDA—Eleventh child and seventh daughter of David and Naomi Gray, born at Ashland, Ohio, January 17, 1844. Died July 13, 1844. Buried in Ashland Cemetery.

GRAY, WALTER—Only son of David S. and Mary Louise Jackson Gray, born at Columbus, Ohio, February 29, 1860. Died there Wednesday, May 23, 1860. Buried, on the breast of his mother, in Green Lawn Cemetery.

GRAY, HELEN [Nellie]—Only daughter of David S. and Mary Louise Jackson Gray, born at Columbus, Ohio, February 29, 1860. Died there Tuesday July 3, 1860. Buried, on the breast of her mother, in Green Lawn Cemetery.

GRAY, INFANT SON—First child of David S. and Eugenia Doolittle Gray, born at Columbus, Ohio, June 30, 1866. Died soon afterward.

GRAY, LOUISE—Daughter of David S. and Eugenia Doolittle Gray, born at Columbus, Ohio, August 12, 1869.

GRAY, DAVID RICHARDS [called Richie]—Son of David S. and Eugenia Doolittle Gray, born at Columbus, Ohio, January 12, 1872.

GRAY, MELDRUM—Son of David S. and Eugenia Doolittle Gray, born at Columbus, Ohio, December 7, 1874.

GRAY, EUGENE—Son of David S. and Eugenia Doolittle Gray, born at Columbus, Ohio, December 24, 1876.

GRAY, WILLIAM D.—First child of Samuel Frazer and Julia Druett Gray, born at Findlay, Ohio, April 4, 1857. Married Minnie C. Roberts, at Clinton, Missouri, November 24, 1883.

GRAY, MARY E.—Second child of Samuel Frazer and Julia Druett Gray, born at Findlay, Ohio, January 3, 1860. Married to James N. Bearnes, by Prof. W. F. Whitlock, Dean of Woman's College, Delaware, Ohio, October 4, 1882.

GRAY, LINDA—Third child of Samuel Frazer and Julia Druett Gray, born at Indianapolis, January 13, 1867.

GRAY, HARRY H.—Fourth child of Samuel Frazer and Julia Druett Gray, born at Indianapolis, July 26, 1872.

GRAY, WM. FRAZER—First child of John Emory and Jane Gray, born at Loveland, Clermont County, Ohio, March 8, 1864. Baptized by Rev. D. Gray, at Findlay, Ohio, July 4, 1864.

GRAY, DAVID RAMSEY—Second child of John Emory and Jane Gray, born at Loveland, Clermont County, Ohio, October 11, 1866. Baptized by Rev. Metz, at Cambridge City, Wayne County, Indiana, April 11, 1869.

GRAY, JESSIE RAMSEY—Third child of John Emory and Jane Gray, born at Cambridge City, Wayne County, Indiana, May 8, 1869. Baptized by Rev. Robert McKaig, at Cambridge City, in 1871.

GRAY, JOHN RUTHRAUFF—Fourth child of John Emory and Jane Gray, born at Cambridge City, Wayne County, Indiana, December 13, 1871. Baptized by Rev. David Gray, at Cambridge City, June 6, 1876.

GRAY, MERRILL ROBERTS—Son of Rev. Wm. D. and Minnie Gray, born at Westerville, Franklin County, Ohio, July 13, 1884.

GRAY, WM. HENRY—First child of George and Jane Barr Gray, born in Sussex County, Delaware, January 31, 1828. Died near Keosauqua, Van Buren County, Iowa, December 1, 1854. Buried there.

GRAY, DAVID—Second child of George and Jane Barr Gray, born in Marion County, Ohio, October 15, 1829. Married Lucinda M. Van Houton, December 14, 1858. Died September 11, 1866. Buried at Pleasant Hill Cemetery, Marion County, Ohio.

GRAY, JAMES K.—Third child of George and Jane Barr Gray, born in Marion County, Ohio, April 16, 1831. Never married.

GRAY, JOHN F.—Fourth child of John and Jane Barr Gray, born in Marion County, Ohio, October 28, 1834. Married Ahinda E. Riley, May 31, 1866.

GRAY, SARAH E.—Fifth child of George and Jane Barr Gray, born in Marion County, Ohio, July 29, 1838. Never married.

GRAY, AMOS B.—Sixth child of George and Jane Barr Gray, born in Marion County, Ohio, April 23, 1841. Married Elizabeth Guthrie, May 3, 1866.

GRAY, MARY A.—Seventh child of George and Jane Barr Gray, born in Marion County, Ohio, July 25, 1843. Married David J. Humphrey, at Scott-Town, Ohio, December 28, 1869.

GODMAN, C. C.—Son of Mr. and Mrs. A. B. Godman, of Marion County, Ohio. Married Linda, daughter of Rev. David and Naomi Gray, at Findlay, Ohio, May 19, 1862.

GODMAN, JAMES GRAY—First child of C. C. and Linda Godman, born at Findlay, Ohio, March 15, 1863. Died March 15, 1866. Buried there with his mother.

GODMAN, LINDA LOUISE—Second child of C. C. and Linda Godman, born at Findlay, Ohio, February 19, 1866. Died February 5, 1867. Buried there with her mother.

GRAY, ERNEST L.—First child of Amos B. and Elizabeth Guthrie Gray, born at Scott-Town, Ohio, April 21, 1867. Died August 30, 1867.

GRAY, ISCAH DELL—Second child of Amos B. and Elizabeth Guthrie Gray, born at Scott-Town, Ohio, October 26, 1868.

GRAY, GRACE—Daughter of Amos B. and Elizabeth Guthrie Gray, born at Scott-Town, Ohio, July 16, 1870.

GRAY, EUGENE—Fourth child of Amos B. and Elizabeth Guthrie Gray, born at Scott-Town, April 27, 1872. Died September 6, 1872.

GRAY, MARY SYBIL—Fifth child of Amos B. and Elizabeth Guthrie Gray, born at Scott-Town, Ohio, September 16, 1879.

GUTHRIE, ELIZABETH—Wife of Amos B. Gray, daughter of Wm. and Lucinda Cleveland Guthrie. Second cousin to President Cleveland.

GRAY, INFANT SON—Son of John F. and Ahinda Riley Gray, born in Marion County, Ohio, April 12, 1867. Died same date.

GRAY, DAVID—Son of same parents, born October 24, 1868.

GRAY, WILLIAM—Son of same parents, born January 15, 1870. Died July 14, 1870.

GRAY, ROBERT—Son of same parents, born July 14, 1873.

GRAY, CORA—Daughter of same parents, born March 4, 1876.

GRAY, EDDIE L.—Son of same parents, born September 1, 1879.

GRAY, FLORA A.—Daughter of David and Lucinda Van Houton Gray, born in Marion County, Ohio, June 28, 1860.

GRAY, CLARA J.—Daughter of same parents, born February 23, 1862.

GRAY, AMOS—Son of same parents, born January 24, 1865; died April 2, 1866.

HIGBEE, LILLIE MAY—Wife of Wm. Morris Brewster, and daughter of Wm. W. and Susan Eichelbarger Higbee, born at Cincinnati, May 16, 1856. Married by Rev. David Gray, April 30, 1879.

HIGGINS, MARTIN LUTHER—Husband of Sarah Catherine Gray, born in Hamilton County, Ohio, May 10, 1831. Married at Maumee City, April 11, 1855, by Rev. Ralph Wilcox.

HIGGINS, CHARLES C.—First child of M. L. and Sarah Catherine Higgins, born at Maumee City, Ohio, June 16, 1857. Married at Columbus, Ohio, October 16, 1880, Rev. Grover, grandfather of the bride, officiating.

HIGGINS, WALTER G.—Second child of M. L. and Sarah Catherine Higgins, born at Findlay, Ohio, November 16, 1858. Married Sarah Shattuck Vance, at Findlay, January 3, 1882.

HIGGINS, NETTIE A.—Third child of M. L. and Sarah Catherine Higgins, born at Findlay, Ohio, April 15, 1861. Married James H. Wheeler December 30, 1882, Rev. Joseph E. Stubbs officiating.

HIGGINS, MAMIE L.—Fourth child of M. L. and Sarah Catherine Higgins, born in St. Louis, Mo., May 14, 1869.

HIGGINS, WARREN GRAY—First child of Charles C. and Anna Higgins, born at Columbus, Ohio, July 4, 1881.

HIGGINS, GROVER BATES—Second child of Charles C. and Anna Higgins. Born at Columbus, Ohio, October 13, 1883.

HIGGINS, BESSIE LOUISE—Daughter of Walter G. and Sarah Higgins, born at Fremont, Dodge County, Nebraska, September 27, 1883.

HEVELOW, JOHN—Husband of Mary Lofland Hevelow, born April —, 1803; died April 23, 1871.

HEVELOW, MARY—First wife of Frazer Gray. Married March 2, 1785; died January, 1795.

HUMPHREY, DAVID J.—Son of Thomas and Mary Philips Humphrey, born April 22, 1841. Married Mary A., daughter of George and Jane Barr Gray, at Scott-Town, Marion County, Ohio, December 28, 1869.

HUMPHREY—Infant son of D. J. and Mary A. Humphrey, born at Marion, Ohio, February 2, 1871; died February 3, 1871.

HUMPHREY, DAVID GRAY—Son of D. J. and Mary A. Humphrey, born at Marion, Ohio, May 4, 1872; died from scarlet fever, July 8, 1880.

HUMPHREY, HARRY AND CHARLIE—Twin sons of D. J. and Mary A. Humphrey, born at Marion, Ohio, January 17, 1876. Charlie died August 9, 1876. Harry died from scarlet fever, June 22, 1880.

HUMPHREY, GLADYS MARIAN—Daughter of D. J. and Mary A. Humphrey, born at Marion, Ohio, November 16, 1882.

JACKSON, MARY LOUISE—Sixth daughter and seventh child of Benj. and Nancy H. Jackson, born in Belleville, Richland County, Ohio, December 27, 1834. Married in same place to David S. Gray, December 27 1858. Died in Columbus, Ohio, March 3, 1860. Buried in Green Lawn Cemetery.

LOFLAND, LYTTLETON—Naomi Gray's grandfather—born in Sussex County, Delaware. Dates of birth and death unknown.

LOFLAND, GRACE—Naomi Gray's grandmother—wife of Lyttleton Lofland, born in Sussex County, Delaware. Dates of birth and death unknown.

LOFLAND, LUKE—Naomi Gray's father—first child of Lyttleton and Grace Lofland, born in Sussex County, Delaware, in 1770. Married Elizabeth Morris first; Elizabeth Evans, second. Died May 23, 1850.

LOFLAND, ELIAS—Second child of Lyttleton and Grace Lofland, born in Sussex County, Delaware. Married daughter of Bivans Morris.

LOFLAND, JAMES—Third child of Lyttleton and Grace Lofland, born in Sussex County, Delaware.

LOFLAND, HEVELOW—Fourth child of Lyttleton and Grace Lofland, born in Sussex County, Delaware.

LOFLAND, WILLIAM—Fifth child of Lyttleton and Grace Lofland, born in Sussex County, Delaware.

LOFLAND, JONATHAN—Sixth child of Lyttleton and Grace Lofland, born in Sussex County, Delaware.

LOFLAND, GRACE—Seventh child of Lyttleton and Grace Lofland, born in Sussex County, Delaware. Married Boze Warren.

LOFLAND, HANNAH—Eighth child of Lyttleton and Grace Lofland, born in Sussex County, Delaware. Married Samuel Hurst.

LOFLAND, MORRIS—First child of Luke and Elizabeth Lofland, born in Sussex County, Delaware. Married Jane Stokely. Died soon after marriage.

**LOFLAND, NAOMI**—Second child of Luke and Elizabeth Lofland, born in Sussex County, Delaware, September 9, 1799. Married David Gray, September 14, 1820. Died April 3, 1876, at Findlay, Ohio. Buried there, in Maple Grove Cemetery.

LOFLAND, MARY—Third child of Luke and Elizabeth Lofland, born in Sussex County, Delaware, April, 1803. Married John Hevelow; died in native county and State, November, 1871.

LOFLAND, SOPHIA—Fourth child of Luke and Elizabeth Lofland, and wife of James Richards, born in Sussex County, Delaware; died in native county and State, July 4, 1883.

LOFLAND, LUKE—Fifth child of Luke and Elizabeth Lofland, born in Sussex County, Delaware; died in youth.

LOFLAND, ELIZABETH—Sixth child of Luke and Elizabeth Lofland, born in Sussex County, Delaware. Married Mr. Houghacre first, and James Hevelow second. Had one child by her second husband. Mother and child both died in Cecil County, Maryland.

LOFLAND, JOHN—Seventh child of Luke and Elizabeth Lofland, born in Sussex County, Delaware; died in youth.

LOFLAND, LYTTLETON M.—First and only child of Luke and Elizabeth Evans Lofland, born in Sussex County, Delaware, September 5, 1820. Married Anna Truitt, August 9, 1842.

LOFLAND, ELIZABETH—First child of Lyttleton M. and Annie Lofland, born in Sussex County, Delaware.

LOFLAND, LUKE—Second child of Lyttleton M. and Annie Lofland, born in Sussex County, Delaware, June 8, 1845.

LOFLAND, ALFRED—Third child of Lyttleton M. and Annie Lofland, born in Sussex County, Delaware, August 9, 1847.

LOFLAND, WILLIAM—Fourth child of Lyttleton M. and Annie Lofland, born in Sussex County, Delaware.

LOFLAND, JOHN—Fifth child of Lyttleton M. and Annie Lofland, born in Sussex County, Delaware, July 1, 1851.

LOFLAND, DAVID—Sixth child of Lyttleton M. and Anna Lofland, born in Sussex County, Delaware, February 6, 1853.

LOCKWOOD, SAMUEL—David Gray's grandfather—citizen of Dagsborough Hundred, Sussex County, Delaware. Dates of birth and death unknown.

LOCKWOOD, ZIPPORAH—David Gray's grandmother—wife of Samuel Lockwood, of Dagsborough Hundred, Sussex County, Delaware. Dates of birth and death unknown.

LOCKWOOD, BENJAMIN—Son of Samuel and Zipporah Lockwood, born in Sussex County, Delaware. Married Louie Long.

LOCKWOOD, WILLIAM—Son of Samuel and Zipporah Lockwood, born in Sussex County, Delaware. Married Phoebe Dingle.

LOCKWOOD, SAMUEL—Son of Samuel and Zipporah Lockwood, born in Sussex County, Delaware. Married Patty Holland.

LOCKWOOD, ZIPPA—Daughter of Samuel and Zipporah Lockwood, born in Sussex County, Delaware. Never married.

LOCKWOOD, ELIZABETH—David Gray's mother—daughter of Samuel and Zipporah Lockwood, born in Sussex County, Delaware, January 27, 1771. Married Frazer Gray, December 19, 1796; died in Marion County, Ohio, June 23, 1853.

LOCKWOOD, RACHEL.—Daughter of Samuel and Zipporah Lockwood, born in Sussex County, Delaware. Married Joshua Robinson.

LOCKWOOD, NANCY—Daughter of Samuel and Zipporah Lockwood, born in Sussex County, Delaware. Married Wm. Schofield.

LOCKWOOD, LEAH—Daughter of Samuel and Zipporah Lockwood, born in Sussex County, Delaware. Married James Tingle.

LONG, JOHN—Second husband of Elizabeth, daughter of Frazer and Mary Hevelow Gray.

LOFLAND, ISAAC—Brother to Lyttleton Lofland, and father of Dr. John Lofland, the Milford Bard.

LOFLAND, PURNAL—Brother to Lyttleton Lofland, and father of Dr. James Lofland, of Milford, Delaware.

MORRIS, WILLIAM—Naomi Gray's grandfather—citizen of Broad-Kiln Hundred, Sussex County, Delaware. Dates of birth and death unknown.

MORRIS, SOPHIA—Naomi Gray's grandmother—wife of William Morris, of Broad-Kiln Hundred, Sussex County, Delaware. Surname before marriage was Lemonde. Dates of birth and death unknown.

MORRIS, WILLIAM—First child of William and Sophia Morris, born in Sussex County, Delaware. Married Mary Hevelow.

MORRIS, ELIZABETH—Naomi Gray's mother—second child of William and Sophia Morris, born in Sussex County, Delaware. Married Luke Lofland. Dates of birth and death unknown.

MORRIS, POLLY—Third child of William and Sophia Morris, born in Sussex County, Delaware. Married John Riley.

MORRIS, BIVANS—Fourth child of William and Sophia Morris, born in Sussex County, Delaware. Married Widow Collins.

MORRIS, JAMES—First husband of Elizabeth, daughter of Frazer and Mary Hevelow Gray; born in Sussex County, Delaware, December 13, 1793; date of death unknown.

POSTLE, JOHN—Son of Luke Postle, born in Sussex County, Delaware, September 30, 1809. Married Mary L., daughter of Frazer and Elizabeth Gray. Died September 6, 1870. Buried in Union Church grounds, Marion County, Ohio.

POSTLE, ELIZA JANE—Daughter of John and Mary L. Postle, born in Sussex County, Delaware, November 23, 1832. Married Irwin Wheeler, February 7, 1856. Died April 10, 1868. Buried in Union Church grounds, Marion County, Ohio.

POSTLE, GEORGE H.—Son of John and Mary L. Postle, born in Sussex County, Delaware, April 15, 1833.

POSTLE, HESTER ANN—Daughter of John and Mary L. Postle, born in Sussex County, Delaware, April 16, 1836. Died in infancy.

POSTLE, MARY E.—Daughter of John and Mary L. Postle, born July 23, 1839. Married R. R. Cameron, in Marion County, Ohio, November 19, 1857. He died August 7, 1866. She married her second husband, Henry Dulebohn, March 18, 1871.

POSTLE, RACHAEL A.—Daughter of John and Mary L. Postle, born in Marion County, Ohio, August 9, 1842. Married J. A. Sappington, May 26, 1868.

POSTLE, ELLA J.—Daughter of George H. and Ann Waples Postle, born June 23, 1856.

POSTLE, MARY R.—Daughter of George H. and Ann Waples Postle, born July 13, 1858.

POSTLE, JOHN E.—Son of George H. and Ann Waples Postle, born July 15, 1861.

POSTLE, GEORGIETTA—Daughter of George H. and Ann Waples Postle, born February 13, 1865.

POSTLE, HARRY B.—Son of George H. and Ann Waples Postle, born August 13, 1868.

POSTLE, LOUISE C. Daughter of George H. and Ann Waples Postle, born July 15, 1876.

PONDER, MARY—Wife of John, second son of Frazer and Mary Hevelow Gray.

PATTERSON, MARY R.—Wife of John Christian Spayd Stubbs. Married at Sacramento, California, August 14, 1871.

ROBERTS, MINNIE Daughter of Thomas and Mary Jane Roberts, born at Rivere-Dee-Loup, near Quebec, Canada, February 9, 1863. Married Rev. W. D. Gray, at Clinton, Mo., November 24, 1883.

RAMSEY, JANE—Daughter of Jesse and Eleanor McKinnie Ramsey, born May 25, 1830. Married John Emory Gray at Loveland, Clermont County, Ohio, April 30, 1863.

RUTHRAUFF, JOHN Husband of Emily McCully Gray, born November 13, 1831. Married at Findlay, Ohio, May 29, 1861.

RUTHRAUFF, HARRY—First child of John and Emily Ruthrauff, born at Findlay, Ohio, July 27, 1862. Died July 4, 1864.

RUTHRAUFF, MARY ELLEN—Second child of John and Emily Ruthrauff, born at Findlay, Ohio, October 15, 1866.

RUTHRAUFF, LINDA GRAY—Third child of John and Emily Ruthrauff, born at Findlay, Ohio, December 23, 1868.

RUTHRAUFF, FREDERICK GRAY—Fourth child of John and Emily Ruthrauff, born at Findlay, Ohio, August 6, 1879.

RAFFENSPERGER, H. J.—Husband of Elizabeth, daughter of William and Elizabeth Brewster. Married at Toledo, Ohio, June 20, 1866.

RAFFENSPERGER, FLORENCE MAY—Daughter of H. J. and Elizabeth Raffensperger, born at Toledo, Ohio, February 9, 1868. Married J. H. Dautermann, August 1, 1885.

RAFFENSPERGER, GRACE ELIZABETH—Daughter of H. J. and Elizabeth Raffensperger, born at Toledo, Ohio, May, 22, 1872.

RILEY, AHINDA E.—Daughter of John P. and Sarah A. Malone Riley. Married John F., son of George and Jane Barr Gray, May 31, 1866.

ROBBINS, WILLIAM—Husband of Elizabeth, sister of Frazer Gray. David Gray went to school to him in Delaware State.

STUBBS, JOSEPH DEYARMON—Husband of Mary Jane Gray, born January 6, 1820. Married by Rev. Elmore Yocum, at Wooster, Wayne County, Ohio, November 5, 1840.

STUBBS, ELIZABETH ELLEN—First child of Joseph D. and Mary Jane Stubbs, born at Loudonville, Ohio, August 19, 1841. Married Jacob J. Dorland, at Ashland, Ohio, April 10, 1865.

STUBBS, FLORENCE HORTENSE—Second child of Joseph D. and Mary Jane Stubbs, born at Loudonville, Ohio, January 20, 1843. Died September 28, 1844.

STUBBS, DAVID DEYARMON—Third child of Joseph D. and Mary Jane Stubbs, born at Ashland, Ohio, April 6, 1845. Married Wilhelmina Winning, November 27, 1873.

STUBBS, JOHN CHRISTIAN SPAYD—Fourth child of Joseph D. and Mary Jane Stubbs, born at Ashland, Ohio, May 31, 1847. Married Mary R. Patterson at Sacramento, California, August 14, 1871.

STUBBS, JOSEPH EDWARD—Fifth child of Joseph D. and Mary Jane Stubbs, born at Ashland, Ohio, March 19, 1850. Married Ella A. Sprengle, July 10, 1873.

STUBBS, MARY NAOMI—Sixth child of Joseph D. and Mary Jane Stubbs, born at Ashland, Ohio, December 19, 1853.

STUBBS, WM. MORRIS—Seventh child of Joseph D. and Mary Jane Stubbs, born at Ashland, Ohio, July 28, 1856. Married Jessie Fremont Sprengle, March 10, 1880. Died at Sacramento, California, November 29, 1886.

STUBBS, JOHN GRAY—First child of David D. and Wilhelmina Stubbs, born at San Francisco, California, October 29, 1874.

STUBBS, MINNIE LOUISE—Second child of David D. and Wilhelmina Stubbs, born at San Francisco, California, April 4, 1876.

STUBBS, WM. DAVID—Third child of David D. and Wilhelmina Stubbs, born at San Francisco, California, December 25, 1878.

STUBBS, JOSEPH DAVID—First child of John C. S. and Mary Patterson Stubbs, born at Sacramento, California, October 14, 1872.

STUBBS, NELLIE LOUISE—Second child of John C. S. and Mary Patterson Stubbs, born at San Francisco, California, February 16, 1875.

STUBBS, MARY SPAYD—Third child of John C. S. and Mary Patterson Stubbs, born at San Francisco, California, March 24, 1876.

STUBBS, EDITH PATTERSON—Fourth child of John C. S. and Mary Patterson Stubbs, born at San Francisco, California, April 29, 1878.

STUBBS, DONALD—Fifth child of John C. S. and Mary Patterson Stubbs, born at San Francisco, California, December 14, 1879.

STUBBS, BUELAH—Sixth child of John C. S. and Mary Patterson Stubbs, born at San Francisco, California, May 16, 1881.

STUBBS, THEODORA WATERS—First child of Joseph E. and Ella Sprengle Stubbs, born at Ashland, Ohio, November 10, 1874.

18—History.

STUBBS, ELIZABETH SPAYD—Second child of Joseph E. and Ella Sprengle Stubbs, born at Ashland, Ohio, October 3, 1878.

STUBBS, RALPH SPRENGLE—Third child of Joseph E. and Ella Sprengle Stubbs, born at Ashland, Ohio, February 3, 1881.

STUBBS, JESSIE—Fourth child of Joseph E. and Ella Sprengle Stubbs, born at Ashland, Ohio, December 9, 1883. Died December 17, 1883.

SPRENGLE, JESSIE FREMONT—Wife of Wm. Morris Stubbs, second daughter of T. Jefferson and Sophia Coffin Sprengle, born July 6, 1856. Married at Ashland, Ohio, by Rev. David Gray, March 10, 1880. Died there June 25, 1883.

SPRENGLE, ELLA AMERICA—Wife of Rev. Joseph Edward Stubbs, eldest daughter of T. Jefferson and Sophia Coffin Sprengle, born at Ashland, Ohio, March 22, 1853. Married there July 10, 1873.

SAPPINGTON, JOHN A.—Son of Elias and Mary Whitcombe Sappington, born October 17, 1839. Married Rachael A., daughter of John and Mary Gray Postle, May 26, 1868.

SAPPINGTON, BERTHA—Daughter of John A. and Rachael Sappington, born June 21, 1870.

SAPPINGTON, JOHN C.—Son of John A. and Rachael Sappington, born June 28, 1875.

SAPPINGTON, CHARLES—Son of John A. and Rachael Sappington, born January 2, 1880. Died January 16, 1880.

TATMAN, MARY—Wife of Wm. Gray, second son of Frazer and Mary Hevelow Gray.

TRUITT, ANNIE—Wife of Lyttleton M. Lofland. Born in Sussex County, Delaware, March, 1812. Married August 9, 1842.

VANCE, SARAH SHATTUCK—Wife of Walter G. Higgins. Daughter of H. M. and Flora Shattuck Vance. Born at Findlay, Ohio. Married there by Rev. Watt, January 3, 1882.

VAN HOUTON, LUCINDA M.—Daughter of David and Tamma Messenger Van Houton. Married David, son of George and Jane Barr Gray, December 14, 1858.

WINGATE, PHILIP—Husband of Nancy, daughter of Frazer and Mary Hevelow Gray. Born in Sussex County, Delaware, August 31, 1789.

WHEELER, IRWIN—Husband of Eliza Jane Postle. Married February 7, 1856.

WHEELER, LINA—Daughter of Irwin and Eliza Jane Wheeler. Born April 7, 1858. Married W. F. Marsh. Now living in Boone, Iowa (1887.)

WHEELER, MATTIE—Daughter of Irwin and Eliza Jane Wheeler. Born June 21, 1859.

WHEELER, FRANK—Son of Irwin and Eliza Jane Wheeler. Born July 16, 1863. Died August 11, 1863.

WINNING, WILHELMINA—Wife of David Deyarmon Stubbs. Married November 27, 1873.

www.ingramcontent.com/pod-product-compliance
Lightning Source LLC
Chambersburg PA
CBHW032145230426
43672CB00011B/2454